MAFIOPOLI

MAFIOPOLI

LIVING AMONG THE 'NDRANGHETA
ITALY'S MOST POWERFUL CRIME ORGANIZATION

SANNE DE BOER

Translated from the Dutch by Eileen J. Stevens

monoray

First published in Great Britain in 2024 by Monoray,
an imprint of Octopus Publishing Group Ltd
Carmelite House
50 Victoria Embankment
London EC4Y 0DZ
www.octopusbooks.co.uk
www.octopusbooksusa.com

An Hachette UK Company
www.hachette.co.uk

Original edition published in 2020 under the title *Mafiopoli – Een zoektocht naar de
'Ndrangheta, de machtigste maffia van Italië* by Nieuw Amsterdam, Amsterdam

Distributed in the US by
Hachette Book Group
1290 Avenue of the Americas
4th and 5th Floors
New York, NY 10104

Distributed in Canada by
Canadian Manda Group
664 Annette St.
Toronto, Ontario, Canada M6S 2C8

ISBN 978-1-80096-212-5 (hardback)
ISBN 978-1-80096-213-2 (trade paperback)

A CIP catalogue record for this book is available from the British Library.

Printed and bound in Great Britain

Typeset in 11.5/17pt Sabon LT Pro by Jouve (UK), Milton Keynes

1 3 5 7 9 10 8 6 4 2

This FSC® label means that materials used
for the product have been responsibly sourced.

This **monoray** book was crafted and published by Jake Lingwood, Mala Sanghera-Warren,
Alex Stetter, Eileen Stevens, John English, Mel Four and Peter Hunt.

Map on page ix by Marcel Groenen/Macareves

This publication was created with the support of the Dutch Fund for In-depth Journalism, www.fondsbjp.nl

The publisher gratefully acknowledges the support of the Dutch Foundation for Literature.

Nederlands
letterenfonds
dutch foundation
for literature

For my father

CONTENTS

CONTENTS

CALABRIA

Milan

ITALY

150 MI
250 KM

Rome

POLLINO

Crati

Cosenza

Tyrrhenian Sea

SILA

Neto

Crotone

Lamezia
Terme

Catanzaro

Isola di
Capo
Rizzuto

Tropea

Vibo
Valentia

Soverato

Rosarno

ASPROMONTE

Ionian Sea

Gioia Tauro

Riace

Palmi

Siderno

Messina

Polsi

Locri

Bovalino

SICILY

Reggio
Calabria

San
Luca

10 MI
20 KM

AUTHOR'S NOTE

Mafiopoli, the title of this book, means a 'society governed by the mafia'. It comes from the Italian word *mafia* and the Ancient Greek *polis*, meaning city or community. The accent is on the first o: Ma-fi-ó-po-li.

The complicated-looking word 'Ndrangheta is surprisingly easy to pronounce: *dráng*-get-ta. If you want to say it the way Italians do, you can ignore the n-sound at the beginning; it's practically silent. The accent is on 'drang', and the g of 'gheta' is like the English g in the word *get*. *Dráng*-get-ta.

The apostrophe is a remnant of the a at the beginning of the Greek word *andragathía*, which is at the root of the name of the Calabrian mafia. Through that word, the term 'Ndrangheta refers (unsuccessfully, as it happens) to good, brave-hearted men.

For the sake of readability, I have stubbornly decided to omit the apostrophe in front of the name 'Ndrangheta in the chapters that follow. Even without an apostrophe, the Ndrangheta is already intimidating enough.

1

HOW IT ALL BEGAN

On Christmas Day 2006, a young mother named Maria was shot in the chest by bullets meant for her husband. At four-thirty in the afternoon, uninvited guests had burst in, disrupting the holiday celebrations at her in-laws' home. Armed with a Kalashnikov, a hunting rifle and pistols, the intruders rapidly fired forty bullets at the family. Maria managed to shield her children from the rain of bullets but died from wounds to her chest. Her husband, a leader of a Ndrangheta clan in the Calabrian village of San Luca, survived.

When I arrived in Calabria four days later, I knew nothing of this family tragedy. I had left Amsterdam to live and work temporarily on a lovely hillside on the outskirts of a village. I was blissfully unaware of the Ndrangheta and surrendered myself to the scent of the fresh oranges I plucked, the warmth of woodstoves and my view of verdant mountains and radiant blue sea.

Maria Strangio's death didn't attract much attention in the media. Still, it was the harbinger of the moment when the Ndrangheta, or Calabrian mafia, would be suddenly thrust into the international limelight. Before that time, the international press hadn't paid much attention to the Ndrangheta's wrongdoings or the challenging spelling of its name. Major Italian newspapers had also ignored the Calabrian

3

mafia, portraying it as a local band of backward hotheads. And yet, even then, the Ndrangheta was already Italy's most powerful mafia, its influence spread worldwide.

The other, 'classic' Italian mafia, the Sicilian Cosa Nostra, had long been famous because of films like *The Godfather*. Cinephiles, however, may not have been aware of what was actually happening in Sicily as the gripping story of the Corleone family was being shot. While the tragic hero was filmed dying a natural death in the garden of his picturesque villa in a safer part of Sicily, the real mafiosi from the village of Corleone were exterminating one enemy after the other. And these enemies could be mafiosi, journalists, judges or policemen. Totò Riina, the boss of all bosses, was also from Corleone; he was responsible for hundreds of deaths and had a penchant for strangling adversaries with his bare hands. Apart from the village of his birth, Totò Riina didn't have much in common with Don Vito Corleone, the more sophisticated fictitious godfather, save for his sagging jowls. And his friends in politics.

In 1992, two years after the release of the final instalment of the *Godfather* trilogy, those friends in politics disappointed Totò Riina and he wasted no time unleashing the ice-cold military violence the Sicilian Mafia was capable of under his leadership. Two courageous prosecuting magistrates, Giovanni Falcone and Paolo Borsellino, were murdered in bomb attacks. Falcone had landed at Palermo Airport one Saturday in May, and he was driving to the city with his wife and his security detail when hundreds of kilos of explosives went off in a culvert beneath the motorway. The first car, carrying three bodyguards, was catapulted into the air, killing all three instantly. Falcone's car then collided with the wall of the massive crater the bomb had left in the road's surface. He and his wife died in the hospital that same evening. Two months later, on a Sunday afternoon, Paolo

Borsellino was ringing the doorbell at his mother's house when he and five of his bodyguards were killed by a massive car bomb. The street was in ruins, as if it had been hit by an earthquake. News of the Cosa Nostra's violence made the front pages of the world's newspapers. But movies and bombings had not yet made the Ndrangheta a household name, and the Calabrian mafia quietly continued building its empire.

2

THERE ARE NO MAFIOSI HERE

During my first summer in Calabria, news spread around the world that the Ndrangheta had carried out a massacre in Germany. In the middle of the night, six young men had been found riddled with bullets on the doorstep of a popular Italian restaurant in Duisburg. The media was quick to link the six murders to a vendetta between Ndrangheta families from the Calabrian village of San Luca.

The term Ndrangheta was familiar to me, but I didn't know much other than that it was the name of the Calabrian mafia. Whenever I asked my neighbours, they'd say, 'No, that's not in our village. Further south, that's where the mafia is.' Indeed, I had noticed that San Luca, the home of both the suspects and the victims of the Duisburg massacre, was about two hours to the south along the coastal road. So why had this reprisal taken place two thousand kilometres to the north, just two hours from my home city of Amsterdam?

The murders in Germany seemed irrelevant to my neighbours in the village. Judging by their lack of interest, San Luca might have been as far away as Duisburg. I wanted to know more, but I needed patience because my limited grasp of Italian stood in the way of reading local newspapers or having meaningful conversations. At the same time,

I wasn't worried, either, because none of the people I knew seemed like mob members. They lived simple, unassuming lives.

In fact, nothing in the village seemed ominous to me, except perhaps the refrigerated vehicle that drove up the hill every Saturday, selling ice cream and frozen food – it announced its arrival with an eery music box jingle that reminded me of horror movies. Unlike many of my elderly neighbours who grew their own fruit and vegetables, I had a car and could drive down the hill to buy groceries. For me, there was no work in the area, but I wasn't looking for a job. I could continue doing my editorial work for Dutch clients remotely. Beyond that, I adopted the local custom and minded my own business, or as they say in the vernacular, 'Fare i cazzi tuoi'. That keeps everyone happy.

Calabrians often seem somewhat guarded with strangers, and not without reason. Throughout history, successive conquering invaders, including the Greeks, Romans, Normans, Spaniards and French, have seized power there, to say nothing of the Ottoman Empire and others circling in wait. And so, when building their villages, the Calabrians avoided the coast and headed for the hills, ensuring they could see the enemy approaching from a distance.

Fortunately, my fellow villagers loved, respected and trusted the expat family from whom I rented my cottage. When we were seen together, people associated me with them, so I was greeted warmly, and it wasn't long before I was invited into local residents' homes. Invitations arrived from the doctor, for instance, and his wife, who taught English at a local school. And from the lawyer, whose mother seemed intent on using her cooking talents to keep her son from ever flying the nest. And from the remarkably spry retirees who passed my cottage on their way home from their vegetable gardens or chicken coops, who sometimes gave me a couple of eggs or draped a bag full of crisp lettuce over my doorknob.

I'd never experienced such warm hospitality as in my tiny Calabrian village. At first, I was afraid that living outside the city limits might be boring, but life was far from dull. Before I knew it, I was looking after an entire family of stray dogs, making honey with a local beekeeper and watching my neighbours butchering wild boars with professional skill. Water was readily available from springs in mountains blanketed in clover and brightly coloured wildflowers. Herds of goats ambled along the steep rocky outcrops, and sheep grazed among trees that kept their leaves throughout the year. I hadn't been prepared for such pastoral romanticism. Ndrangheta or no Ndrangheta, I immersed myself in this earthly paradise.

I had been in Calabria for about nine months when, one warm September night, something shook me out of my idyll. The entire street woke up with a start: a car was on fire. Everyone rushed out in their pyjamas to help extinguish the flames. The vehicle belonged to a young woman who worked for the municipality. She seemed shocked, but she said nothing and looked resigned. Neither the fire brigade nor the police were called.

The following day, at her kitchen table, it became clear to me that she had a pretty good idea who had set her car on fire. Everyone who applied for a building permit where she worked was subject to the same regulations. But apparently, some villagers found that unacceptable. They demanded certain privileges, and when they didn't get their way, they threw their weight around, no matter what anyone else thought. I asked my neighbour if she planned to report the arson attack to the police. No, she said, that would only make matters worse. Instead, she was going to look for a different job because she didn't want to work for the municipality any more, knowing she would eventually have to bow to pressure. She didn't mention the suspected perpetrators' names and I didn't press the issue. Instead, I loaned her my car.

Meanwhile, more than a hundred German and Italian detectives had been working on solving the multiple murder case in Duisburg. Some fifteen years earlier, the Italian authorities had warned their German associates that the restaurant – not a humble pizza place, but a classy joint with lobster on the menu – was run by a Calabrian mafia clan. Now, evidence was mounting, in the form, for example, of a scorched prayer card depicting the Archangel Michael, one of the Ndrangheta's patron saints. The card was found in the pocket of one of the victims, Tommaso, a culinary school student doing an internship at the restaurant. He had just turned eighteen that day, and all signs indicated that his boss, Chef Sebastiano, had seized the opportunity to induct Tommaso into the clan after closing time.

As required by the rules of the induction ritual, Tommaso had pricked his finger, allowing a drop of blood to fall onto the prayer card before setting it alight. But he hadn't burned the entire prayer card, just the angel's face. The image was still clear: an angel aiming a sword at a creature that was half human, half dragon, lying prone on some smouldering rocks. The angel's large white wings and long red cape were also visible, starkly contrasting with the clear blue sky and green hills.

Perhaps Tommaso had hoped to keep the card as a memento of the night's events. Once the prayer card had cooled, he had tucked it into his wallet, which he put in his back pocket. At 2am, he left the restaurant with his 39-year-old boss Sebastiano, the boss's 16-year-old nephew and three other men in their twenties: two of the other

Calabrian waiters and Marco, who had just arrived from the home province. Shortly after that, the police discovered the six bodies in a black Volkswagen Golf and a white van, pierced by bullets. Tommaso had been hit fourteen times, including four shots to the head.

It was a German woman who had raised the alarm. She'd passed two men heading towards the restaurant's car park. A short while later, she heard what she thought were fireworks, but when she walked back, she saw the same two men disappearing down an alleyway. Detectives based their search for the killers on her witness statements and footage from security cameras. They knew almost immediately that they were dealing with the Ndrangheta clan of the Nirta and Strangio families because that clan was engaged in a fierce battle with the clan of the Pelle and Vottari families, who happened to run the Da Bruno restaurant. The rival clans had been waging a vendetta in and around San Luca for sixteen years – ever since a carnival night ended with the first lethal shooting, the two clans in Calabria periodically faced off with pistols and Kalashnikovs.

The owner and chef of Da Bruno, Sebastiano Strangio, who despite his name was not a member of the Nirta–Strangio clan, had been unarmed when he left the restaurant with his boys that night. Still, he was well-prepared for the next chapter of the vendetta. In a restaurant storage room, police discovered an automatic weapon loaded with ninety bullets, and a formidable array of other ammunition. No one would have suspected such a thing behind the gleaming facade of the famous restaurant in the Silberpalais, Duisburg's largest office building, near the central train station. According to its website, the Silberpalais was 'an ideal place for national and international companies to do business'.

It transpired that Da Bruno was both the Pelle–Vottari clan's weapons repository and their regular meeting place. A special room had been set up for that purpose; it was a windowless space hidden behind a panel. Some of the servers and, presumably, most of the guests were unaware of the existence of that hidden room. It contained a statue of Archangel Michael and a solid wooden table surrounded by twelve grand chairs; the one at the head of the table had a higher backrest. This was exactly the right kind of setting for solemn rituals like Tommaso's initiation.

It turns out the two shooters from the Nirta–Strangio clan were also fond of symbolism. They may not have been aware that Tommaso had turned eighteen that evening, or that he was being welcomed into the fold. Nevertheless, they had carefully chosen the date of their blood revenge. It was the night of 14–15 August 2007, meaning the sun would rise on the feast day of the Assumption of the Blessed Virgin Mary, a Catholic holiday that, to Italian families, is as important to a feeling of togetherness as Christmas. The killers intended to permanently ruin the day for members of the Pelle–Vottari clan, forever linking it with memories of the bloodbath and the loss of their boys' lives. Just as Christmas would never be the same again for the Nirta–Strangios after the death of Maria Strangio, who was killed on Christmas Day in San Luca by bullets meant for her husband. Did they really believe that Maria's spirit could finally ascend to heaven, now that her death had been avenged by six new souls?

3

A SENSE OF FAMILY

During my first year in Calabria, my most loyal friend was Peppina, a woman in her seventies. She was the salt of the earth. She served coffee in miniature beer steins and her headscarf hid a schoolboy's haircut. And while she no longer washed her clothes by the river, as she'd done for decades, she still drew water from the municipal tap on the street. That's where she seemed at home, partially shaded by the walled fountain, standing under the pious watchful eye of the statue of Mary guarding a niche above the tap.

Her husband Antonio was close to eighty, but he still climbed the hills to his vegetable patch early every morning, carrying a few empty plastic bags and an axe slung over his shoulder. After a few hours, he would return, his bags full.

At least once a week, Peppina would call out to me from the street around noon. Her tone was stern and alarming, but nothing earth-shattering had occurred. She was simply summoning me to their table. 'Come, sit,' she said when I arrived at her door, which opened directly into her comfortable eat-in kitchen. 'It's time for lunch.'

There were also days when Antonio used their landline to call me on my mobile phone and convey a short but urgent message: 'Peppina has made *minestra*.' Minestra wasn't a vegetable soup but a code word for wild chicory with white beans. This simple dish was heavenly in Peppina's hands. To accompany it, Antonio poured his own wine, which was orange and slightly cloudy. Often, he also offered me some slices of their homemade *soppressata* sausage. He usually ended lunch with a hand gesture and a proud gleam in his eyes: '*Perfetto.*' Then, following a tiny beer stein of coffee – complete with a splash of anise liqueur – Antonio dozed on the sofa or next to the woodstove.

After the meal, Peppina would often retrieve pictures of her children and grandchildren from the glass display cabinet. We hadn't known each other very long before the tragic news arrived from Canada that her son had died. He had been seriously ill, and they had recently come back from paying him one last visit. The evening he passed away, neighbours and family gathered silently in a large circle in Peppina and Antonio's kitchen. From then on, Peppina always dressed in a black skirt and a black jumper, with a black scarf covering her short black hair.

Their daughter had also emigrated to Canada in her teens. There wasn't enough work in Calabria, and stories from relatives on the other side of the ocean were hard to resist. A woman now, she returned to Italy every August to spend the summer holiday at her parents' home. Seeing Peppina's daughter so out of place in the village where she was born saddened me. She had become the child of a different world.

Luckily, one of Peppina's two sons had remained in Calabria. When he and his wife and children visited from the provincial capital of Catanzaro, Sunday lunch at Peppina and Antonio's lasted almost the entire day.

Many years earlier, Antonio had also worked in Canada, on a railway line. He asked me to check the monthly letter accompanying his

Canadian pension because he'd never learned to read and write very well. And although Antonio understood Italian, he preferred to speak his Calabrian dialect. Antonio was not much of a talker, but he had a way with words, making him a good teacher. He and Peppina guided me as I made my first steps in the local language.

All of Calabria's conquerors left their linguistic mark on the region's dialect, whether it was Greek or Spanish, French or Germanic. This makes the Calabrian dialect sound almost like Esperanto, with some words taking you on a guided tour of your language memory. My favourites are the onomatopoetic verbs. *Scialarsi*, for example, is pronounced with two long aahs and roughly translates to 'experiencing extended pleasure'. Or *spagnarsi*, to be afraid. *Ti spagni?* means 'Are you afraid?' It sounds familiar to me and is easy to remember, because of the Dutch expression *Spaans benauwd*, which means 'with Spanish fear'. A history of terrifying Spanish rulers is something the Dutch and the Calabrians have in common.

Sometimes, my ability to understand the Calabrian dialect was even more direct. The first time Peppina asked me if I wanted some grated *kasu* on my pasta, I couldn't help beaming. I replied, 'Kasu? *Formaggio*? Like the Dutch word *kaas*, for cheese!'

Otherwise, our meals were mostly consumed in silence. Peppina sometimes grumbled about her neighbours or warned me that not everyone was as trustworthy as she was. When she cursed, saying *cazzo*, I'd repeat the word and ask what it meant. She'd smile slyly and clutch her forehead, half ashamed. *'È parlare, figghia.'* That's just how I talk, my girl, don't take it seriously.

One thing Peppina did take seriously was the evil eye. According to her, jealous glances could leave a person feeling listless and ill. If someone was extremely tired or had a headache, the curse of the evil eye had to be broken with a secret magic spell. She would softly murmur her incantation while making the sign of the cross on my forehead with her thumb. If she started yawning, she said, that meant it was working.

Women from generation to generation were allowed to pass down the ancient chants, but only on high holidays: Christmas, Easter or the feast day of the Assumption of the Blessed Virgin Mary. And so, one Christmas Eve, Peppina taught me her spell. I was honoured that she included me in her family with this and other rituals. I wrote down and carefully saved her esoteric legacy. And if someone were to ask me for the formula, I would remain faithful to the rules of tradition. It would spoil the magic if I revealed more than that the spell is rich in rhyme, rhythm and Catholic figures.

Over the years, as my grasp of Italian improved and I learned more about the local mafia, it became increasingly clear that the Ndrangheta had appropriated crucial aspects of Calabrian culture to suit their needs. In Ndrangheta circles, warm hospitality is twisted to become an oppressive dependency. A sense of reserve leads to *omertà*, the iron-clad code of silence. And the occult is used to guarantee a lifelong blood oath, never to be broken. The extraordinary way the Ndrangheta deals with the central place of the family, especially the pivotal position of the mother, is evident from a telephone call the Italian police tapped on the day of the shocking massacre in Duisburg.

'*Pronto!*' says a young man in San Luca, cheerfully answering his phone. It's a little past noon on Ferragosto, the feast day of the Assumption of the Blessed Virgin Mary, characterized by lavish outdoor family lunches.

'*La mamma è jocu?*' asks the young man on the other end of the line, using the Calabrian dialect. He's calling from Duisburg. 'Is Mamma there?' His voice is shaking.

'No. What's happened?' asks the young man in San Luca.

'Spread the word,' the other one says through tears. 'My brother is dead, my nephew, your brother, all of them are dead . . .'

On first hearing, there's nothing remarkable about what the police overheard during this conversation, except, of course, for the sad news. You'd easily be forgiven for thinking that *La mamma* was the mother. But with the Ndrangheta, things aren't always straightforward. In this case, 'La Mamma' referred to Antonio Pelle, the boss of these two young men and the leader of the Pelle–Vottari clan. He had to be the first to be told which of his men had died that night in the clash with the hostile Nirta–Strangio clan, even before the victims' own flesh and blood mothers.

The Ndrangheta's coded language is rich in metaphors. Religious terms are used to gently disguise criminal traditions. For example, a new member's initiation is called a 'baptism'. You must be at least fourteen to undergo such a baptism, complete with a few drops of blood on a prayer card. However, boys born into traditional Ndrangheta families already have a title even before their baptism ritual. With a Ndranghetist father, you automatically become a *giovane d'onore*, a 'young man of honour'. That's your birthright, or rather, your birth duty.

For daughters, there are no such hereditary titles. Women can play an essential role behind the scenes for the clans, but they cannot undergo a Ndrangheta initiation. The only honorary title they can hope to achieve is the relatively passive-sounding *sorella d'omertà*, or silent sister. Many daughters of Ndrangheta families are married off within the clan or to someone from a different clan if that's better for business, and women fulfil the clan's expectations by having children and raising them to live by the Ndrangheta's moral code.

During their Ndrangheta initiation, young men pledge to hold the clan's interests above those of their parents, brothers or sisters. 'From now on, you are my family,' they swear. 'The punishment for making a mistake is death.'

Whether inborn or cultivated, this sense of family lies behind the Ndrangheta's success. You don't betray your family – especially when you know a death sentence is hanging over your head.

Among the first things I heard from Calabrian friends and aquaintances about the Ndrangheta's crimes were accounts of the horrific kidnappings they had carried out in the 1970s and '80s, some of the longest abductions in Italian history. The area around the imposing Aspromonte mountains in the hinterlands of San Luca was notorious for its huts and underground bunkers, where one kidnapped victim after the other was held in chains, sometimes for years. Victims were regularly moved from place to place, but when the police came looking, no one would admit to having seen anything. That's because San Luca and other nearby villages with only a few thousand inhabitants have historically been the home of several long-established Ndrangheta families. By violently enforcing their fellow villagers' code of silence and obedience, those families, working with neighbouring clans, could successfully carry out mind-boggling criminal operations.

Cesare Casella was the 18-year-old son of a wealthy car dealer. He was kidnapped in the northern Italian city of Pavia in the late 1980s and held captive in Calabria for more than two years. The kidnappers initially demanded eight billion lire – roughly four million euros – for Cesare's release, but his parents did not have that kind of money. In desperation, Cesare's mother paid two visits to San Luca. On her first trip, she asked the village priest to plea for her son's release during mass. The second time, she appealed directly to the women of San Luca and begged them to help. She walked around in chains and slept in a tent on the village square to draw attention to her son's plight. After 743 days, the family paid one billion lire (500,000 euros) and Cesare was finally released.

The 17-year-old grandson of oil magnate John Paul Getty was also kidnapped by a group of Ndrangheta clans working together. Getty, one of the world's wealthiest men, showed less compassion than Cesare's mother. Ultimately, the kidnappers received about a tenth of the seventeen million dollars they demanded. Thanks to Getty's hard-handed negotiating techniques, his grandson Paul waited five months for his release. He was subjected to additional mistreatment when a large chunk of his right ear was hacked off. It's little wonder that for the rest of his brief life, Paul was addicted to alcohol and drugs.

Ironically, Ndrangheta clans used their ill-gotten millions to invest in drug trafficking. They became the largest importers of cocaine on the Western market. That's how members of the Ndrangheta stealthily conquered the world: by transforming themselves from furtive masters of kidnapping to closed-lipped masters of the narcotics trade.

Keeping quiet is as highly valued when dealing with the outside world as it is within the Ndrangheta itself. During large-scale and complex operations, including international drug trafficking, various clans must collaborate and share certain information. But as a rule, individual clans work independently and operate within their territory. A clan – or *ndrina*, the Pelle–Vottari clan being just one example – is usually named after a family or group of families who have collaborated for an extended period and may be connected through marriage. These clans are formed by fathers, grandfathers, sons, grandsons, brothers and male cousins, supplemented by those who marry into the family: strategically chosen sons-in-law and brothers-in-law.

The longer someone is involved, the more power and responsibilities that person acquires. A rank within the pecking order is called *dote*, an Italian word meaning both dowry and talent. And while higher echelon Ndranghetists know the status of clan members below them, the converse only applies to a limited extent. This way, members lower down the ladder don't know who exactly has the most power, and that limits the risk of betrayal or a coup.

Rites are associated with every rung of the ladder, each having a specific playbook and elaborate incantations. No one is allowed to write down these Ndrangheta spells, so members must memorize them, and higher-ups pass them down as needed to newcomers. Strangely, detectives have found many pages of handwritten codes of conduct and rituals in barns and villas, and also in bunkers that had been used by fugitives. There are pictures of these written descriptions in some of the books about the Calabrian mafia that fill my bookcase. The barely legible handwriting of these rituals and spells is often riddled with spelling errors. A few have been patiently chronicled in secret code, lending the incantations a peculiar air of composure and serenity.

The ground rules are the same for all the clans. A member of the Ndrangheta swears allegiance to his own clan family and to the board of supreme leaders. The leaders of the most powerful clans from the province of Reggio Calabria, on the southernmost tip of Calabria, are all members of that board, which is called *la Provincia,* or the Province. A surprisingly transparent other name for this executive board is *il Crimine*, or the Crime. A committee meets annually near San Luca to elect the board of leaders who will, for the coming year, decide on matters affecting the entire criminal organization. For instance, a clan needs permission from la Provincia, the provincial executive branch, to claim a particular territory, even if that clan operates in another part of Calabria, Italy or the world. In short, all the family lines are connected by an umbilical cord leading to the province of Reggio Calabria and the Ndrangheta's ceremonial birthplace, San Luca. Hence, Ndranghetists worldwide refer to the headquarters in San Luca as *la mamma*, and the chief of the provincial executive board is sometimes called *mammasantissima*, or most sacred mother.

Could the Ndrangheta be using these metaphoric mother figures to soften its image among its members? An intriguing idea – so many armed men with one mother who gave birth to them and nurtures them, who punishes them when they disobey, but who also comforts her sons and brings them together.

Unsurprisingly, the most important traditional venue for Ndrangheta gatherings is near San Luca, in the Sanctuary of the Madonna of Polsi. There, a statue of one of their most valued patron saint, the Madonna della Montagna, is a tangible symbolic mother to every member of the Ndrangheta. The Madonna is found in a church in a remote valley deep within the Aspromonte mountains. She wears a pale pink gown, a light blue veil and a large golden crown. The naked baby Jesus sits on her lap; he also wears a large crown and plays with a golden orb. Replicas of the statue can be found everywhere Ndranghetists live, work, hide or gather, including in secluded Calabrian farmhouses or in bunkers hidden beneath luxurious villas. The image was also on display in the Da Bruno restaurant dining room in Duisburg, a port city in one of Europe's busiest industrial areas.

In Polsi, at the sanctuary of the Madonna of the Mountain, leading members of the Ndrangheta gathered to discuss the blood feud in Duisburg, which had suddenly thrust the Calabrian mafia into the European spotlight. Criminal organizations thrive in the shadows, so the situation had to be diffused quickly. At the Sanctuary of the Madonna of Polsi, less than two weeks after the nearby burial of the six murder victims, the vendetta between the families from San Luca, which had gone on for more than sixteen years, was miraculously called to a halt. The Calabrian police overheard one of the Ndrangheta leaders enthusiastically report, 'Everyone was dancing and shaking hands. The friendship has been restored.' Since the reconciliation of those two warring clans from San Luca, business for the Ndrangheta has only improved.

4

'ARE YOU GOING TO WRITE THAT IN THE NEWSPAPER?'

Hardly anything had yet been written about the Ndrangheta in the Dutch press when one of Europe's most wanted fugitives was found in the Netherlands. Giovanni Strangio, from San Luca, was a suspect in the massacre that had occurred nineteen months earlier in Duisburg, Germany. At the time of his arrest, he was living with his wife and three-year-old son in a small apartment in Diemen, just outside Amsterdam. Strangio's brother-in-law, another fugitive who had been convicted of cocaine trafficking and membership of the Ndrangheta in the late 1990s, was staying with them. When they searched the house, police found three fake passports, a bulletproof vest, three wigs, eleven mobile phones, a money-counting machine and half a million euros in cash. A loaded pistol was hidden in a shoe rack by the front door.

At the time of the arrest, I had been living in Calabria for more than two years. I no longer had a home in Amsterdam to return to; the apartment building where I rented the top floor had been sold to some property developers hoping to make a quick buck. They'd had their eye on the building for some time. They wanted to split it up, renovate it and flip it for profit. But I didn't want to leave. The apartment was lovely, and I had a long-term lease, in sharp contrast to the endless stream of temporary digs I'd occupied during my student years. I held on until I was the only remaining tenant in that large building in the De Pijp neighbourhood. Visits from the slick, scooter-riding property developers became more frequent until they finally offered me a healthy sum to soften the inconvenience of forced relocation. I saw it as a golden opportunity to kick start the foreign adventure I had dreamed of. In hindsight, my journey could easily have led me to Brazil or Japan. But by chance, it took me to Italy's deep south – a place I found so fascinating I wanted to stay forever. Of course, I could have stayed in Amsterdam and blown my moving bonus on another temporary rental. However, I decided to use the money for something different. Because in Calabria, I could buy a house of my own with endless views of the Ionian Sea.

The charming village where I bought a house lies spread across three hills at an elevation of roughly a thousand feet. The sea is a short drive away, and the newer part of the village lies along the coastal road, where most of the approximately two thousand inhabitants live. Higher up the hills in the older town centre are a couple of small grocery stores and cafés. There is also a primary school, a monastery, a retirement home and a tiny but lively pizzeria run by a friendly owner.

I love the quiet around my house. The contrast, therefore, is even greater on high days and holidays, with processions and bursts of fireworks, when church bells peel much longer and more merrily than usual. Brass bands echo through the alleyways, audible in every corner of the village. The organizers of these traditional Calabrian celebrations like to go overboard: church bells, a brass band and fireworks, all at once, in the middle of the day. It's all about the commotion, since nothing can be seen of the fireworks, except for a few wisps of smoke in the sunny sky.

On other days, the slow, mournful tones of funeral bells ring out. The average age of the village's inhabitants is relatively high; I try not to think about what that means for the future. The town has a good internet connection. I tell myself that a younger generation of Italians and foreigners will, like me, one day discover that this region is a beautiful place to work from home.

Despite the village's dwindling population, it still makes a prosperous impression. So, of course, I couldn't help wondering if any of my fellow villagers belonged to the mafia. One thing was clear: nobody would volunteer that type of information. What I did know, however, was that there wasn't any evidence of a permanent Ndrangheta base in the village, which meant it didn't fall under specific families' traditional sphere of influence. All I could do was trust my intuition and avoid suspicious characters or those who looked like bullies.

I'm lucky the village has so many builders and contractors because the house I bought is a fixer-upper. The windows need repairs, the pipes and flooring need replacing and the roof needs patching. Of all the places for sale, mine certainly didn't have the most kerb appeal. Maybe that's what attracted me to the place: the outside wasn't pretentious, but inside, it contained a cosy labyrinth of interconnected rooms, and all the windows offered a spectacular view of the coast. The previous occupants, a carpenter and his wife, had lived there into their eighties. They had painted the walls in various hues and covered them with family photographs.

Once, the neighbours told me, each of these small rooms had housed an entire family – some even kept a pig – and the village's alleyways were forever bustling with children and busy workshops, but that was many decades ago, before masses of Calabrians had left for northern Italy, Germany, America and Australia. My cantina, the 'cellar' on the ground floor, still contained the dusty remnants of all that long-ago activity, quite hard to imagine now: everything you need to produce homemade wine, plus all kinds of painting supplies and, of course, a collection of lumber and tools. There were nails in every shape and size and a couple of iron crucifixes. There's no avoiding it: here, the previous occupant had built cupboards, tables and beds – and also coffins.

By now, almost all the craftsmen have left the village. This region on the Ionian coast of Calabria is clearly pinning its economic hopes on tourism. For two months every year, the area transforms from an out-of-the-way refuge into a popular holiday destination. At the end of June, beach pavilions, parasols and lounge chairs suddenly appear, only to disappear again when the holidaymakers flee on the first weekend of September. Hardly any tourists come from outside Italy. Apart from Calabrian accents, you can mostly hear Milanese and Roman accents at the seaside in July and August. These Calabrians have 'emigrated' to other parts of Italy, and every summer they return with their children to the sun-dappled sea of their youth.

On the streets, people seemed gratified when they heard that I had decided to move to their village; I plan to stay year-round and not just visit from the distant north for the summer. I say hello to all the new faces and usually receive a friendly greeting in return. Calabria has the highest unemployment figures in Europe, so many Calabrians around my age still live with their parents. That's if they haven't followed their classmates and gone to look for work up north. News about me travels fast: everyone knows I live alone and work for a living. *Poverina, lavora al computer* – the poor girl works at a computer, I overhear one neighbour telling another.

I am the first Dutch person to live in my village. When I register my residency at the municipality, the woman at the counter asks what I do for a living. At a loss for words, I say I mostly do freelance text work, editing books and articles, and sometimes translating from English into Dutch. Translator? Not really. I consider using *editrice*, but that's ambiguous – much closer to publishing than editing. Then the woman at the counter pronounces decisively, *giornalista*. Journalist. The label feels slightly uncomfortable, but people are waiting behind me, and it doesn't seem worth taking up more of their time. I agree.

Italians love titles, and they enjoy cheerful greetings like *maestro!*, *dottore!* or *avvocato!* It's their way of acknowledging the other person's status and showing respect. My fellow citizens must have easy access to the municipality's administrative system because soon everyone seems to know about my somewhat uncomfortable professional title, *giornalista*. Fortunately, no one addresses me as such, but some people approach me of their own accord with their stories. That can lead to some extraordinary conversations, like the ones I had with Totò, a man in his late forties. He had been in a car accident, after which he spent a long time in a coma. Ever since waking up, he has talked about nothing but God.

Totò enjoys preaching on the streets, in the village square. He's a much livelier ambassador of the faith than the dreary local priest. To judge by the strait-laced priest's tone of voice, whether it's a funeral or a high holiday, it always feels like doomsday is just around the corner. With his fire and brimstone sermons, I am astonished that he attracts such a loyal daily following among the over-fifty female population. However, attendance may be boosted by the lure of four friendly nuns from the Philippines and India who help keep the monumental village monastery running.

Totò, in his unique, disarming style, likes to call me 'Sa' for short.

After we'd run into each other a few times, he started belting hymns at the top of his lungs every time he saw me. Bystanders chuckled, but I found his honesty refreshing.

'Sa, I am like a child. God made me a child again. When I was in a coma, I saw Him. All the saints were there, and my grandparents, too. Do you see that sunbeam? That is God. Do you believe in God, Sa?'

I don't want to burst his bubble, and his sunbeam appeals to me, so I nod. 'You have to pray and follow the Ten Commandments. Are you going to write about what happened to me in the newspaper, Sa? The world can't see it, but the light of the world is God. Are you going to write that in the newspaper?'

I don't know if such upsetting events would ever have penetrated Totò's radiant cognitive world, but suddenly, there was news of a mafia killing that had taken place on a nearby street. A 34-year-old man was shot dead in front of his house in the newer part of the village, down along the coast. He had just parked his BMW when two masked men opened fire. I didn't know him personally. The paper said that his uncle – who had been killed a few weeks earlier by two helmeted men on a scooter – was the leader of the Ndrangheta clan in the next village. No other information about the boss was forthcoming, except that his official profession was 'contractor'.

5

DIGNITY

If contractors could be mafia bosses, could some of the builders I saw driving their rusty pickup trucks through the village also be connected? Who could I confidently allow to work on my house, and who should I try to avoid? After a lot of hemming and hawing, it seemed best to hire an independent bricklayer, electrician and plumber.

People warned me that renovating my house with independent tradespeople would be slower and less efficient than working with one of the larger building firms that arrange everything at once, and they were right. However, the larger firms were intimidating, even without their suspected connection to the clans. I wouldn't say I liked the idea of my quirky, slanty-walled house being turned into an over-restored designer showplace. This was my first chance to renovate an old house, and I wanted to restore it step by step, with input from the professionals I had hired.

I hadn't anticipated that allowing several self-employed tradesmen to work together would go against the grain of certain expectations. Because even the independent bricklayers behaved like contractors, assuming they could bring along a friend who was a plumber or an electrician. And the plumber and electrician thought they could do the same. They all wanted to escort me to a buddy's bathroom supply store or give me the number of a cousin who happened to be a plasterer or tiler. I had hired these tradespeople independently, so they had never worked together before, and they found the situation awkward, to say the least. I quickly realized that professional life in Calabria revolves around quid pro quo. If no favours are exchanged, a job is deemed to be a lot less prestigious.

In hindsight, my renovation would have provided excellent material for a comic reality show, because everyone wanted to be in charge. And although it was my house and I was the one footing the bill, as a woman – and a foreigner to boot – I was the last person those gentlemen expected to behave like a project manager. So, instead, they fervently slagged off each other's work, hoping to prove their skills were the best.

I tried to understand that their pride was at stake. With my naïve Dutch faith in cooperation and consensus-building, I endeavoured to foster team spirit by photographing the entire crew. But that only made matters worse. They looked so despondently into the lens that from that day forward, I decided to have the men come to the house one at a time, to keep them from giving each other dirty looks or worse. That way, each, in turn, could feel like the lord and master of the renovation. And although it took much longer than it should have, I am happy with the results.

While the renovation progressed at a snail's pace, I stumbled across another contrast between the mindset in the Netherlands and that in southern Italy. As a woman alone in a Calabrian village, I would be asked: *A cui appartieni*? To whom do you belong? The question wasn't always expressed in so many words, but you could usually feel the subtext hanging in the air. Because here a single woman is an anomaly that evokes pity or suspicion. In rural Calabria, a woman is expected to remain in her parents' home until marriage. She 'belongs' to her parents, to her spouse or to her children. Here, the concept of belonging to no one is viewed as typical of northern individualists, who underestimate the importance of the family.

When I fell in love with N, a young Calabrian man, I no longer had to walk the streets alone and was spared all those pitying glances. N was from Soverato, a more worldly and modern town on the same coast as my village. He had worked abroad and in northern Italy but had returned because he missed Calabria. Life with N was happier and more relaxed, so I turned a blind eye to his Calabrian pride, stubbornness and machismo. Of course, it helped that he didn't expect me to play a traditional role. At least not in the kitchen, because the meals he prepared for me were out of this world.

It was with N that I started attending public meetings about the Ndrangheta. We had to drive a long way to the meetings, which were usually held near Cosenza, the largest Calabrian college town. It was a breath of fresh air to hear people talking openly – and into a microphone – about a subject that was never mentioned in my village. I learned about the Calabrian mafia's past and current activities. Some of the speakers had been victims of extortion and had risked their lives by becoming whistle-blowers. They showed incredible dignity and inspired me to start writing about the Ndrangheta. One man whose story I found especially moving was Gaetano Saffioti, an entrepreneur specializing in concrete products and excavation works. I visited him again some years later.

Gaetano Saffioti is a bear of a man. He has a slight paunch, a dark beard, a bulbous nose and gentle eyes. He's in his fifties, but when he talks about his diggers – a few are parked on his business premises – his eyes light up like a child's. 'When I look at them, it feels like they're smiling at me.'

Saffioti grew up surrounded by tractors; his father worked in agriculture, and by the time Gaetano was eight, he was hooked. As a teenager, he'd become so obsessed with these vehicles that his friends teased him, calling them his girlfriends. 'I talked to the machines, cleaned them, and looked after them lovingly.'

Of course, Gaetano Saffioti was aware that he lived in an area run by extremely violent families. Palmi was a city on the southern tip of the Tyrrhenian coast; it had been the domain of those 'men of honour' for over a century. Everyone – including Saffioti – knew who those families were. But he didn't know that those families were also putting pressure on his father. When their olive mill caught fire one day, a 'short circuit' was blamed. And when Gaetano went on his first school trip, his father suddenly appeared and asked him to come home, saying that he missed him too much. It wasn't until after the good man had passed away far too soon, due to an illness, that Gaetano learned these strange incidents were linked to extortion and intimidation. He was fifteen, his older brother nineteen, and the youngest of the four younger siblings was still an infant. His mother was in tears, waiting beside the telephone, which never stopped ringing. Finally, she admitted, 'It's the Ndrangheta. They want money.'

Gaetano Saffioti had never heard that name. 'The Ndrangheta, what's that? A business? A person?' In the 1970s, it wasn't widely known that all those families everyone had to bow down to were also referred to as 'Ndrangheta'. His mother explained that their father had long been extorted for *pizzo,* or protection money. Moreover, the extortionists had committed arson and were threatening to harm Gaetano and his brothers and sisters – which is why he'd been abruptly dragged away from that primary school trip. And after his father died, they had continued badgering his mother, a widow with six children.

'Why didn't we go to the police back then?' Saffioti wonders aloud. 'The police avoided confronting members of the Ndrangheta because the risks were too high: around here, they slaughtered each other. Every day, we woke up knowing something bad would happen, but not who would be killed or where the next bomb would go off. Above all, most people were convinced that you just had to pay, that it was part of the deal. We lived and worked in their territory, and they made the rules.'

Saffioti took odd jobs with his tractor until he was called up for military service when he was eighteen. He was eligible for a paid position in Palmi, his hometown, in the local high-security prison. No one else wanted to be a guard there; the facility housed the most dangerous criminals, including many local Ndrangheta bosses. But he decided to take the job and act as if he didn't recognize them.

When Saffioti turned nineteen, his term of service ended, and he started his own company. 'Ploughing earth with the tractor; the work doesn't pay well, but I enjoyed it. However, there were places where I wasn't allowed to work because even then, the clans had control over other people's land. They said, you can work here, but not there.' Nevertheless, Gaetano Saffioti's company flourished. He acquired excavators, trucks, bulldozers and concrete mixers, and took on more and more employees. 'If you love your work, success comes naturally.'

Unfortunately, in Calabria, more profits lead to increased obstacles. Saffioti received anonymous letters and phone calls detailing how to hand over money, and how much. 'Dearest Gaetano, you must help us. If you refuse or if you warn the police, you'll be in even bigger trouble. Come to the fountain on 29 April at precisely midnight with thirty million lire in small denominations. Take the stairs leading down to the beach. Carry the money in a sturdy plastic bag in your right hand. There will be someone you can hand the bag to without fear. If you don't show up, we'll come and get you and tie you up in a dark place, and we'll make sure you starve to death, all alone. So think it over carefully.'

Saffioti was forced to tear up invoices for some of his most lucrative contracts. He knew he wouldn't be paid because friends of well-known families expected him to cut them a deal. And he'd almost grown used to the obligatory harassments, like coming home to find that vandals had squeezed glue into his door locks. 'Sometimes, a guy would show up, acting like a friend, offering to clean up the mess. You had to pay those guys, and they pretended they'd done you a big favour, but they'd caused the damage in the first place, you know?'

They often threatened to kill him or his little son, or to torch the place. 'When they set one of my machines on fire, I went to the police. But the officers told me I'd be better off keeping my mouth shut. That doesn't necessarily mean the police were corrupt; maybe they genuinely meant it for my own good. They knew that my problems would only multiply if I spoke up. Nevertheless, I pressed charges. But nothing came of it.'

Gaetano Saffioti tried to persuade other entrepreneurs to join him in standing up to the Ndrangheta. 'They told me I was out of my mind, and were afraid we'd all be killed.' He gradually made his peace with the status quo, and despite everything, his company grew. He won large contracts, constructing motorways and ports, and that brought him into contact with more and more Ndrangheta families from the surrounding area. Several clans held power over the Tyrrhenian coast. Sometimes, Saffioti had to pay *pizzo* three times for the same contract: first to a family in Palmi, where his company was based, then to a clan ruling the area he had to drive through and finally to the clan in the municipality where he carried out the work.

In the 1990s, Saffioti's passion for heavy machinery led to an appearance on an Italian television show dedicated to stunts and competitions. During the programme, a small fork was attached to the end of Saffioti's digger. He was challenged to pick up three olives from a small dish and eat them individually while sitting in the open driver's cab. 'That was the first time I'd ever done anything like that!' He succeeded and even used the mechanical arm to neatly put one of the olive pits back on the dish within the allotted time. And while he enjoyed being in the spotlight for a night, the next day, it was back to business as usual.

Unfortunately, the extortion continued, year after year. Saffioti noticed that, with time, the Ndranghetists were growing increasingly arrogant. They tended to be young men, the boss's errand boys. 'They didn't try to disguise what they were doing and dropped in without an excuse, to collect the money. As if no one could touch them.'

They didn't shy away from committing arson in broad daylight. 'They forced one of my employees at gunpoint to pour gasoline over a truck and hold a lighter to it.'

That was in 2000, when Saffioti was almost forty, and his patience had run out. The provocations had also started coming from the authorities. On local television, one public prosecutor had labelled all Calabrian entrepreneurs 'cowards' and even 'accessories to the mafia'. That was enough to make anyone bitter, or drive them to desperation, because the Ndrangheta clans had started to refine their extortion techniques. As a victim, Saffioti ran a genuine risk of being arrested, for instance, as a straw man or cover. 'The extortionists wanted to register some properties in my name to keep them out of the prosecutor's hands. But I managed to wriggle out of that. I said, Let's not go there. My business could go bankrupt, and everything would be confiscated or sold at auction. After that, they were stupid enough to register things in the names of people who had nothing. Like a schoolteacher who, on paper, supposedly owned a building worth a million euros. Or an unemployed person with a hotel! The prosecutors got wind of the scam, and now the clans have stopped doing it. These days, they take over your company.'

They wanted to create a monopoly by investing in Saffioti's business. 'I was an ideal candidate because I had no criminal record and was a successful entrepreneur. When I refused, they said I was nuts. "There are people who beg us for this kind of deal." In retaliation, they forced employees on me – I had to pay people who never showed up. Or I had to buy their choice of building supplies: I owned a quarry but was forced to buy my stone from a different one.'

Saffioti's only option was to patiently gather evidence of the things he resisted and all the things he couldn't refuse. His extortionists believed they were untouchable; they sometimes looked directly into his office security cameras while counting their pay-off. Did they assume he would never dare to use those images?

In a wry twist, one of his extortionists was a former employee who had resigned. 'Sometime later, he dropped in when I was expecting a representative from the clans. I was happy to see him because I'd always liked him. We chatted, and I told him I was waiting for someone. He said he was the one who had been sent to collect the money. Stunned, I tried to open his eyes. "Don't you realize what you're doing? You've backed the wrong horse. You're facing a sad, violent future." But he said it was the life he wanted. He didn't have to get up early or work hard. He didn't have to pay for drinks at the bar, and girls were lining up, waiting to go out with him . . . When I told him that sooner or later, he'd end up in jail, he said, "Prison is where you become a real man. That's where you get to know the real men." They'd brainwashed him.'

Other confrontations could have cost him his life. 'A few times, they brought me to see bosses who were in hiding. There was no need, because they could easily have passed any orders from these fugitive leaders on to me, but no. They take you to see someone like that in person because they want to show you how worthless you are; your existence is in his hands. I bought a special micro-cassette recorder to document these encounters. You could record thirty minutes on each side of those little cassettes. It was the most discreet option before the days of digital devices.'

During these meetings, Saffioti would hide the tape recorder in the chest pocket of his shirt, and he'd wear a fisherman's vest on top. 'If they'd ever found it, I would've been dead. One time, it was touch and go. I looked at my watch and noticed the half-hour was almost up; the cassette was about to run out. I knew that when it did, it would stop with a loud click that everyone would hear, but I couldn't turn off the recorder without attracting too much attention. The fugitive boss of the most powerful family from Palmi was facing me, holding a weapon on his lap. I was so close I could read the word "Kalashnikov" on the barrel. Luckily, we were in the countryside, surrounded by olive trees. Dry branches were scattered all around. I started pacing nervously, breaking twigs with my feet. I hoped it would be enough to mask the click from the tape recorder and that I would take the decisive step at just the right moment. By some miracle, it worked.'

In 2001, Gaetano Saffioti walked into the Palace of Justice in Reggio Calabria carrying a box full of evidence. His first words to the public prosecutor were, 'I'm not a coward.' The prosecutor couldn't believe his eyes: hard evidence of systemic extortion and other crimes carried out by eight different Ndrangheta families from ten different cities, handed over on a silver platter.

Saffioti was aware of the fact that a handful of arrests would not solve the problem, because when one goes to prison, another carries on in his place. 'So, we decided to go big. We had to prove that the state runs the show here, not the Ndrangheta.' A legal investigation was opened. 'The prosecutor said we couldn't meet at the courthouse any more because the walls had ears . . . and that was later confirmed. The investigation was fully underway when they found a leak, and everyone had to be arrested earlier than planned.'

First, Saffioti met clandestinely with investigators for a year to clarify details and collect even more evidence. He had to wear a disguise for the meetings, and the magistrates and detectives were in plain clothes and drove regular cars. They met on remote mountain roads or, in the winter, near the beach at night. 'I had to laugh because we ran into some amorous couples in the car park near the beach one night. One of the cars turned on its high beams to see who was pulling in. The policeman I was with said, "If he recognizes you, he's going to tell everyone in town that you're cheating on your wife!"'

Saffioti's wife knew nothing; he hadn't told her about his plans or activities. 'I didn't want to saddle her with it, and what's more, I knew she would ask me to stop because she was afraid. But I hoped she would understand that everything I did was also for her and my son.'

In fact, Saffioti's wife didn't discover what her husband had been up to until the day of the arrests, 25 January 2002. Forty-eight Ndranghetists from Palmi and the surrounding areas were rounded up in the small hours. 'That morning was earth-shattering, apocalyptic,' Saffioti said. 'The silence was deafening. My employees didn't show up. There were no cars on the roads; people were expecting a shoot-out. Even the birds were quiet.'

The only visitors to the premises of Saffioti's home and work were sitting in a car with tinted windows. They were the bodyguards who would keep him, his wife and their 12-year-old son under 24-hour guard from that day forward.

Meanwhile, his clients started phoning the office, telling him not to bother showing up any more. 'They didn't want to risk being associated with me. "Otherwise, we'll be in trouble," they said. Or they gave some other lame excuse.'

At noon, Saffioti turned on the television to watch the news. 'The presenter described the arrests. "Thanks to the bravery of businessman Gaetano Saffioti . . ." The public prosecutors had promised me they wouldn't release my name, but they hadn't managed to keep it out of the press. My wife shouted: "That's impossible, there must be some mistake!" But no one in the world has the same name as me. She cried when she saw the names of all the families that had been arrested, each more notorious than the next. I patiently explained everything to her: the protection programme and my motivation. I told her there was a deeper reason behind my accusations, that I wanted to prove it's possible to stand up to them.'

The Italian authorities offer witnesses like Gaetano Saffioti a new identity and a chance to relocate and receive a monthly stipend. That's hardly an excessive luxury when you receive letters that say things like, 'Before you know it, you'll be hit by forty-five bullets. You will disappear. Not only from Palmi but from the face of the earth.' Saffioti showed me the letter, laughing at the words scrawled across the page. 'It's a message, meaning: one bullet for every arrest. But three of the forty-eight are missing! Maybe this guy wasn't friends with those other three.' Despite the constant threats, Saffioti remained in his home and near his business in Palmi, Calabria. He wanted to show there was an alternative, to prove you could continue living and working in Calabria without being held down by the Ndrangheta.

It soon became clear he'd been too optimistic. His turnover plummeted to a tenth of what he'd made previously. He went from sixty employees to five. No one would hire him in Calabria, and he also ran up against Ndrangheta clans in northern Italy, where they continued to harass him. One night in Tuscany, seven of his machines went up in flames. And when he sought respite elsewhere in Europe, he discovered that wasn't safe, either. 'In France, we worked on a length of track for the TGV and on a runway for Charles de Gaulle airport. The clans approached my employees and said, "Remember when one of your co-workers was forced to set a truck on fire? That could happen here, too." The construction companies that worked with me were told it would be better if they stopped.' He also faced threats from the Ndrangheta in Spain and Germany.

And so, to ensure his business could grow again, Saffioti had to search for countries where Ndrangheta clans hadn't yet established a base. 'I didn't see them in Tunisia or the United Arab Emirates. Maybe they do business there in other fields, like money laundering. But they let people get on with their work. And that's something.'

By now, Saffioti is proud to employ hundreds of people worldwide. But his eyes tell another story: back in Calabria, he's still haunted by social and economic isolation. 'The security guards here are expensive. To the government, I represent a bitter defeat. They're embarrassed because a citizen of a democratic European country has to live like this. It proves that the state is weaker than the Ndrangheta. But the Ndrangheta hasn't laid a finger on me, because that would attract too much attention. What they do instead is worse: they marginalize people. They spread the word that I'm the one who has misbehaved. People no longer drop in or invite me anywhere. At the bank, they said, "You can't offer us enough guarantees, so we're closing your account." With that, they're doing the Ndrangheta a favour. People always used to ask me to sponsor religious processions. I used to support sports clubs and village festivals. But after I became a state witness, people stopped asking. The municipality and the province scratched me off their list of trusted companies, the ones they call for emergency repairs. Even when I offered to work for free, they never contacted me.' After the earthquake in Amatrice, Saffioti went to the disaster area in the middle of Italy, offering to clear away rubble for free. He was turned down, with the excuse that he would be taking work away from others.

He did take on one job, pro bono and with glee: to demolish a villa belonging to the Pesces, the most notorious Ndrangheta family from the neighbouring city of Rosarno. 'The villa had been built illegally on a plot that belonged to someone else, and there were archaeological artefacts on the site too. But nobody dared get rid of that villa. Even the army refused. Or rather, they gave the municipality a ridiculously high quote to show their lack of interest.' When tearing down this Ndrangheta memorial, Saffioti himself sat at the wheel of the bulldozer.

Gaetano Saffioti went on to testify in four other major legal investigations following that first case, and he hasn't stopped yet. Thanks to his evidence, countless Ndranghetists have been arrested, seven mafia-owned businesses have been shut down and 150 million euros have been seized. However, Saffioti has never seen a penny of the 2.8 million euros he was forced to pay the Ndrangheta during the twenty-two years of his extortion. 'That was never my motivation. But I do think the government should make it possible for me to work here and serve as an example. Because I do my work well, follow the rules, and pay my employees what they are entitled to.'

Although some of Saffioti's employees initially quit out of fear, many eventually returned. 'Not because they were brave. They had seen that the outside world was different. I wasn't doing anything special, but in this context, I did something extraordinary: I paid them every month. I paid overtime and holiday pay – normal things that are unusual here. So, my employees said, OK, he's an outcast, but at least he pays our wages. With other companies, they were paid poorly or nothing at all, or they were paid under the table. That's why they came back.'

The premises of Gaetano Saffioti's company are near the four-lane motorway along the Tyrrhenian coast. This road offers breathtaking views of the glittering sea and the countryside's vibrant green hills. But it also has a bad reputation due to ongoing repairs. The roadworks sometimes made headlines as far away as the UK or the US because billions of euros in European subsidies have disappeared here into a seemingly bottomless mafia pit. It took nineteen years to broaden and modernize a scant hundred kilometres of motorway.

The repairs to the road began before Saffioti had brought charges against his extortionists. According to Saffioti – and several verdicts support his hypothesis – the roadworks were carried out by mafia-linked construction companies. Saffioti asserts large-scale fraud was carried out through skimping on materials, for example, or using substandard products. The primary contractor for the job was Impregilo, a company originally from northern Italy responsible for constructing motorways, dams, harbours and airports worldwide. It also has an office in Amsterdam's Zuidas financial hub. As a primary contractor, Impregilo included an extra three per cent under the heading 'security' or 'environmental tax' in their estimate. That's a euphemism for *pizzo*, the protection money they would be expected to pay the Ndrangheta. And it's in writing.

Saffioti thinks that's outrageous. Moreover, he's not convinced the company actually had to surrender three per cent, as they subcontracted the work to companies that were linked to local clans. 'Impregilo didn't shift a single grain of sand themselves; they let subcontractors do all the work. One of them even hired me for a job. At a certain point, he wanted to know who was backing me. I told him that nobody was backing me, that I opposed that sort of thing. He tore up the contract and said, "You can't give me any guarantees." I said there wasn't a problem and that I would cover the expense of any possible damage. He said, "We only want to work with the *amici*, the friends, because they know how to turn a blind eye." '

A verdict from the Calabrian court states that Impregilo 'had a thorough understanding of the Calabrian mafia's working methods' and had asked an engineer who had made 'agreements with the Ndrangheta' to distribute the subcontracts. The engineer didn't face any legal consequences, although the Ndranghetists with whom he made the deals were convicted. According to Gaetano Saffioti, 'Impregilo is a mafia-type company that has been legalized.'

The walls of the office where Saffioti once filmed his extortionists are now lined with awards: framed tributes to his resistance. The excavators and bulldozers parked on the premises are visible from the balcony. A security vehicle is parked in the courtyard between the house and the office. The grounds are surrounded by thick walls topped with steel bars. During the day, the gate is kept open. After all, four agents keep the area under constant supervision, and there are five different alarm systems with fifty-three cameras linked directly to the police station.

Gaetano Saffioti shows me a few more threatening letters and then some graphs tracking his national and international turnover. An old recording from his security camera shows a young Ndranghetist in a tracksuit coming to collect a payout. There are photographs of burned-out trucks and of him as an 18-year-old soldier working in the high-security prison. He laughs again. 'You could make the mistake of thinking that I'm imprisoned behind these walls. The truth is *they* are the ones who are locked out. I am a free man.'

6

THE WORST KIND OF DISGRACE

Until about ten years ago, definitive court decisions revealed little about the structure of the Ndrangheta. For decades, the main bosses had been acquitted on appeal or cleared by courts of cassation. The legal evidence regarding the hierarchy among Calabrian mafiosi collapsed again and again, and the connection between various clans remained elusive. But then, a group of mafia prosecutors in Reggio Calabria rolled up their sleeves and decided to change the situation as soon as possible.

They aimed to prove that the Ndrangheta clans weren't individual criminal families but members of the same mafia organization. The prosecutors needed to uncover how the Calabrian mafia was run, establish which internal laws applied and determine who was in charge. To reach that goal, detectives used bugging devices to infiltrate places where clan bosses met to discuss their most carefully guarded secrets. Then, in 2009, a significant breakthrough occurred when a video from the Sanctuary of the Madonna of Polsi showed the Ndrangheta appointing a new leader.

The new boss was Domenico Oppedisano, an eighty-year-old retired farmer. Anyone who wants to know more about his inauguration to the top position in the Ndrangheta can find the video on YouTube. When it comes to the privacy of suspects, Italian law is lax. Following the arrests, the images were immediately made public without masking anyone's identity. The video shows a group of primarily older men and a few younger ones gathered in broad daylight around a statue of the Madonna of the Mountain on a white pillar. There isn't much talking. Instead, the men greet each other with a kiss on each cheek or a handshake, and then they form a circle. Their actions speak louder than words, conveying their agreement with the new balance of power. They have chosen their new *Capocrimine*, Domenico Oppedisano.

Some of the Ndranghetists can be seen looking nervously over their shoulders, wary of uninvited eyes or ears. Others lean back casually, resting their crossed arms on their protruding bellies. They are all plainly dressed in cotton trousers and simple shirts or jeans with faded sports jackets. Domenico Oppedisano wears brown trousers and a brown and white short-sleeved shirt. Nothing in his attitude or demeanour hints at his being the head of an international criminal organization.

The successful criminal proceedings against Oppedisano and more than a hundred other Ndranghetists were given the name Crimine, the same name the Ndrangheta uses for its top provincial management. The Calabrian prosecutors had filmed the Ndranghetists symbolically confirming their choice of leader by forming a circle around their patron saint. In addition, they had listened in on the negotiations that led to Oppedisano's appointment.

The previous Capocrimine, the 77-year-old fugitive Antonio Pelle from San Luca, had been arrested in June 2009 when he was admitted to hospital for an operation. He was facing twenty years in prison, and even if he were to escape again, poor health meant he could no longer function as Capocrimine. A new leader was needed to succeed him as the head of the Ndrangheta, and fast.

The decision fell to representatives of the most powerful clans in the province of Reggio Calabria. The Ndrangheta had divided the area into three districts: the Ionian district in the east of the province, the Tyrrhenian district in the west, and the territory around the provincial capital of Reggio Calabria, on the extreme tip of the Italian mainland. Giuseppe Pelle, the son of the top man, wanted the highest function to remain in the hands of his district on the Ionian coast – the region around San Luca, the home base of the oldest criminal families, the Ndrangheta 'royalty'. Naturally, the Tyrrhenian clans didn't agree and felt that their stake in the organization was equally important. Vincenzo Pesce, the clan leader from Rosarno on the Tyrrhenian coast, threatened to walk out, taking many clans from his district with him.

Senior Ndrangheta representatives from Reggio Calabria needed to broker a compromise between the Ionian and Tyrrhenian clans in order to avoid a risky loss of capital and human resources. And so, as the police and prosecutors continued to clandestinely listen in, negotiations went on for several months in locations where clan leaders felt shielded from observation, ranging from orange groves to launderettes. Finally, a breakthrough came during the extravagant wedding of then-Capocrimine Antonio Pelle's granddaughter from San Luca to a Ndrangheta prince from the neighbouring village of Platì. In the end, Rosarno, in the Tyrrhenian area, won the day with Domenico Oppedisano's appointment. He became the new Capocrimine, the head of the Crimine, the most important provincial governing board. And while 'Don Mico' Oppedisano was relatively unknown within the Ndrangheta, at eighty years old, he was one of the oldest and most experienced members. No one could object to his appointment as the wisest.

In recordings secretly made by detectives, Oppedisano comes across as a democratic leader: 'The Crimine belongs to everyone'. Although the retired farmer wasn't much of a speaker, he liked to reminisce about important Ndrangheta members with whom he had shared special moments. 'We met in the mountains that night with more than a thousand men. I remember Peppe and Antonio Nirta were there too. They had me stand between them.'

Oppedisano was the first to have been elevated to the high rank of Vangelo, which literally means Gospel. That made him well-suited to the position of Capocrimine, because his job was to ensure that members followed the gospel of the Ndrangheta, in other words, its dogma, rules and rituals. With the help of his fellow executives, Chief Oppedisano's primary responsibility was to maintain the unity of the organization and approve new, high-ranking appointments. His express wish was that important promotions would occur only three times a year – at Easter, at Christmas and on Assumption Day. Like his predecessors, Oppedisano left the practical, day-to-day criminal management to the clans.

If one or more collaborating clans want to establish new headquarters, they need permission from the top. A minimum of forty-nine men are required to set up such a new operational base, called a locale in Ndrangheta parlance. To keep the peace, a Capocrimine such as Oppedisano ensures that the Ndrangheta clans in the area are all on board. Only then is the locale sanctioned, and its boss – called a *capolocale* – may, along with his group, hold criminal sway over a particular area, village or section of a city.

In recent decades, new *locali* have sprung up primarily in northern Italy. So much so that in Lombardy, the region around Milan, and in Liguria, where Genoa is located, 'control rooms' have been set up with similar tasks to the Calabrian Crimine to monitor harmony between the clans. There are also local control rooms in Canada and Australia. However, prosecutors discovered that when major conflicts arise, Ndranghetists throughout the world are still expected to obey the verdict of the Crimine in Calabria. Allegedly, delegates from the most important Italian and international clans still gather near the Polsi sanctuary every year.

If the Crimine had its way, the umbilical cord connecting the Ndranghetists with *la mamma* – meaning San Luca and the Madonna of the Mountain – would never be cut. Those who show insufficient respect for the authority of the Calabrian governing board meet a tragic end. In 2009, prosecutors investigating the Calabrian mafia discovered this when collaborating with colleagues in Milan. They were studying the clans there and at the same time trying to solve the recent murder of a capolocale named Carmelo Novella. It was evident from the information they gathered that Novella's separatist ambitions proved fatal. Wiretaps confirmed that Novella planned to break free of Calabria's watchful eye, taking sixteen other Ndrangheta clans from Lombardy with him. Don Mico Oppedisano had become aware that Novella was overstepping his bounds, trying to introduce new ranks and initiation rites in Lombardy. For instance, with boundless ambition, Novella had invented the rank of *Infinito,* or 'Infinite'. The top management simply couldn't tolerate such insubordination, and Novella was shot dead while sitting at a plastic patio table at a café in a village outside Milan. The hitmen returned to Calabria the next day and were warmly welcomed with champagne and pastries.

In 2011, a year after Oppedisano's arrest, it emerged that the village where I lived was also controlled by a Ndrangheta locale. Among my neighbours, the one I intuitively mistrusted the most was a guy with piercing eyes, an alpha-male posture and a gleaming pickup truck.

It turned out he was a member of the Ndrangheta. He lived with his wife and three daughters about 150 metres from my house. The police, however, refrained from handcuffing him at home and arrested him instead at his usual table at a restaurant in a tourist resort near the beach. He'd grown accustomed to eating there for free. He also dictated which of his family members and friends would be on the resort's payroll without ever having to lift a finger and, in collaboration with other clan members, he forced the owners to get their fruit and vegetables from specific suppliers and made the restaurant pay protection money. His message for the owners of the resort was: 'You are all guests in my domain.'

According to reports, my neighbour reached for his loaded pistol when officers approached to arrest him, but no shots were fired. Later, he had to appear before the judge, charged with extortion and Ndrangheta membership. Four others were also accused of participating in the extortion, including his wife and 18-year-old daughter, who were placed under house arrest.

I recalled that one of the men arrested had once forced me to dance with him during a tarantella party in the village square. After twirling an involuntary pirouette under his arm, I managed to break free of his grasp as calmly as I could; a man like that wouldn't stand for any open resistance.

Yet again, the arrests were not spoken of openly in the village, but the sense of relief was palpable. It was reassuring to know that the suspected Ndranghetists were in pre-trial detention. Still, I did not fool myself into thinking this would liberate us from the mafia's territorial claims.

The house arrest of the local boss's wife and daughter drew my attention to the role of women within the Ndrangheta. I requested an interview at the Palace of Justice in Reggio Calabria with mafia prosecutor Alessandra Cerreti, a charismatic Sicilian woman in her early forties with close-cropped hair and a steady gaze. She had recently wound up a highly successful case against one of the mightiest Ndrangheta clans, the Pesce family from Rosarno – the same family that had lobbied for Oppedisano's appointment as Capocrimine. The case against the Pesce clan was called 'All Inside', and the judge's sentence lived up to that name, primarily due to Cerreti's efforts to win a key witness's trust. That witness was named Giusy Pesce, and she was one of the first female informants to help the authorities.

Mafia prosecutor Alessandra Cerreti explained that, for a long time, people believed that women played a minor role within the Ndrangheta. However, they were often active within the criminal family circle. These women could be of interest to the justice system without having committed serious criminal offences because they also gathered important information from more modest positions, by delivering messages to imprisoned or fugitive Ndranghetists, for example, or by taking part in money-laundering or guarding the safe.

As a young woman, Giusy Pesce was arrested on suspicion of money laundering and transmitting messages for the clan. It would be an exaggeration to say she had an immediate rapport with the public prosecutor. 'Giusy didn't trust me at all. To her, I was the enemy: I locked her up and separated her from her three children.' And yet, Giusy asked to speak to Cerreti: 'She missed her children terribly. I explained that she could do a great deal for them, especially in her present situation. If she wanted her children's lives to be different from hers, now was the time to make that happen.'

Giusy was aware that, according to her family's rules, she would face certain death for cooperating with the justice department. Moreover, according to the regulations of the Ndrangheta, her father, brother or son would have to carry out the honour killing. But it gradually dawned on Giusy Pesce that another world was waiting outside of the realm of the mafia, one with different rules. She decided to tell the authorities everything she knew. Her information led investigators to bunkers where men from the Pesce clan were hiding out, and it helped the authorities seize more than two hundred million euros.

According to Alessandra Cerreti, when women break the code of silence, it's the worst kind of disgrace for male mafiosi. 'For such men, not being able to control their women is a terrible loss of face. They aren't particularly afraid of being sent to prison – that's one of the profession's risks and can, in their eyes, even boost their standing. But when a woman exposes family secrets, her man's social standing plummets dramatically. It's a serious threat to their power.'

Thanks partly to Giusy's testimony, forty-two members of the Pesce clan were sentenced to more than five hundred years in prison. Giusy's mother was sentenced to thirteen years, her father twenty-seven years, her sister twelve years and her husband to twenty-one years in prison.

Giusy Pesce was sentenced to four years of house arrest, to be carried out at a secret location, under a new identity, together with her son and two daughters. Her brave break with her criminal family made her a national hero. Would other Ndrangheta women dare to follow her example?

7

THE SCENT OF MIMOSA

When I think of Rosarno, the town where the farmer and Ndrangheta chief Oppedisano brought vegetables to market in his three-wheeled pickup, I sometimes recall police photographs of dinners in his orchard, where murders may have been plotted. Then, the same sense of suffocation hits me, the one I felt the few times I drove over the town's bumpy roads. In Rosarno, the control of the clans is so strong you can almost smell it. But when I think of that town, I think first and foremost of Maria Concetta Cacciola.

'I am with my friend Giusy,' said the cryptic message Maria Concetta left for her father and brother. They would know how to interpret it. She wrote a much longer, heartfelt plea to her mother.

'Give my kids a better life than the one I had. I got married at thirteen because I thought it would give me more freedom. I thought anything was possible, but I ruined my life because, as you know, he didn't love me, and I don't love him. I beg you not to make the same mistake with my children . . . give them the space they need. If you lock them up, they'll feel trapped and go down the wrong path. Give them what you never gave me.'

Maria Concetta asked her mother to forgive her for what she was about to do, for the shame she would bring on her family. 'I slowly came to realize that I was alone, alone with everyone and everything. I didn't want luxury or money. I longed for the peace and love you feel when making a sacrifice that gives you satisfaction. My life has been full of suffering. My children are the most beautiful thing I have, and I carry them in my heart. It pains me terribly to leave them. No one can ease that pain.'

She hurriedly finished the letter because a police car was waiting outside. 'Hug my children the way you always do and tell them about me. Don't give them away; my children are worth more than that. Farewell, mamma, forgive me if you can. I will never see you again because that is not allowed according to our family's laws of honour. You have lost a daughter. Goodbye, I will always love you. Please forgive me. Farewell.'

Two weeks earlier, Maria Concetta Cacciola had walked into the Rosarno police station to pay a fine for her 15-year-old son, whose scooter had been confiscated. She seized her chance and decided then and there to follow in the footsteps of her childhood friend, Giusy Pesce. She told the carabinieri that she wanted to talk about her family.

Maria Concetta had been going crazy at home, living like a prisoner in her parents' house since her husband's arrest eight years earlier for mafia-related crimes. However, she had never enjoyed much freedom. When she was thirteen, she became engaged to Salvatore. They were quickly married, and when she was fifteen, they had a son. When Salvatore was sent to jail, her son was seven and her eldest daughter was four. Maria Concetta became pregnant with their youngest daughter shortly before her husband went to prison.

Cetta, as she was known in Rosarno, was a beautiful, well-groomed woman of thirty. She had gentle eyes and jet-black, shoulder-length hair that she blow-dried straight. She lived on the top floor of her parents' house; they kept a watchful eye on her activities outside the home, so she turned to the internet for diversion. She had recently become acquainted with a few men on chat sites. When her brother found out, he beat her up. He wouldn't stop kicking her, even when she collapsed in the corner of her room. She had fractured ribs, but her parents wouldn't allow her to go to hospital. In the Cacciola family, such matters were resolved at home with the help of a doctor who regularly provided 'extra' services to Ndrangheta families.

Before he went to prison, her husband Salvatore had been the one who physically abused Maria Concetta – from the time she was thirteen until she was twenty-two. Once, he even aimed a pistol at her face. When she told her father, he said, 'That's your marriage. You must deal with it for the rest of your life.'

Now that Salvatore was in jail, her father and brother took it upon themselves to keep her from cheating on her husband. As a result, she was rarely allowed outside the house on her own or even in the company of a girlfriend. Running errands required an escort from her immediate family or one of her in-laws, who lived on the same street. Concetta's mother or sister-in-law usually accompanied her. When she brought her children to school, she had to return home immediately. She often noticed that she was being followed by her brother Giuseppe or one of her cousins.

Cetta wanted more than anything to divorce her husband and get to meet her latest online love interest, but her parents would never allow it. If she ran away, she was sure her brother would eventually track her down and murder both her and her new lover. And if her brother ever discovered what she had already told the police, she was convinced that he wouldn't let her live either. Clearly, if she wanted to testify against her family and tell the police everything she knew about the business affairs of the Rosarno clans, she would have to make a run for it, and quickly.

The carabinieri had scheduled her escape for a Sunday night at the end of May 2011. While everyone was asleep, she wrote her letter to her mother. She left it in her bedroom, slipped out of the door and got into the police car that headed out of Rosarno, where she had lived her entire life. The carabinieri followed inland roads towards the northernmost part of Calabria, taking Maria Concetta to an *agriturismo*, a farm nestled in the foothills of Mount Pollino that rented accommodation to tourists. There, just a few hours away from her claustrophobic past, she could do whatever she pleased for the first time in ages.

As soon as possible, Concetta had her first real-life meeting with her internet boyfriend, Pasquale, who lived in Naples. Meeting a man who worshipped the ground she walked on was a new experience for her. He stayed for a few nights. Cetta also enjoyed chatting with the hotel's other guests and staff, and she delighted in the large outdoor swimming pool and the garden filled with palm trees and purple bougainvillea.

Meanwhile, back in the Cacciola home, all hell had broken loose. The family was furious with Maria Concetta: by running into the arms of the police, she had unforgivably damaged the family's reputation. Her mother started dressing in black as if she were in mourning. Her brother let his beard grow and refused to leave the house. In Rosarno, the hometown of the Ndrangheta's Capocrimine Oppedisano, residents are acutely aware of every shift in power between the various Ndrangheta clans. The Bellocco family, with whom the Cacciolas had close ties, may have been both shocked and secretly pleased by the recent disgrace of the Pesce family, their rivals, over Giusy's talks with the police. But Cetta's father, Michele Cacciola, was the brother-in-law of boss Gregorio Bellocco. Now that Maria Concetta had endangered the affairs of the Cacciolas as well as the business of her uncle Bellocco, her family feared not only jail time but also reprisals from their in-laws and clan mates. Therefore, it was even more important for the family – and everyone in Rosarno who respected the laws of the Ndrangheta – to publicly condemn Cetta's choice.

Luckily, Cetta was safe among the tourists in her comfortable rural holiday lodgings. Her bodyguards were always nearby, and she didn't have to do much aside from occasionally talk with public prosecutors, who drove up from Reggio Calabria with their bodyguards to record her deposition. One of those prosecutors was Alessandra Cerreti, the woman who had interrogated Cetta's childhood friend, Giusy Pesce.

Giusy Pesce had known much more than Cetta about the Ndrangheta's practices in and around Rosarno. That's because Giusy's activities had gone beyond laundering drug and extortion money or acting as a messenger for prisoners and fugitives. Giusy also understood how different lengths of motorway along the Tyrrhenian coast, stretching from Rosarno and Gioia Tauro to Palmi and Reggio Calabria, were divided among the clans. She knew which members of the Pesce clan had close ties with local politicians, and she knew which judge her family could rely on for an acquittal on appeal.

Unlike Giusy, Cetta didn't play an active criminal role within her family. She was unaware of the fact that her family imported cocaine through the Netherlands, for instance. But her information did lead the police to the Cacciolas' weapons stockpile and one of the Bellocco family's secret bunkers. Cetta primarily passed along things she had overheard at home or on the streets of Rosarno about her family's extortion and loansharking activities, as well as the identity of a suspected murderer. Although Cetta delivered less information to the public prosecutor than Giusy had, her testimony was still important. Her brave step could also be just as inspiring as Giusy's in offering alternatives to women born into the emotional prison of Ndrangheta families.

It remained to be seen if Cetta could safely conclude delivering her deposition, especially after what had happened two years earlier to another witness, Lea Garofalo. Lea was also the daughter of a prominent Ndranghetist. Like Cetta and Giusy, she was one of a handful of Ndrangheta women strong enough to break the bonds of silence, of omertà. Lea's father had been killed when she was still a baby, and she grew up surrounded by blood feuds and family betrayals in the hinterlands of the Calabrian province of Crotone. Still in her teens, she fell in love and moved to Milan, where she hoped to begin a new life far from the Ndrangheta environment familiar to her. However, she soon realized that Milan was the heart of the drug distribution centre for the Calabrian mafia. Her husband Carlo had lied to her and was only using her to climb the clan's hierarchy. Lea left him, taking their small daughter with her, and decided to collaborate with the authorities. But after seven years, she walked out of the witness protection programme and reconnected with her ex, Carlo, because she wanted her daughter to have a father. One day, Lea disappeared, and there was no trace of her for a long time. It eventually emerged that Carlo had murdered her and and that her body had been burned, until nothing but ashes remained.

Alessandra Cerreti asked Maria Concetta if she wanted her three children to join her in the witness protection programme. Not yet, Cetta replied. She thought they were still too young to be suddenly and permanently torn away from the rest of their family. Cetta felt that for now, her children were safe with her mother. She first had to build up her courage to finish giving her testimony. In time, she would allow her children to choose between staying with their grandparents or moving in with her and assuming a new identity.

Cetta was a guest at the sunny tourist farm for two months, but sadly, she could not stay there forever. It would be safer for her to leave Calabria and travel further north in Italy. So, at the end of July, she packed her bags and was driven to Bolzano, a city in the Alps. Shortly after that, she had to move again, this time to Genoa.

Did Cetta's successive moves and northern Italy's foreign atmosphere trigger her homesickness and her longing for her children? In the witness protection programme, she was forbidden from contacting family members and yet she sent a text message to her eldest daughter, Tania. The 12-year-old, the spitting image of her mother, showed the text to her grandmother. Suddenly, there was a breach in the protective wall surrounding Maria Concetta. Before contacting her daughter, she had only used her new SIM card to phone her boyfriend, Pasquale, and her best friend, Emanuela. During all that time, she hadn't spoken with anyone else in Rosarno. But now, Tania was begging her mother to phone home.

In early August, Maria Concetta called her mother, Rosalba. She said she missed her, trusted her, and told her where she was. Her parents immediately drove to Genoa. Cetta got in the car with them to return to Calabria and her three children.

A few weeks earlier, however, the police had planted a hidden microphone in the Cacciolas' Mercedes, enabling them to listen in on talks between Cetta and her parents. They had heard, for instance, that when Cetta admitted talking to the police about a murder, her father Michele and mother Rosalba were furious. But then they did an about-face, adopting a calmer tone. Her father said she didn't have to worry about repercussions; everything would return to how it had been before. 'You can walk your kids to school together with your mother. Nothing has to change.' She didn't have to worry about other people's opinions of her. 'Have I ever harmed you?' he demanded. 'Have I ever abandoned you? I want my daughter at home with me. I'm not going to leave you to those filthy dogs. You must understand that nobody is better than your father, your mother and your brothers.'

'I know,' Cetta mumbled from the back seat.

Her mother repeated the litany. 'No one is better than your mother and father, remember that. If I have to make sacrifices for my daughter, I do so. Because you are my blood, do you see? The most important thing for you is to stay with your mother, your children, and your husband. Because those people you are talking to already know about what we are doing! They don't need your help to come and arrest me, do you understand?'

Her parents promised that everything would be fine if Cetta retracted her statement. But something felt off, and her parents didn't seem to trust her, either. When Cetta went to use the toilet at a petrol station, her father sent her mother after her to keep her from secretly phoning the police. And yet, when the family stopped for the night, halfway to Calabria, Cetta did manage to contact the carabinieri. They picked her up at five in the morning and took her back to Genoa.

'*Mannaia la Madonna della Montagna!*' That morning, when Michele Cacciola realized that Cetta had fled, he cursed the Ndrangheta's patron saint, the Madonna of the Mountain. He screamed at his wife as they drove back to Rosarno. 'I didn't send her to school so she could fill out police reports for that whore. What a tragedy. Doesn't that woman realize that the girl knows nothing? What could a woman from my household possibly know?'

With 'that whore' and 'that woman', Michele Cacciola was referring to prosecutor Alessandra Cerreti. 'Can you picture how that whore – that *puttana* – laughs as she's breaking your heart and your daughter's? Because she wants to see us dead. Don't you get it? They are the murderers! This is their way of getting rid of us. And then they have the nerve to say *we* are the bad guys! They'll laugh their heads off in their offices when we're all killed off.'

Cetta and her mother were only fifteen years apart in age. They were both fifteen when they had their first child, and as young girls, they each married a member of the Ndrangheta. Cetta thought of her mother almost like a sister, and a fellow sufferer. Once she was back in Genoa, Cetta phoned her mother to ask if she had arrived safely in Rosarno. She could hear her father whispering in the background, telling her mother what to say. 'The police and magistrates only want to hurt us, Cetta. They are using you. Come back home.' Her mother told her a lawyer was on his way to take her wherever she wanted. She didn't have to return to Rosarno; she could stay with an aunt. But she had to withdraw her testimony; only then would she be allowed to see her children again. 'You have to meet the lawyer and give a statement saying you know nothing.' Cetta was even told that she would be rewarded. Her mother said she would send her enough money to live independently, far from Rosarno, reunited with her children.

Rosalba reproached Cetta, telling her how deeply disappointed her children were when she didn't return home. 'Tania hasn't stopped crying, did you know? And the youngest has stopped talking. They are dying without you. You must make a choice.'

The message was clear: if Cetta wanted to destroy her family, she was going about it the right way. Her mother said it was time to choose, 'You're either with us or with them. *O cu nui o cu iddi.*'

Before she hung up, Cetta was forced to promise she would call the lawyer. 'If you don't, you can forget about me,' her mother added. 'I'm finished, Cetta. I'm dying.'

'Leave me alone, mamma. I already said I'm going to call him.'

There were two people Cetta could turn to: her boyfriend, Pasquale, and her friend Emanuela. Emanuela still lived in Rosarno and knew Cetta's parents and brothers. During a lengthy phone call with Emanuela, Cetta explained her dilemma. 'I want to see my children. My parents will never send them to me because they know that would mean the end; they would lose me forever.' Cetta said she had no choice but to go home. Yet she was terrified of her father and her aggressive brother Giuseppe, whose temper was legendary throughout Rosarno. Cetta regretted phoning home; since then, she hadn't been able to get her family out of her mind. 'I don't trust them.' She knew full well how they operated. 'What would you do if you were me, Emanuela? Let yourself be killed?'

'I can't tell you whether you should go home or not,' Emanuela replied. 'You know them better than I do. You know what you're facing.'

'My mother says they won't lay a finger on me, at least not as long as she's alive.'

Emanuela told Cetta that her mother looked terrible, just skin and bones. And, in any event, it would attract too much attention if they tried to do something to Cetta right away.

'Is it worth going back and only living for a year or eighteen months?' Cetta wondered aloud, stressing that they never forgave matters of honour.

Cetta's next call was to Pasquale. She confessed to him that she still phoned her family. 'You are too good for them,' he said. He reminded her that her brother had once broken her ribs, but he also believed Cetta could trust her mother because she too was a victim of the men of the family.

Cetta needed time to think. Her daughter Tania had told her that her father and brother had recently stopped talking whenever her mother entered the room. That wasn't a good sign. 'My stomach hurts,' she said. 'I'm afraid to go home.'

Pasquale told her he would come and pick her up in Rosarno if she felt unsafe. In return, Cetta warned him, 'The street is filled with families like ours.' Pasquale tried again to ease her mind – 'You can count on me,' he said.

Two days later, on 8 August, Cetta's mother, Rosalba, returned to Genoa with Cetta's brother and her daughter, Tania. On the phone, Cetta hesitated to tell them where she was, but when her mother held her phone up to Tania, who was crying hysterically, Cetta relented and gave them a location to pick her up in Genoa. They were driving a car that hadn't been bugged and the police lost all contact with Maria Concetta.

A few days later, Pasquale received text messages from Cetta in Rosarno. 'They found a couple of lawyers and are pressuring me to withdraw my statement. They're saying I was heavily medicated and only went to the police because I was angry with my father and brother.' She hid her phone, only turning it on to send a short message and then quickly turning it off again.

On 14 August, she managed to phone the police. Unfortunately, Gennaro, her contact there, was away for a few days, as it was the day before Assumption Day, a national holiday. Cetta finally reached him on 17 August and said things were going from bad to worse; going home had been a mistake. The family had forced her to read out a statement drawn up by the lawyers, withdrawing her testimony. Still, Cetta reassured Gennaro that she hoped to continue collaborating with the justice department.

This time, it would be harder for her to get away from her family than it had been two and a half months earlier. Now, the family never let her out of their sight; she couldn't leave the house except sometimes with her mother, and she didn't want to run away on one of those occasions because she feared the reprisals her mother would face. Couldn't the police pretend they were coming to arrest her? That would be tricky, Gennaro explained. Couldn't she sneak out of the house like she did the first time? Cetta agreed to a date, but later phoned to postpone it for a few days because one of her daughters was ill.

On 18 August, Cetta was sitting with her mother in the bugged Mercedes. The people they passed on the street were giving her dirty looks. Finally, she said she couldn't take it any more. 'I'm getting out of here, mamma!' she cried, desperate.

The next signal the police received arrived two days later when an unconscious Cetta was loaded onto the back seat of the Mercedes and driven to the hospital by her parents, along with an empty litre bottle of hydrochloric acid that had been found near her body. Soon after they arrived at the hospital, Cetta was pronounced dead.

The autopsy indicated there was no way Maria Concetta could have swallowed so much hydrochloric acid on her own. She would have vomited after the first sip; the amount she ingested burned through her intestines. Bruises and other marks on her body suggested that at least two people had forced her to swallow the deadly liquid.

*

Years after her death, I stand before Maria Concetta's tomb, looking into her smiling face. I am amazed by what I see. It's a very different picture than the pale passport photo used by the media, which shows her in a lavender hooded sweatshirt with a mournful look on her face. In the photograph affixed to her tomb behind Plexiglas, her smile is radiant. Her large, diamond-studded earrings and gold sequinned evening dress glitter in the sun. Her hair is pinned up, her makeup is flawless and her perfect teeth are visible between lipstick-red lips. Her eyes are smiling, too, and she looks genuinely happy.

Her name is engraved on a copper plate beside the photograph. Maria Concetta Cacciola, born on 30 September 1980, died on 20 August 2011. If I had been born in Rosarno, she and Giusy Pesce might have been my classmates. We are less than a year apart in age.

In addition to her radiant photograph, the most striking feature of her resting place is a gilded heart-shaped plaque atop the marble tomb, with an engraved text signed by her mother. 'Lord, You gave her to us to bring us great joy. Now we give her back to You, with no angry words but with a broken heart. She left behind a world of pain to enter a kingdom of peace.'

The words confuse and disgust me. The woman who wrote them has since received a final conviction for her role in the mental and physical abuse leading to her daughter's death. In their verdict, the judges stated that a murder had been committed, although there was not enough conclusive evidence for a specific person, or specific persons, to be convicted of that crime. There was, however, sufficient proof of the abuse that had led to Maria Concetta's death. Her father and brother were sentenced to more than seven and eight years in prison respectively; her mother was sentenced to seven years of house arrest. In addition, the Cacciola family's two lawyers were jailed for a few years for forcing Maria Concetta to give false testimony in service of the clan.

I have read everything in the criminal file, which included wiretapped conversations, letters and witness statements. Giusy Pesce was one of the witnesses called to testify against Cetta's family. She wept as she described how afraid Cetta had been of her brother from an early age. But Cetta wasn't weak, Giusy said. 'She was strong and optimistic. She had a sunny disposition and laughed all the time. And she took great care with her appearance.'

As young girls, Giusy and Cetta had gone to the same school. They remained close until they both became engaged at the age of thirteen. After that, each had a household to manage, a husband and, before long, children. They ran into each other when picking their kids up from school, or when Cetta went grocery shopping in the Pesce family's supermarket, where Giusy worked. 'We couldn't meet the way we would have liked. We weren't free to say, let's grab a pizza or go for ice cream.' The only day of the year they were sometimes permitted to go out with a group of girls was Women's Day, on 8 March, *la festa delle donne*.

The tragic death of Maria Concetta Cacciola received a great deal of media attention in Italy, as did the death, two years earlier, of Lea Garofalo, the witness who had been incinerated in Milan. The unimaginably cruel blood vengeance within Ndrangheta families may have deterred others from following in Giusy Pesce's successful footsteps. However, the courage of these three women is still honoured.

'Three photographs and a mimosa' was the name of an initiative started by the editor-in-chief of *Il Quotidiano della Calabria*. On 8 March 2012, he called on all Calabrians to honour the strength of

Maria Concetta Cacciola, Lea Garafalo and Giusy Pesce. In Italy, it is the custom to give women a sprig of mimosa blossom on Women's Day. The delicate yellow flowers, one of the first harbingers of spring's arrival at winter's end, symbolize solidarity. 'This year, every sprig of mimosa should bear their pictures,' wrote the editor of the Calabrian newspaper. 'That way, we can show the military branch of the Ndrangheta as well as the white-collar branch (who unfortunately are also among us) whose side we're on.'

Mimosa. With my nose buried in the fragile blossom, I think of pine, talcum powder and honey. And, ever since that year, I also think of hydrochloric acid, ashes and courage.

8

THE MAFIA BOURGEOISIE

It's August, and the beach is dotted with brightly coloured umbrellas. Increasing numbers of holidaymakers have been arriving every day since late July. I think back wistfully to the previous months when N and I had this untamed stretch of beach all to ourselves. We declared a corner at the edge of the dunes our 'summer kitchen' and furnished it with large chunks of driftwood to sit on. We'd even left behind a mini barbecue so others could use it too. That has recently disappeared. Instead, in the middle of the beach, there are remnants of a colossal campfire, complete with charred plastic rubbish and a partially incinerated umbrella.

Fortunately, the bright blue sky and a dip in the warm, crystal-clear sea help curb our annoyance at the casual indifference of those with whom we share one of Calabria's most beautiful beaches. The surf gleams with shimmering grains of golden sand and a smattering of small silver fish. N heads off to fetch something to drink at a beach pavilion some distance away. I'm still drying off under our beach umbrella when a man suddenly appears beside me.

'*Salve*. You're the *giornalista*, aren't you?' he says, using the formal term of address.

'Good afternoon. Why do you want to know, sir?'

'Could you please write an article about the outrageous way the government deals with sewage on this coast? It's all in the hands of the mafia. The treatment plants don't work, so all the tourists' sewage is discharged directly into the sea. This morning, the water was covered with a layer of foam. The current has already washed it away, but seeing all that filth has ruined our day at the beach. We're leaving.'

A short distance away, I can see a woman dragging a small girl and boy towards the eucalyptus trees marking the entrance to the improvised car park.

Although I wonder how much use this information would be to the Dutch media, I don't want to rebuff the man out of hand. The local sewage treatment problem is well known. During peak season, the pollution occasionally forms a subtle layer of whitish foam on the surface of the sea. So, I truly understand this man's frustration.

'It's such a gorgeous coast, but the mafia's ruining it. Think of all the little kids getting sick from the filth in the sea. No one here dares say anything, because of that bloody omertà.'

I find my notebook and pen to write down what he's saying.

'I really must go now,' he says.

'If you give me your name and a way to contact you, maybe I can ask you some more questions later?'

The man tells me his name and says he lives in Milan but spends his holidays here every summer, in the village where he was born. After briefly explaining where he's staying in town, he hurries towards his car, trying to catch up with his wife and children.

It's the first time someone from the village has asked me to write about the mafia. My 'title' of *giornalista* usually sets off a different set of expectations, for example, when the mayor or developers of coastal holiday homes try to get me to boost the area's popularity among my Dutch compatriots.

In the meantime, new visitors to the beach have moved into the spot next to mine. They've set up their parasol, some folding chairs and a cooler and are already frolicking in the sea. As I scan the surface of the water for suspicious-looking foam, one of my new neighbours spontaneously sticks both thumbs in the air. After mulling over the invisible health risks of faulty sewage plants for a while, I see to my surprise that the man I spoke with earlier has returned to the beach. He is heading my way.

'*Scusi*,' he says. 'If you plan on writing that article, please don't use my name.'

That takes me aback. Hardly ten minutes have passed. The man must have changed his mind on his way home, or maybe his wife told him off, forcing him to make a U-turn.

'Don't worry, sir,' I reassure him. It seems he wants me to put my name to an accusation he's afraid to back up himself.

'This is not about protecting myself, you understand, I'm asking for my family,' he says. I nod politely as the man slinks off.

While we were facing minor annoyances at the beach that summer, a few hours away to the north a much greater environmental disaster was taking place, and those affected had long since passed the stage of suffering in silence. For decades, toxic waste had been dumped on a massive scale near Naples, in the Campania region, in collaboration with the Camorra's local mafia clans. There, agricultural land had become so contaminated that young children were dying of cancer. When their mothers decided to take to the streets to protest the silence and impunity, I made a report about it for an in-depth Dutch television news programme called *Nieuwsuur*.

Before that item was broadcast in the Netherlands, awareness among the broader Dutch public had been limited to images of odorous mountains of uncollected rubbish lining the streets of Naples. In Italy, those bags of rubbish also managed to divert the public's attention from what was taking place twenty kilometres away, namely the dumping of industrial, toxic and radioactive waste. Such dumping was carried out both surreptitiously and in plain sight, along the side of the road.

In fact, it's possible to walk for miles along roads stacked with household and bulk waste, electrical appliances, car parts, asbestos, scraps of dyed leather, lead and chemicals. How did the situation deteriorate to such a point? Companies can choose between paying the total cost of processing their special waste or succumbing to the temptation of having the Camorra deal with it for them – including transportation and all the necessary paperwork – for a fraction of the price. To add insult to injury, the government doesn't clean up the illegal dumping grounds; instead, criminals set them ablaze. The smouldering heaps of rubbish are adjacent to fields of tomato plants, fruit trees and greenhouses filled with strawberries. Gradually, the groundwater, air and food have become so toxic that it's impossible to ignore the high incidence of cancer among area residents.

In a sad twist, much of the illegally dumped industrial waste doesn't come from local companies; instead, it's from northern Italy or countries beyond the Italian border. And like its sources, the toxic consequences of this pollution are not limited to one place. The area's tomatoes and other produce aren't exclusively meant for local consumption. In fact, major food producers buy them for their tomato sauces and frozen vegetables, which are subsequently sold in supermarkets in the rest of Italy and abroad.

Looking around Naples the day after filming for *Nieuwsuur*, I saw almost no rubbish on the streets of the city. However, I did see plenty of charming and exuberant Neapolitans, heavenly pizzas that cost next to nothing and majestic buildings lining the glorious waterfront.

Years later, I'm still in the habit of checking the origins of my produce whenever I visit a greengrocer. The handwritten description usually reads *origine locale* or *Italia*. The crates rarely bear the name Campania, although that's hardly reassuring. It would be naive to think contaminated agriculture doesn't exist in other Italian regions, just as it's absurd to believe that no healthy vegetables are grown in the area surrounding Naples.

In Italy, they call it the *ecomafia*, a type of mafia whose trademark is environmental pollution. Contaminating the environment has proven a lucrative and highly sought-after line of business for criminal organizations, whether it involves illegally dumping rubbish along the road, releasing unfiltered sewage or burying barrels of toxic waste in quarries, fields, lakes, rivers or the sea. For many years, it has proven to be a vital source of income.

When I first delved into this stomach-churning subject, I quickly discovered that the Ndrangheta had developod a favourite method of dumping deadly substances in the 1980s and '90s. They would sink freighters full of industrial, toxic and radioactive waste along the Italian coast or in international waters. And the profits were extraordinary: instead of disposal costs there was a hefty payment for the disappearing act, plus insurance compensation – up to seven figures – for the loss of a ship.

According to former members of the Ndrangheta, since turned informers, such was also the fate of a ship called the *Rigel*, which made its final voyage in 1987. The official documents stated that the vessel was transporting hundreds of tons of marble dust. Marble happens to have the capacity to shield radioactive material so scanners can't detect it during port inspections. Allegedly, the *Rigel* sank somewhere between Italy and Greece, but curiously, the wreck has never been found.

Investigations into the *Rigel* and more than twenty other 'toxic ships' have been systematically obstructed. In the mid-1990s, a young captain named Natale De Grazia was determined to locate those sunken ships. During one of his many research missions, he was poisoned and died. The truth was not allowed to surface.

Ilaria Alpi, a 32-year-old journalist for RAI, the Italian public broadcasting network, was investigating the story of the mysterious toxic shipments; the trail led her to Somalia. In 1994, she discovered that the former Italian colony, ravaged by civil war, was receiving not only humanitarian food aid but also illegal cargoes of weapons and toxic and nuclear waste. Were arms being exchanged for the opportunity to dump the hazardous waste? The waste was sometimes discharged into the sea and sometimes buried in places where highways were being constructed. Ilaria Alpi was no stranger to Somalia, and she didn't pay attention to warnings that it would be better if she turned a blind eye to certain international deals. She and a cameraman were driving a pickup truck near the Mogadishu police station when gunmen surrounded them; both were shot dead. Soon it would turn out that somebody had also broken into their hotel rooms to steal her notebooks and the videotapes of the footage they'd been working on.

The Italian authorities maintained that the murder of the investigative journalists was motivated by robbery. A Somali man, Hashi Omar Hassan, was convicted of the murders following a dubious trial plagued by lost evidence. Hassan had spent seventeen years in an Italian prison when a TV production team tracked down another Somali who had testified against him; he regretted accepting money from the Italian government for making a false statement and pointing the finger at Hassan. Hassan was released, but to this day it remains unclear who murdered Ilaria Alpi and her cameraman and who gave the orders.

For twenty years, Italian television's most critical pieces of investigative journalism were awarded a prize named after Ilaria Alpi. After the twentieth ceremony, Ilaria's mother asked that the name of the award be changed. She said she found it too painful, because there was still no justice, even after so many years.

Italy remains fascinated by the toxic ships and the lack of justice associated with them. Where are those shipwrecks located? How many rusty steel drums of harmful waste and radioactive materials are waiting like time bombs on the seabed? Or have their deadly contents already scattered throughout the water? What are the dangers to marine life and humans? Environmental organizations continue to raise the alarm, and new parliamentary committees are formed each time to investigate.

Emilio Di Giovine is a former leader of a prominent Milan branch of the Ndrangheta. He has numerous convictions for trafficking in drugs and arms, but since 2003, he's become an informant. Shortly after he agreed to testify about the toxic ships, he was involved in a curious accident. 'I escaped by a hair's breadth. They found me in the middle of the road, almost across the street; I'd been catapulted a few metres through the air. People were screaming; they thought I'd been killed.'

How did Emilio Di Giovine come to have information about the ships? Through a Dutchman, Theodor Cranendonk. 'I lived with his daughter for a while; a beautiful lady, a model for Chanel, *una bellissima donna*. Her father, Cranendonk, had an asset management company in Klosters, Switzerland, near Davos. He was brilliant and he knew important people around the world, especially in Russia and in the secret services of the former Yugoslavia. He was friends with ex-president Milošević.'

Emilio Di Giovine grows nostalgic as he explains to the parliamentary committee in February 2010 how he met Cranendonk's daughter Marie Louise in 1990: 'I was on a flight from Barcelona to Zurich. She was much taller than me, but I plucked up my courage and decided to make a move. I said I wanted to marry her. Two weeks later, we were officially a couple, and she took me to meet her parents.'

For Di Giovine, those were happy times. He was a millionaire and he had a chauffeur – who would later turn him over to the police, but who was still driving him through the Swiss Alps back then. Di Giovine was in awe of Cranendonk's wealth: 'To me, he seemed like a bank director, the type you read about in the paper. The whole family was attractive, from his wife to his kids. Beautiful people.' They owned a professional riding stable and an arena for show jumping; Cranendonk's daughter was an excellent horsewoman.

Before the parliamentary commission, Di Giovine decides to elaborate on his complicated love life. Marie Louise wanted to marry him, but he had neglected to mention that he was already married. Surprisingly, when he came clean about his marriage as well as his criminal activities, she didn't bat an eyelid. It wasn't a problem, and she urged him to talk with her father.

And so Di Giovine told Cranendonk that he was looking to buy bazookas and send them to Calabria: rocket launchers that could pierce armoured cars. Cranendonk had been a commando in Burma and knew his way around, so he ordered thirty bazookas in Croatia. Somebody later smuggled them across the Slovenian border into Italy. For the equivalent of fifty thousand euros, Cranendonk had government documents falsified, stating that the weapons had been ordered in Kenya and were to be shipped through the port of Genoa. Of course, the bazookas never left Italy. Instead, the Ndrangheta used them in Calabria for a clan war that claimed more than seven hundred lives over six years.

Following that successful arms deal, Theodor Cranendonk asked Emilio Di Giovine if he would like to invest in the toxic waste business. 'At the time, I was dealing hashish: I made 1.5 billion lire for a thousand kilos of hash. That was a piece of cake.' Di Giovine wasn't interested in trying his luck. 'But Cranendonk told me you could earn much more with garbage than with drugs. He explained how it went: toxic waste got loaded onto ships officially headed for Mozambique, but the vessels would then sink along the way.'

According to Cranendonk, all the pieces were already in place: the ships and contacts with engineers and Italians who handle particular types of waste. Anyway, the scheme stood the test of time. 'A goldmine, he told me. Much more lucrative than hashish!'

Theodor Cranendonk is also mentioned in Emilio Di Giovine's published memoirs. According to him, Cranendonk had many talents, including money laundering and oil dealings. Di Giovine explains that sometimes, the Dutch entrepreneur combined various activities, such as supplying weapons in exchange for oil, which he could then sell through the Rotterdam oil company he owned.

Di Giovine was offered the chance to make a lot of money with the toxic ships. Still, he tells the parliamentary committee that he wanted nothing to do with Cranendonk's proposal. And that's all he can say about the toxic vessels. Moreover, while Di Giovine's relationship with Cranendonk's daughter ended, the two businessmen remained close for a long time. To illustrate this, Emilio Di Giovine describes for investigators the operation he'd asked Theodor Cranendonk to set up to help him escape from a Portuguese prison. The attempt failed, but it was anything but child's play. 'He bought a helicopter for me – worth 1.5 million dollars – and loaded it onto a truck heading for Portugal, along with machine guns. The court knows all about it.'

And indeed, the court was aware of Cranendonk's efforts. In 1998, an Italian court sentenced Cranendonk to eleven years for collaborating with the Ndrangheta, for planning Di Giovine's attempted escape, and for the sale of thirty bazookas. The Italian authorities had him arrested in Switzerland. According to reports in the Italian press, investigators found documents in Cranendonk's house detailing the maritime transport of toxic and nuclear waste.

In February 2010, when Di Giovine described his relationship with Theodor Cranendonk, the Dutch entrepreneur was a free man, but not because he'd completed that eleven-year sentence. In the late 1990s, shortly after he arrived in the heavily guarded prison in Milan, he was transferred to a private clinic because of psychological complaints. Prison authorities sent him to the Le Betulle clinic in Como, a luxurious facility surrounded by greenery. Cranendonk later admitted to a Dutch newspaper that he'd ordered a bottle of red wine the minute he arrived. He'd been given back his passport and security at the clinic seemed lax, so nothing prevented Cranendonk from walking out and going back to his wife in Rotterdam.

As the parliamentary committee was rounding off its questioning of Emilio Di Giovine, they briefly touched on the road accident he had survived a short time earlier. 'It was an unusual accident because I was hit when I had almost reached the other side of the road. Nevertheless, a vehicle hit me, I was thrown in the air and I landed on the other side. The lane was clear, so you can't claim the car hadn't seen me or that I was suddenly darting across. I had almost reached the pavement.

The truth is a lot of people are bothered by my testifying about this, and I've been pressured in other ways, too. Maybe they're worried I know more than I do. But this is genuinely everything I know about the subject.' Whether true or not, the informant refused to reveal anything more.

In March 2010, one month after Emilio Di Giovine testified before the commission, Theodor Cranendonk was arrested in Rotterdam at Italy's request. Italy wanted the Dutch to extradite him, but according to Dutch authorities, Cranendonk could no longer serve time in Italy. However, there were possible grounds for incarcerating him in the Netherlands; a new trial would be needed to decide. Cranendonk, at eighty, was not considered a flight risk, so he awaited the court's decision at his own recognizance.

The Dutch radio programme *Argos* followed the case, revealing that in the late 1990s, a Dutch diplomat visited Cranendonk in Rotterdam shortly after he had left the private Italian clinic. That's odd, because in the eyes of the Italian authorities, Cranendonk was a fugitive at the time. The diplomat, Charles O., was a vice-consul at the Dutch Consulate in Milan and he told *Argos* that his visit to Cranendonk meant little. He had assisted during Cranendonk's incarceration in Italy, and the two had become friends. 'Once, I happened to be in Rotterdam, and I dropped by with a bunch of flowers.' The vice-consul said it had never crossed his mind to mention the private visit to his colleagues in the Netherlands or Italy. Inquiries made by the Dutch Parliament regarding the diplomat's social contact with the refugee remained classified.

After two years, a Dutch judge had the job of deciding Cranendonk's sentence, interpreting crimes committed in Italy under Dutch law. Although the public prosecutor requested eight years, the judge reduced the sentence to five. In practice, it meant that Theodor Cranendonk was released on probation. The empathetic Rotterdam judge said, 'Imprisonment would pose too great an emotional burden on Mr Cranendonk.'

Did the Netherlands fail to pick up on Cranendonk's links with the Ndrangheta, or was he given special protection? Maybe a bit of both. During those years, the Dutch National Police Force compiled what they knew about the Calabrian mafia in the Netherlands. In their hundred-page report, the police concluded they had little insight into the Ndrangheta's interests, presence and contacts in the Netherlands.

Theodor Cranendonk's name didn't appear in that publication, and the issue of the toxic ships was only briefly touched upon. However, the text revealed another interesting relationship that involves the Ndrangheta's powerful Di Giovine family in the Netherlands. This time, the focus was on the love life of Emilio Di Giovine's younger brother. In 1992, Emilio Di Giovine was doing time in a Portuguese prison – the same one Cranendonk had tried to help him escape from – after being arrested with his brother's girlfriend. She was a twenty-year-old Dutch woman, Barbara F., who later went on to become a trainee agent with The Hague police force.

Portuguese authorities had suspected Barbara of being involved in the Di Giovine family's activities, namely smuggling and trafficking large shipments of hashish from Morocco. Her boyfriend, Filippo Di Giovine, was also a suspect in the case, but he had managed to elude the Portuguese police. Barbara, however, had to stay in Portugal for a year and a half in pre-trial detention; when she was released, it was on the condition that she did not leave the country. The Portuguese authorities held her passport while the case was pending, but she asked the Dutch embassy in Lisbon to issue her a new document, allowing her to cross the border. Barbara subsequently moved to the Amsterdam suburb of Diemen, where she lived with her fugitive boyfriend, Filippo Di Giovine, and they had a child. It wasn't long before Filippo was arrested in Morocco and extradited to Italy, where he was sentenced to fourteen years.

That information didn't stand in the way of Barbara being accepted by the Dutch police force for training in 2008; apparently, the details of her Portuguese arrest had been erased from the Dutch police and justice systems. But in Italy, as became painfully clear on a holiday during her second year of police training, there was still an outstanding search warrant in her name. Moments after Barbara checked into her hotel in Genoa, local police arrested her and brought her to the nearest women's prison. It was then that the Dutch police found out that Barbara had concealed her criminal past – and they sacked her immediately.

The anonymous authors of *The Ndrangheta in the Netherlands*, the Dutch National Police Force's publication in which this peculiar story appears, remain diplomatic. They refer to a Europol analyst, who calls it 'extremely curious that Barbara F., with her background, had applied to join the police force'. The authors write that 'the analyst suspects that she knew in advance that no information about her criminal history would be found in the police system. He refers to the phenomenon of the "mafia bourgeoisie", a circle of individuals in the upper world or legitimate society who are not actual members of the mafia themselves, but who do lend them a hand. This group includes municipal and provincial civil servants and employees in the banking sector, of housing associations and energy companies. They can monitor individuals in their systems, alter data, or provide other services.'

That proves that the mafia bourgeoisie exists outside of Italy's borders. And so, while living in Calabria and delving into the Ndrangheta's connections, I had my eyes opened to a different side of my seemingly safe and reliable home country, the Netherlands.

9

PEPPINO'S MAFIOPOLI

The entire world knows and celebrates Italy's historical geniuses in the fields of art and music. The compelling work of contemporary Italian filmmakers and novelists also has no trouble reaching an international audience. But for the heroes of journalism, it's a different story. With few exceptions, their fame stops at their country's borders. Sadly, that also applies to journalists who have died for their endless dedication to the truth, such as Ilaria Alpi, the RAI journalist from Rome who perished in Somalia after she uncovered the secrets of the international ecomafia and arms-trafficking industry. Her commitment, and that of the many other fearless journalistic watchdogs who make up Italy's rich history, is nothing less than awe inspiring.

Sometimes, these journalists inspire people to shout from the rooftops – perhaps with the words, 'The mafia is a pile of shit!' Admittedly it does sound better in Italian: *'La mafia è una montagna di merda*!' Those winged words were reportedly penned by the legendary Peppino Impastato, who likely shouted them in the 1970s in Sicily, where he was leading the resistance against the mafia in his village. His unique story is a benchmark in the history of Italian anti-mafia activism.

Peppino Impastato grew up in Cinisi, a town of roughly eight thousand inhabitants near Palermo. His father was a member of the mafia, and when Peppino was fifteen, a car bomb killed his uncle. Peppino and his younger brother went to the site of the explosion. 'Is this the mafia?' he said, staring at the wreckage. 'If this is what the mafia does, I will spend the rest of my life fighting it.'

At home, Peppino didn't hear any mention of the mafia or Cosa Nostra. Instead, it was called the *onorata società*, the 'society of honour'. Peppino kept his word and turned his back on his family's expectations. At seventeen, he and a group of friends set up a mimeographed newspaper. In it, he wrote about links between members of the mafia and his village's corrupt politicians. His father, furious, threw him out of the house.

Living independently, Peppino soon opened a cultural centre. With his friends, he created exhibitions about the ugliness the mafia caused in the area, using pictures and descriptions of illegally built seaside villas and unfinished construction projects in which much public money was wasted. But Peppino's group didn't hang their exhibition panels on the walls of the cultural centre; instead, they carried them to the busiest parts of the village. When customers at an outdoor café or residents sitting on a bench in the town square tried to turn their heads, Peppino's crew would force them to look, holding the panels in front of their noses.

The boss of the village of Cinisi was Don Tano Badalamenti, who, thanks partly to friends and family in Milan and America, had become a linchpin in the international heroin and cocaine trade. He had done a brief stint in a Palermo prison, but that hadn't diminished his standing in the eyes of the citizens or the police of Cinisi. Don Tano continued to stroll calmly down the main street, surrounded by his bodyguards, sometimes pausing for a quiet exchange with a local policeman. Don Tano may have been a man of the world, but he kept a close eye on his interests in and around Cinisi.

In 1977, Peppino and his friends set up a radio station. They began broadcasting a satirical radio play called *Onda Pazza*, which roughly translates as 'Wave of Madness'. It was an irreverent and sharp-edged programme about mafia-related and governmental abuses of power in and around Cinisi. Peppino gave everyone and everything in the satire a nickname: Cinisi became 'Mafiopoli' and Don Tano Badalamenti became 'Tano Seduto', or 'Sitting Tano', reminiscent of the name of a tribal chief.

Wave of Madness zoomed in on public contracts and other issues relevant to the municipal council; background noises included gunshots, war whoops and the soundtracks of Westerns. When the municipality sold a stretch of beach to Don Tano's cronies for development with municipal funds, Peppino spoke theatrically: 'These are the words of Sitting Tano, Mafiopoli's big chief. A magnificent harbour will arise, from whence all our heroic merchandise will depart unhindered, and from whence all our business will flourish in perpetuity.'

Peppino knew that making the mafia look ridiculous was the best form of attack. And there was plenty of inspiration for his satirical programme, including, among other things, a tribute to the big boss at a village fete, the Church's role in corruption and cocaine-snorting mob entrepreneurs – Peppino spared no one. The radio programme attracted scores of fans, who initially listened behind closed doors. But in time, even a few baristas dared to tune their café's radio to the programme, and children on the street started mocking 'Sitting Tano'.

These developments enraged the boss, and he put his foot down. The residents of Cinisi had always been afraid of Don Tano, and had treated him with respect. To keep the peace, they had given him free rein to pursue his criminal activities. But now, a bunch of hippies on the radio were turning him into a laughing stock. Don Tano spoke with Peppino Impastato's father, and his message was clear: 'Your son has to stop. Otherwise, we'll kill him.'

Peppino's father begged Don Tano not to murder his son. He knew he could do nothing to stop Peppino. His only option was to kick him out of the house and stop talking to him, but he'd already done that.

Shortly thereafter, Peppino's father was killed, hit by a car. At the funeral, Peppino refused to shake hands with Don Tano and his cronies. Peppino's mother and brother supported him. He continued with his satirical radio show and became a candidate for the municipal council elections.

At the end of April 1978, *Wave of Madness* began with the words, 'Once upon a time, long ago, there was a village far, far away, called Mafiopoli. It was a peaceful village where there were many friends, *amici, amici,* friends here and friends there. And in that village, the municipal council had made many of their friends happy. But their term of office was over; elections were coming. And what would happen in the village of Mafiopoli, which was so peaceful, so *tranquillo*? Whose names appeared on the ballot for the new municipal council? The friends, the friends of the friends, the friends of the friends of the friends, the friends of the friends of the friends of the friends and then again, the friends of the friends of the friends of the friends of the friends.'

Peppino ironically described the parties on the ballot from left to right. Fascists, republicans and communists. 'And then there are a few troublemakers, proud, ambitious kids, who want to solve problems. But what problems are there to solve? They're just rabble-rousers, sticking their noses into other people's business.'

Finally, he arrived at the *Democrazia Cristiana*, the Christian Democrats, for years the largest party. 'Upstanding Catholics, who will pray for us. And then there are the friends, who will also pray for the victory of the Christian Democrats. Friends like Don Tano, who is also a very pious man, a man of immense faith, who fully believes in the divine, the saints, God's peace and eternal rest. Don Tano, who donated two million lire to the festival honouring the village's patron saint, who paid for the entire celebration. Don Tano is also praying.'

On 8 May 1978, Peppino left the radio station, where he had been all afternoon. He had planned to meet his friends that evening to campaign for the municipal elections, but never showed up. His worried friends immediately launched a search.

His body was found the following morning by the railway tracks between Cinisi and Trapani. Or rather, small pieces of his body that explosives had blown apart. Nothing was left of him but his hands and one foot.

His mother, brother and friends believed they knew who was responsible, but the police turned a deaf ear. Detectives concluded that Peppino died while attempting to carry out a terrorist attack on the train. The only other possibility they were willing to accept was that Peppino had taken his own life.

The police didn't question Don Tano, but they searched the homes of Peppino's friends, some of whom even spent the night in jail, suspected of conspiring to carry out a terrorist attack. The mood of the times worked against them: Peppino's remains were found the same day Aldo Moro's body was discovered in Rome. Moro, a former prime minister of Italy, had been kidnapped by the Red Brigades, a violent communist organization founded by students. The Red Brigades had given left-wing activism a terrible reputation, lending credence to the theory that Peppino had been planning a terrorist attack.

The following day, Peppino's loyal group of friends gathered the pieces of his body scattered in the trees, shrubbery and high-voltage pylons along the railway tracks. They also found blood-covered stones in the grass, and splatters of blood on the walls of an abandoned barn nearby. Had Peppino been beaten in the barn, pelted with stones and then tied to the tracks with explosives? His friends begged the police to investigate the bloodied walls and rocks for possible evidence. But they never did.

Peppino Impastato posthumously won a seat in the municipal council election. Still, that tribute could not prevent the Christian Democratic party from gaining a majority again.

In 1987, Don Tano Badalamenti, the boss of Cinisi, was convicted in the Pizza Connection case in New York. He was sentenced to forty-five years in prison for his part in a drug and arms trafficking racket involving at least 1.65 billion dollars, using pizzerias in various American states as a front.

After more than twenty years, Peppino's mother, brother and supporters finally convinced the Italian Public Prosecutor's Office to reopen the murder investigation. Former members of the Sicilian mafia who have become informers now admit that Peppino was kidnapped and tortured until he lost consciousness, and then tied to a pile of explosives on the tracks.

In 2002, twenty-four years after Peppino's death, Tano Badalamenti watched via a video link from a prison in the US as an Italian judge sentenced him to life in prison for ordering the murder of Peppino Impastato. The verdict didn't alter Don Tano's fate. He died of a heart attack two years later, at the age of eighty, in that American prison. For those curious about the extent of Don Tano's relationship with the Christian Democrats, all was revealed by the Italian supreme court the year he died: Don Tano not only maintained 'friendly ties' with the mayor of Cinisi, but also with fellow party member Giulio Andreotti, seven-time prime minister of Italy.

Peppino Impastato only lived to be thirty. After his death, he was widely described in newspapers as a fervent 'left-wing extremist' who had clumsily blown himself up. It seems that Peppino not only had to die, but that his reputation also had to be destroyed. Such efforts were in vain. Today, Peppino's name is known by almost everyone in Italy, and many students watch *I cento passi*, a heartrending film about his life, in school. The title refers to the short distance, just one hundred steps, between the house of the Impastato family and that of Don Tano.

Painfully enough, Italy still has countless Mafiopolis: villages and cities controlled by the criminal interests of a mafia-friendly minority. Yet many people have wholeheartedly embraced Peppino Impastato's aspirations. Some have shouted that the mafia is a pile of shit, *'una montagna di merda'*. But no one since has matched Peppino's courageous irreverence. Why would anyone dare, after his horrific death?

10

'ONE DAY, THIS PLACE WILL BE BEAUTIFUL'

June nights in Calabria are warm and delightful – not yet too warm, as some nights in July and August can be. In the historic town centre of Lamezia Terme, sharply chirping swallows dart through the sky. They fly over the stages set up for a unique Italian festival centred on books, music and movies about the mafia. Every year since the festival was first held in 2011, the mafia has been the topic of discussion in Lamezia Terme for five days and nights at the end of June, preferably outdoors, in the town square.

Before each event, police dogs trained to detect explosives snuffle the stages. That's certainly no extravagance at this festival, where many of the speakers have received death threats. Their armed bodyguards are always nearby. While visitors shouldn't expect satirical humour in the style of Peppino Impastato, the writers, journalists, entrepreneurs, mayors and public prosecutors who come to speak here do tend to avoid the mirthless moral high ground. Instead, there is laughter, heartfelt storytelling and words of encouragement. The audience is attentive and diverse. As midnight approaches, you can still spot a few children sprawled on their parents' laps.

The festival is called 'Trame', the Italian word for narratives, storylines and schemes. The logo is a raised right hand, its palm cross-hatched with lines. Large-scale, brightly coloured versions of the hand are displayed on the stage and around a large fountain. The image also adorns the T-shirts of dozens of high school students who are volunteering at the festival. This raised hand is everywhere, and its meaning intrigues me. It's a hand that greets, maybe poses an impertinent question – and more than anything, it's a hand that says 'stop', setting clear boundaries. For those so inclined, it's also a palm that someone can read.

It goes without saying that in Calabria, a festival like Trame could never be large-scale, so the vibe remains friendly and intimate. Occasionally, loud music blaring from a nearby café breaks the idyll. As expected, some of the locals don't support the festival; they'd rather people didn't talk about the mafia so openly. The neighbourhood's opposition swings from harassingly loud to suffocatingly quiet, and that seems to lend the speakers' voices an extra emotional charge. I had heard some of these speakers before, on television or in other public venues. Yet here, outdoors on a city square in Lamezia Terme, the audience's concentration seemed more focused, the stakes higher, the words more urgent and the listeners more critical.

On the opening day of the third iteration of the festival, I spoke with the man who had launched it, investigative journalist Lirio Abbate. He explained why he believed that Trame should take place in a Calabrian city and not, for example, a Sicilian city like Palermo, where he was born. 'In many places in Calabria, today's situation mirrors what it was like thirty years ago in Palermo. People hardly dare to utter the word "mafia" aloud. We want to break the silence, especially here, by giving writers, journalists and magistrates a platform. We want to unleash a virtual earthquake in the heads of Calabrians and strengthen solidarity with everyone who does dare to speak out.'

Lirio Abbate, a stocky, handsome man with blond curls, is the first journalist I've met with round-the-clock protection. In Palermo, his work sparked the wrath of some hostile mafiosi; since then, he's lived in Rome, where he continues to expose criminal networks.

We sat in an empty, white room in the former convent that serves as the festival's headquarters. I asked him about a statement he made in 2007, the year death threats made bodyguards a necessary part of his life. 'In the interests of public opinion, the "civil society", you try to do what's right by shedding light on the dark and filthy corners of the courtyard. But then you discover that you've been naive. No one wants to look in those corners. People prefer to turn their heads away, even when you grab them by the lapels.'

Optimistically, I asked him if anything had changed in the meantime. After all, we were attending a multi-day festival that revolved around those same 'dark and filthy corners of the courtyard', and a respectable number of interested people had turned up. 'No, nothing has changed,' the award-winning investigative journalist soberly replied. But he didn't sound downhearted or bitter. 'Most people don't want to look. And the same things keep happening, over and over.'

History repeats itself, not only in the expected places, but also in new territories. In late 2012, Lirio Abbate revealed a network of mafia clans in Rome with links to corrupt businesspeople and government officials, up to and including the Roman mayor. Was Rome another Mafiopoli? The trial that resulted from Abbate's journalistic investigation into the mafia in Italy's capital caused quite a stir in the entire country.

Speaking with me at the festival headquarters, Lirio Abbate said, 'When you write about the mafia that shoots and carries out bloody attacks, everyone applauds, including polititicians. But journalists can also reveal connections between the mafia and politicians, for example by taking pictures of a mafioso dining with a mayor, and writing about it. Of course, having a meal together isn't a crime. But if a public prosecutor decides to investigate such a politician, suddenly the path is blocked. There are new laws, there are threats. The same applies to former mafia bosses who have become informants. If they want to talk about murders, fine. But if they start blabbing about a politician, they run into trouble, and no one listens to them. Politics will always protect itself.'

President Giorgio Napolitano sprang to mind. In 2013, the 88-year-old Napolitano became the first head of state in the history of the Italian republic to be elected for a second term. On the day of his second inauguration as president, he ordered the destruction of certain legal evidence. The legal case to which the evidence pertained was centred around negotiations between the Sicilian mafia and the Italian state in the early 1990s. That trial opened many people's eyes to the historical relationship between the mafia and the Italian government, making President Napolitano's actions even more humiliating.

Lirio Abbate didn't mince words: 'There were recordings of phone calls between Napolitano and a suspect in the case. According to the prosecution, the tapes weren't relevant to the trial. And so, legally, they had to be destroyed. But only after they had been made available to everyone involved in the case, something President Napolitano wanted to avoid. The tapes were destroyed before anyone else could evaluate their relevance. And that is forbidden by criminal law. Napolitano could have written a new law stating that if the president is wiretapped, the evidence should automatically be destroyed. However, that would have violated the Italian Constitution. And so, the matter was resolved in a way that spared the president's image.

Lirio Abbate noticed my shocked reaction. He nodded gently and said, 'We still have a long way to go.'

Trame, like Abbate's work, focuses on the economic and political power of the mafia rather than its gun-toting, violent side. That's familiar territory in Lamezia Terme, where mafia infiltration had already once caused the city's municipal council to be dissolved. However, the speakers at Trame stress that the Ndrangheta's political influence is felt not only here in Calabria but throughout Italy. For instance in Ventimiglia, a prosperous coastal village in northern Italy, near the French border. It is a favourite destination for many foreign tourists, and an example of a northern Italian municipal council being dissolved because of a Ndrangheta takeover. In Ventimiglia, the Ndrangheta not only manipulated the city council elections and construction bids, they also dumped waste and extorted individuals. It may sound harsh, but for Calabrians, this is almost comforting to hear, because the fault clearly lies outside their region. The Ndrangheta is like a weed that can take root anywhere, a political-economic pestilence that also infests places where the local citizens aren't underprivileged or systematically silenced.

Café de Paris in Rome is another unexpected haunt of the Ndrangheta. The place was once frequented by world-renowned film director Federico Fellini, who re-created its terrace in a studio for his film *La Dolce Vita*. However, the grand café's more recent history was less captivating: it was the setting of a Ndrangheta boss's meeting with the Italian minister of agriculture and the vice-president of the data protection authority. The minister of agriculture went on to become the mayor of Rome, and he was later convicted of being a political linchpin for the capital's mafia.

And here's another example: the managers of a thriving call centre company in Milan asked the Belloccos, an infamous Ndrangheta family from Rosarno, to 'motivate' people in Calabria to repay their loans. The Belloccos were happy to lend a hand, but in exchange for their services, they demanded shares in the business. Gradually, they took over the whole company and ruined it. The Italian media referred to this as Ndrangheta infiltration, but at Trame, a subtle distinction was pointed out: if you invite a clan to get involved in your business, how can that involvement be called 'infiltration'?

Nicola Gratteri is Trame's biggest crowd-pleaser by far. As a Calabrian mafia prosecutor, he enjoys a status like that of his iconic Sicilian predecessors Falcone and Borsellino, who were brutally murdered with their bodyguards in the 1990s. Gratteri makes frequent television appearances and publishes at least one bestseller about the Ndrangheta every year. He has also become the face of the fight against the Calabrian mafia beyond Italy's borders. He's relentless in his message about how the Ndrangheta has slowly but surely taken root throughout Europe, from America to Australia, and from Asia to Africa. *Fratelli di sangue* (Blood Brothers), the overview of the Calabrian clans Gratteri wrote with his regular co-author, Antonio Nicaso, has been translated into several languages.

Gratteri appears at Trame surrounded by his usual circle of permanent bodyguards. He seems relaxed, and for once, he isn't wearing a suit. Instead, he is dressed in a light blue checked shirt and khakis. His most recent book is about the Ndrangheta's traditions and laws, of which the best known is the omertà, the code of silence, although there are many others. Gratteri is not a modest man. He says that Ndranghetists are regularly overheard in wiretaps bragging about their clan's prominent place in his best-known book, *Fratelli di sangue*. 'The book sells well because there is a copy on every Ndrangheta family's bookshelf and in the barracks of every carabinieri unit.'

According to Gratteri, the Ndrangheta is successful because of two crucial factors: blood ties and an obsession with rules. 'When a Ndranghetist breaks the rules, there are always penalties. Even if he's just fifteen minutes late for a meeting, the rest will immediately decide which punishment to mete out. The others might urinate on the offender's leg or give him a "swirly", holding his head in the toilet while flushing. The humiliation is intended to teach transgressors a lesson. A Ndranghetist addicted to drugs or alcohol will be barred until he's clean. It's that level of rigour that makes the Ndrangheta the preferred partner of the Mexican and Colombian cartels. Because the clans are so reliable, they can buy cocaine for the lowest price. In parts of the Amazon where the army doesn't dare to show its face, members of the Ndrangheta feel right at home.'

Rules are rules, even when it's a matter of life or death. When a member of the Ndrangheta kills someone, they believe they have no choice. 'The Ndranghetist tells himself death is the consequence of breaking a rule. Before carrying out the murder, he makes the sign of the cross, prays to God and asks the Madonna for protection. He must respect the rules at all costs. But be careful,' Gratteri says, 'before we romanticize the members' obedience to those ghastly rules, we must remember that the rules don't apply to the bosses themselves if they happen to be temporarily inconvenient. They only apply to the idiots who do the boss's bidding. Young men so brainwashed, they think it's the only way to command any respect in their hometown.'

The Ndrangheta calls new or low-ranking members *picciotti*. 'The morning after a boy goes through initiation to become a *picciotto*, he heads to Lamezia Terme's most popular bar. A patron offers him a coffee. No one bought him coffee yesterday, so right away, he feels different. In every village and city in Calabria, people meet at the bar every morning for coffee and a cornetto, a croissant, *il rito del caffè*; people on their way to work or civil servants who've already clocked in at the office. The coffee ritual involves making the other person feel important or confirming your status. The postal worker insists on paying for the lawyer's coffee; the mayor pays for the doctor, and so on. Of course, a capolocale is there too, surrounded by picciotti who've started walking differently, assumed a proud stance, and started puffing out their chests. This ritual is the starting point of the deception that later produces war machines, hitmen and drug runners. Young men who travel from Lamezia to Milan to smuggle cocaine, returning home via Bologna. A typical picciotto will earn 1,500 to 2,000 euros, about what a plumber pulls in for a good-sized job. So, what's the difference? On average, the plumber will only be paid for four out of five jobs. He might become angry, lose sleep and pick a fight with his wife before he forgets all about it. A drug runner, on the other hand, visits Milan's most exclusive restaurant and orders the most expensive dish on the menu. Maybe lobster, because he's heard people talk about it. And a bottle of champagne for the same reason. He finds a prostitute and spends a few hundred euros on her. It's not that he takes pleasure in all the so-called luxury. It's about bragging about it back in his village in Calabria and seeing his friends' jaws drop. He wants to feel important and respected. Maybe he'll make ten trips trafficking cocaine. By then, he's started attracting attention with his new car and designer-label clothes, and he finds a sweetheart, a young girl who's still in high school. Now, he can buy everyone a round of coffee at breakfast in the bar. Not out of generosity, but as a way of displaying his power. Watch me as I pull a hundred euros out of my pocket to pay for three coffees.'

I wonder if there are guys in the audience who recognize themselves in Gratteri's words. Although it seems unlikely, a journalist from the local paper, the *Gazzetta del Sud*, has told me that he sometimes spots members of the Ndrangheta in the audience at this festival: 'They are sent here to listen to what's being said and to see who else is here.'

Gratteri, Italy's most famous living mafia prosecutor, continues describing the life of the average Ndranghetist: 'His criminal philosophy leads him to marry young and start a family, not for love, but because children mean power. Once they're older, girls can be married to boys from other Ndrangheta families to form an alliance and consolidate power. That's the way royal families did business centuries ago. And, for Ndranghetists, sons are like atomic bombs: ammunition during wartime.'

Finally, Gratteri steps into his narrative. 'What if, during the young man's umpteenth trip as a drugs courier, we tap his telephone? We then have enough evidence to convict him of trafficking and membership of a mafia organization. He'd be sent to prison for ten years, far from home, locked up during the best years of his life. He'd be held in pre-trial detention while his very young wife was stuck at home with the kids, unemployed and, as often happens, addicted to sleeping pills and antidepressants. A lawyer from Calabria might rush to the prison to defend the young man in question. These lawyers are often watchdogs for the clan, saying, "Don't worry, so-and-so sends his best wishes. We'll get you out of here, rest assured." But by then, that young man is struggling; his world is crashing down around his shoulders, and maybe he's tempted to cooperate with the public prosecutor. But how could he dare open his mouth? That would mean betraying dozens of family members and friends.'

There they are again: the blood ties that guarantee the silence of individual Ndranghetists. And the rules, like the law of blood vengeance hanging over an informant's head for the rest of his life, an execution that a family member must carry out. These things seem to have kept the Ndrangheta running like clockwork for over a century.

Someone asks Nicola Gratteri if the relationship between members of the Ndrangheta and politicians has changed in recent years. 'Twenty years ago, a mafioso might offer a politician a certain amount of votes in exchange for a public procurement contract. Today, the politicians, the election candidates themselves, visit mafia bosses at home to ask for votes in exchange for awarding public contracts. We have witnessed this ourselves using cameras and eavesdropping equipment. A crucial part of public administration and of the economy, the stock exchange, has long been in the hands of the mafia. Why do politicians turn to mafia bosses? Because the mafiosi have more credibility with the public than they do. If, for instance, a municipality's road needs to be resurfaced, five men will work on it for twenty days. That puts bread on the table, and when the elections come around, all five will vote for the candidate who is the mafia boss's favourite. Where the mayor and the municipal employment agency failed to find work for those five men, the mafia boss succeeded. He wins public procurement contracts; then, he decides where the materials will be bought and who will be employed. In other words, the mafia boss holds the welfare of that community in his hands.'

The clans use these techniques to keep entire villages and cities under their thumb: the Ndrangheta decides who is allowed to work and who will sit on the municipal council. On a more extensive, international scale, the Ndrangheta bases its economic power on cocaine trafficking, perhaps the most lucrative trade today. According to Gratteri, 'Ndrangheta clans import eighty per cent of the cocaine entering Europe. They buy cocaine in South America at a cut-rate price. Instead of eighteen hundred euros a kilo, they pay a thousand, for ninety-eight per cent pure coke. Each kilo is cut to produce four and a half kilos, and the consumer pays fifty euros a gram.' Off the top of my head, I calculate that a kilo costing a thousand euros ends up selling for more than two hundred thousand, based on Gratteri's figures. 'Those astronomical profits give the Calabrian clans unbelievable economic power: they can buy anything. And it's not just South America that lives off profits from cocaine: the sale of cocaine also fuels the European economy. The luxury seen on the streets of London or in Germany is made possible in part by laundered cocaine money.'

In Italy, a special anti-mafia law prevents the Ndrangheta from blithely investing because the clans risk having their assets discovered and seized by judicial authorities. However, according to Gratteri, the rest of Europe is 'a large green pasture where the Ndrangheta can graze without anyone bothering them. It seems that the EU is unprepared to deal with the Ndrangheta, and I have no idea how we'll be able to resolve the problem. We have a clear picture of the *cappa*, the oppressive bell jar placed over our lives by the mafia; it's taken away our smiles. And we understand the consequences of their suffocating influence on the economy and democracy.'

Nicola Gratteri grew up with the Ndrangheta, observing clan members at close range when he attended school with their kids. At the start of his career in the 1990s, he used his own money to buy eavesdropping equipment for the court in Locri. Despite a lack of adequate funding, he was keen to use new techniques in his legal investigations. The Calabrian public prosecutors' office still suffers from an unrelenting shortage of money; nevertheless, they are leaders in the national and international fight against the Ndrangheta.

'Dozens of grandiose magistrates work hard behind the scenes, writing until their fingers are worn to the bone. But you don't see them; I'm the only one on TV and in the papers. I'm the showgirl.' Gratteri receives a burst of applause for his self-mockery.

After Gratteri's talk, I blink to clear my vision – am I seeing things? But yes, a line of carabinieri, dressed in their elegant uniforms, are waiting for Gratteri to sign their copies of his book. He doesn't allow a long queue to form, and after a few minutes, he stands up and leaves with his bodyguards. I decide to approach him.

'*Dottor* Gratteri, how did it go yesterday in Brussels?' I asked. I'd read that he had visited the European Parliament, where a special committee was drafting a resolution to strengthen the international stance against the mafia. 'The trouble is that European members of parliament are blind to the fact that the Ndrangheta is active in their countries. They say: nothing happens, there are no shootings, there are no bodies or burned-out cars on our streets. I say, you're right, they don't need to use violence for money laundering and cocaine trafficking. I try to explain the nature of the problem to them. The Germans, especially, are hard-headed. They won't admit that the Ndrangheta is firmly rooted in Germany. I usually have a good working relationship with the justice department in the Netherlands. But recently, staff shortages have kept them from fulfilling our requests for legal assistance, and that's disappointing, mainly because the Ndrangheta favours importing cocaine through the ports of Rotterdam and Amsterdam. Many drugs arrive in the Netherlands, and so many fugitives live there: there has to be a network of people offering to protect them. The Netherlands must watch out.'

*

At the end of the evening, I pass the historic entrance to Trame's headquarters and paused to revisit those raised hands. Red, yellow and blue, the hands are painted on a gigantic sheet of paper and covered with the words '*Questa terra diventerà bellissima*': one day, this place will be beautiful.

11

IS IT SOMETHING YOU EAT OR DRINK?

To pay for my journalistic mission and the renovation of my house, I earned money primarily through editorial and translation work. I'd work through the weekends to allow myself a few days during the week to dig deeper into the Calabrian mafia, a subject I found increasingly fascinating. My boyfriend N supported my efforts wholeheartedly. He'd set up a marketing business with a friend and was eager to make video reports about Calabria. To help me prepare for an item about the port in Gioia Tauro, traditionally the domain of the Ndrangheta's Piromalli family, he showed me an old television clip on YouTube. It immediately illustrated why trying to get a response out of a Ndrangheta boss is maddening.

The video shows Giuseppe Marrazzo, a journalist famous for his interviews with convicted mafiosi, holding a microphone to the mouth of a man in his sixties lying in a hospital bed. The faded colours indicate that the clip dates from the 1970s. 'Don Mommo Piromalli, King of the Gioia Tauro plains, and *super-padrino* – how do you feel about being given such titles?'

Mommo Piromalli, the man being questioned by Marrazzo, is dressed in a pale orange jacket and baby blue pyjama bottoms pulled up around his waist. The camera angle makes his belly impossible to ignore. 'I never had those titles and never asked for them. The police, who call me that, just want to stir up trouble. I am neither a padrino nor a boss of the Calabrian mafia. I am a *padre di famiglia*, a family man, wrongly persecuted and tormented.'

'And yet, it's reported that you own the two hundred lorries used for excavations around Gioia Tauro.'

'I don't even own a bicycle.'

'People say no one can work in Gioia Tauro without your permission.'

'I haven't set foot in Gioia Tauro for four years because the judiciary is prosecuting me and because I'm ill.'

'Is it true you maintain close ties with key politicians?'

'Absolutely not. Of course, some local politicians know me, and when they say hello to me on the street, I politely return their greetings. And if I need something, I ask them for help, like everyone else.'

'It's reported that although you don't officially own anything, you are, in fact, a billionaire.'

'Where are these billions of lire supposed to be? I certainly don't have them.'

'How do you support yourself?'

'I worked hard for twenty years growing oranges.'

'But surely the strories about the Calabrian mafia are not made up?'

'It's only recently that I've heard people mention this mafia, but I have no idea what they're talking about. Is it something you eat or drink?'

While it's certainly not unusual for mafiosi to deny the existence of the mafia, Don Mommo Piromalli, lying in the hospital bed in his high-waisted baby blue pyjama bottoms, takes the cake with his 'something you eat or drink?' Whether or not you believe his act, Mommo Piromalli had been a key figure in the Ndrangheta. His family used profits from the illegal sale of cigarettes to buy large tracts of land in what is called the Gioia Tauro plain: the flat, fertile region along the Tyrrhenian coast of Calabria, whose main crops are oranges and olives. But agriculture was just a sideline. His Ndrangheta family was more interested in the opportunities and contacts their territorial dominance gave them.

In the 1970s, when Don Mommo was the 'king of the plains', the Italian government announced plans for extensive public redevelopment to boost the Calabrian economy. The projects included, among other things, constructing a massive port near Gioia Tauro and building highways through the Aspromonte and along the Tyrrhenian coast. According to the Calabrian courts, Mommo Piromalli's strategic position during that time meant more wealth and power for the Ndrangheta. He accomplished that by modernizing the Ndrangheta's business model and ensuring that more and more funds from government support became available to his family and to all the Calabrian clans.

Mommo Piromalli had served time for murder, and he'd been tried for ordering the kidnapping of the grandson of oil magnate John Paul Getty. The 16-year-old victim was ultimately left along the side of a motorway after his family paid almost two million dollars in ransom; the boy had withstood five traumatic months in captivity and the bloody agony of having his ear cut off. And even though the courts acquitted Piromalli due to a lack of evidence, he decided it was time the Calabrian clans stopped kidnapping and shifted their attention to drug trafficking. While he was at it, he also wanted to transform the Ndrangheta's rules. He realized that in order to build an efficient network within the upper echelons of society, Ndranghetists, like members of the Sicilian mafia, had to be allowed to maintain closer ties with the political elite and join the Freemasons.

To change the rules, Piromalli first had to convince his associates in the highest ranks of the Ndrangheta. The most important of these were Paolo De Stefano, who controlled the clans around the city of Reggio Calabria, and Antonio Macrì, who ruled the Ionian coast. But Macrì, the former Capocrimine from Siderno, wasn't keen to start trafficking in drugs or to change the time-honoured rules. And so, one mild winter evening, when he had just finished a game of bocce ball, Macrì was shot and killed. In fact, before Piromalli could change the rules to suit his needs, two hundred additional Ndranghetists had to die in what became known as the First Ndrangheta War, which lasted three years.

Together with his supporters, including the De Stefano family of Reggio Calabria, the Strangios from San Luca, and the Pesces and Belloccos from Rosarno, Piromalli decided on the new official rules of the game. They set up a new internal society called *la Santa*, or 'the Holy', intended to prevent upstart Ndranghetists from knocking on the doors of the Freemasons or state representatives. Experienced Ndranghetists invited to join this secret society were given certain privileges. Santisti, as they were called, were permitted to establish confidential relationships with police agents and judicial authorities. They were allowed to enter the Freemasons, helping them develop cordial ties within the realms of politics, banking and business. And if it was in the Santa's interests, the new rules made it possible to betray other lower-ranking Ndrangheta members.

Of course, Don Mommo Piromalli was among the first to achieve the Santista status. He was still serving time in 1979 when he died in the hospital in Gioia Tauro, surrounded by his wife and children. Six thousand people came to pay their respects to the so-called 'family man' at his funeral.

In 1975, it was Don Mommo Piromalli's cousin who welcomed Minister Giulio Andreotti to Gioia Tauro by offering him a cup of coffee. Andreotti would serve seven terms as prime minister, and it was later proven in a Sicilian court that he had close links to members of the mafia. But when the Piromalli family was plying Andreotti with pastries and espresso at the Euromotel they ran, Andreotti was still the minister in charge of the *Cassa del Mezzogiorno,* public funds available for distribution in southern Italy. And the Piromallis and their associates were eager to get their hands on that cash. After coffee, Minister Andreotti was invited to the harbour's construction site to lay the first stone. He then gave a mollifying speech about the boundless economic opportunities the port would bring to Calabria.

The container port on the Tyrrhenian coast became the largest in the Mediterranean. But, not unlike the motorway and other public works on the Gioia Tauro plain, construction of the harbour took considerably longer than expected. It wasn't until 1994, after almost twenty years, that the port finally became operational. During construction, the Piromallis secured many of the subcontracts, and they pressured the container terminal managers to agree to a kickback of a dollar and a half for every container the port handled. Because, as the Piromallis reasoned, Gioia Tauro belonged to them. In no uncertain terms, they told the harbour's managers, 'We are the past, the present and the future.'

Prophetic words: for decades, the Piromallis extorted the management of the container terminal for a percentage of the profits and forced them to hire Ndranghetists. That helped the family keep an eye on the shipments and allowed other clans as far away as the

Ionian coast to benefit from cocaine and arms smuggling. In 2011, the police apprehended an employee of the container terminal driving a van loaded with 560 kilos of cocaine.

At that time, approximately three million containers per year passed through Gioia Tauro. Because many imports coming through Calabria were destined for the United States, the US government ordered a special investigation into the port's security. According to investigators, it wasn't a lack of control capabilities that made Gioia Tauro so attractive for drug smuggling and illegal arms shipments. The presence of corrupt personnel working for customs and within the harbour police was deemed to be an important factor.

The Americans decided to tighten inspections of their own cargo to and from Gioia Tauro. But that proved no easy task; inspectors received letters containing bullets, and some were even shot. At the conclusion of the investigation, the Americans were pessimistic: 'Because the mafia controls the port and can easily use it to import drugs or weapons, it risks becoming the gateway to even more dangerous materials.'

The nature of those 'dangerous materials' was left open. Even so, in 2014, the United Nations and the US Navy decided to ship eighty containers of the world's most deadly substances to Gioia Tauro. The containers carried a stockpile of chemical weapons from Syria, where President Bashar al-Assad had used mustard gas and sarin to attack his own citizens, killing or seriously injuring many. The UN Organization for the Prohibition of Chemical Weapons, winner of the Nobel Peace Prize, had seized Assad's supply of chemical weapons to quash well-based fears that he might reuse them for further attacks. The mustard gas and sarin had to be shipped to a safer place and converted into less hazardous waste.

In Calabria, while few doubted the UN mission's urgency and

good intentions, the choice of Gioia Tauro raised eyebrows. Of course, finding a suitable port would not have been easy for the UN. Options within Europe were limited after Norway, France and Belgium refused to allow ships carrying chemical weapons to dock. Following fierce protests, the Albanian government also withdrew its offer.

Italy had initially suggested a port in Sardinia for the UN transhipment, but local council members vetoed the plan. In the end, the Italian government decided to ship the eighty containers of chemical weapons to Gioia Tauro and transfer them there to another vessel, to be taken elsewhere and rendered less harmful.

With memories of the vanished toxic ships still fresh in their minds, the outraged people in Calabria took to the streets, even though it was too late to stop the arrival of the dangerous cargo. Local mayors demanded a disaster contingency plan, at the very least. Calabria was, after all, an earthquake zone. What if a container of mustard gas fell and broke open? A residential area and a primary school were just a few hundred metres from the port. The fire department was also dismayed because they didn't have suitable equipment for dealing with such a disaster. The staff of the nearest hospital, half an hour away, added their voices to the uproar, saying they had no idea how to treat potential victims.

Fortunately, the containers of Syrian chemical weapons were transferred at Gioia Tauro without incident; the Veolia Group, one of the largest multinational companies in the world, was responsible for treating the extraordinary waste. The company's name was already well known in Calabria, thanks to the rust-coloured water running from the taps of hundreds of thousands of residents. I remember being warned not to drink the water when we visited a friend of N's in Vibo, the largest city near Gioia Tauro. Apparently, the water contained harmful substances. The manager of the provincial water service was later charged with negligence, and the Veolia Group promptly sold off its forty-seven per cent share in the Calabrian water company.

A few months after the shipment of chemical weapons arrived in Gioia Tauro, police carried out another in its endless series of operations against the Ndrangheta. This one targeted the clans' involvement in various business activities in the port, including money laundering, fraud and tax evasion on a grand scale. The military police dispatched two hundred soldiers, describing the Ndrangheta's 'suffocating hold' on virtually all the activities in the port area. It seems some clan members used their friends at customs to ensure the free passage not only of drugs but also of such things as counterfeit designer goods made in China.

Don Mommo Piromalli clearly had keen foresight, but in the late 1970s, would he have dreamt of Chinese business partners? We'll never know. According to the justice department, the current generation of Piromallis, spread from Calabria to Ecuador, invests in waste management, water treatment and shopping centres. They ship cocaine directly from Colombia to the ports of Rotterdam or Genoa, or to their home base, Gioia Tauro.

However, some members of the Piromalli family still draw on the family's agricultural roots. These include Antonio Piromalli, who moved to Milan, where, according to Calabrian mafia prosecutors, he ruled over Italy's largest fruit and vegetable market, the Ortomercato. As expected, the oranges there came from Gioia Tauro. They were picked for a pittance by stateless Africans trying to survive in muddy Italian refugee camps. Antonio Piromalli's fruit was exported throughout Europe. And in America, he sold residual oil, chemically extracted from olive kernels and waste pulp, labelled as the purest *extra virgin olive oil*.

12

REGRETS AND MORE REGRETS

'I am a child of mamma Ndrangheta.' Luigi Bonaventura was in his early forties, compact and stocky, with dark blond hair, pale eyes and a treble voice with dark, husky undertones, evidence of heavy smoking. His family founded the first Ndrangheta 'locale' or base of operations in Crotone, a seaside village in north-eastern Calabria. At the end of 2013, Luigi Bonaventura started to follow me on Twitter. He then sent me a message to ask if he could 'friend' me on Facebook. I saw the words *Collaboratore di giustizia* adorning his profile. Who was this justice collaborator or informant? And why did he want to get in touch with me?

Based on his social media posts, Luigi could prove valuable for my research. So we quickly set up a Skype session. 'I was a member of the mafia from birth, just like my father and grandfather, who, like me, were destined to follow in their fathers' footsteps,' he explained. 'The Ndrangheta is like a tribe with a unique religion and lifestyle. You're raised with it and indoctrinated from childhood. It's like military training. I grew up in a highly violent world because my family was embroiled in two clan wars simultaneously.

'I remember firing a gun when I was ten. It was New Year's Eve; where I grew up, people used to shoot into the sky on that night.

Although it probably wasn't the first time I had used a gun, that moment stuck with me because when I pulled the trigger, I hurt my thumb. In any case, from a very early age, I was exposed to the weapons my father and uncles brought home. I loved watching them handle those weapons; I was fascinated. I wasn't so different from other boys, except that the guns in my house weren't toys.

'On that New Year's Eve, when I was ten, I put my thumb in the wrong place, and it hurt like hell. I don't remember the pain so much as my shame, because I had always been told I had to do everything perfectly. You had to be at least as good as your forebears. My grandfather Luigi was one of Calabria's most important bosses; I was named after him and had to live up to his reputation.

'You don't realize your home life is abnormal when you're a kid. I accepted my world and learned the code of conduct that went along with it. To bullies in the neighbourhood, I'd shout, "Who's in charge here?" I'd beat up anyone who tried to challenge me. Afterwards, I'd say, "From now on, I'm the boss." That's the behaviour of a mafioso, but I wasn't old enough to recognize it.'

Luigi's words kept flowing; he seemed to have a deep need to talk about his past. Any earlier reluctance or shame had turned to outrage. 'We tell ourselves that there are no child soldiers in Europe. They're in Africa, OK, but we find it almost impossible to acknowledge that there are also child soldiers in Italy, especially in Calabria, Sicily and Naples. I'm not just talking about kids who are trained from an early age to go to war for mafia organizations, but also children who move cocaine or weapons from one place to another when they're eight or ten, or stand watch for drug dealers. Those kids are also child soldiers.

'I vividly remember the beatings my father gave me. Sometimes, he'd use a big whip, the kind used to keep herds of cattle in line. I experienced mortal fear before I was ten, because I was terrified of my father and uncle. There comes a point when you either go insane or learn to cope. As a teenager, I toughened up and stopped feeling the fear.

'I learned my way around increasingly dangerous weapons. At the age of twelve, I started dealing with specialized weapons, ranging from AK-47s from the Kalashnikov family to pistols, machine guns, and the classic sawn-off shotgun. Have you seen *Gomorrah*, the film about the Neapolitan mafia, with those two teenagers on the beach firing randomly? We did that, too, on cloudy or rainy days at the beach. We'd stash the guns in the trunk because, when the weather was bad, fewer police officers were guarding the roads. Actually, we never shot off rounds at random. We always aimed at a target: bottles, cans or barrels. We'd lean them against the rock face and practise hitting them with various weapons. My dad or uncle showed me how to do it, how to stand, take aim and use your arms and legs. I was intrigued by how the different bullets hit their target, and would inspect the holes they left in the rock.

'My father and uncle used bottles to get me accustomed to the idea of a target. But later, that target would be a human being. The reality of that hits you like a ton of bricks the first time you see someone lying on the ground, dead. Then you realize – the only difference between you and the target is that you're still standing.'

During those Skype sessions, Luigi Bonaventura revealed his vulnerable side. I was struck by the way he'd occasionally interrupt his grim monologue with something to lighten the mood. Sometimes, when my boyfriend N was sitting beside me, Luigi would confess to being homesick for Calabria, the food, the mountains and the sea. Occasionally, his wife and children would briefly appear on screen to say hello.

'After I completed my weapons training, I started a new phase.

I had reached the age of majority and had to build up experience outside of Calabria, in northern Italy. I had to make myself invisible, like a spare round of ammunition. The Ndrangheta often keeps extras in reserve, people who can stay under the police's radar but are ready to be recalled in case of a clan war or a covert mission. They often work for a while in northern Italy, like I did, or abroad. I worked for two different construction companies associated with my family, first in Veneto and Emilia Romagna, and then in Tuscany. The idea is to become accustomed to being away from your family. As a clan member, you grow up in a sheltered social circle: all your friends are either your cousins or the sons of other clan members. But when you're working far from home, you get used to them not being around. That way, the clan prepares you for the future, because you will probably end up in prison at some point or hiding in a bunker as a fugitive.

'The clan wouldn't allow me to commit any crimes in the north. Even minor violations were forbidden; my criminal record had to remain pristine. Making sure you keep your nose clean and stay under the radar is all part of the Ndrangheta's strategy. At the same time, in the north, you can pick up different social customs. You must learn how to behave; you can't remain an uncivilized back-country bumpkin. Otherwise, you won't be able to gain access to high-class society. So you work, but you're a mole, an infiltrator, at the same time. You learn the language and the etiquette. You learn how to use other people's weaknesses and fears to further the Ndrangheta's business interests. In short, you're sent to a different region to learn the local customs, to assimilate and become one of them, so that later, you can go back as a colonizer to build the clan's political and economic power. In the Ndrangheta's eyes, Calabria is the homeland, and all the other regions and countries are there to be colonized.

That could mean northern Italy, but also Germany, Belgium and the Netherlands.'

In 1990, Luigi was ordered to return to Calabria. Feuds and arrests had weakened his family, so he had to get used to being a soldier again. 'Some guys had turned up, threatening my family and trying to take over. I went back to Calabria right away. We were preparing our reprisals when a young man around my age was shot and killed. His father was a member of our clan, and the victim had been born the same year I was, even in the same week.

'My family decided our revenge had to send a clear message. So, to show them we had power and guts, we picked the Piazza Pitagora in the heart of Crotone. It was always crowded, so our enemies would believe we couldn't touch them there. Our message was that no place was safe for those who attacked us. And that's the way it played out. One afternoon that autumn, we killed the self-proclaimed boss and two others right there on the square. A few bystanders were also injured. From that moment on, my family was able to rapidly increase its investments, such as those in waste processing and the football club. We would never have realized such growth if the other clan had had their way.

'Incidentally, I wasn't the one who pulled the trigger during that hit on the Piazza Pitagora. That time, I was just keeping watch. I committed my first actual murder a year later when I was nineteen. Then, my cousins and I were ordered to eliminate four individuals. Not just pull the trigger, mind you, but take care of all the surrounding details. We were only given the targets' names and approximate addresses. I didn't even know the boy I was supposed to kill. They pointed him out to me once.

'I did everything by the book. I kept my heart rate under control, pulled the trigger, fired five rounds and saved one bullet for myself in case someone came after me. Then I left the scene, slowly at first, then running. I had carried out the perfect murder, but I felt like killing someone had brought me to the lowest point of humanity. It's almost like killing yourself.

'But when I returned home, my father was clearly pleased with how I had carried out the mission. I had been seeking his approval for ages, hoping to get his blessing for other things. My uncle and other clan members were there, too; they kissed and embraced me. That evening, we had a meal together, even though there were still specks of the victim's blood and brains on my shoes. I was confused by the satisfaction I saw in my father's eyes; I couldn't understand why he was validating me at that specific moment. Maybe I would have been happier if my father had seemed pleased after I'd carried out a successful robbery with no fatalities. You might not believe me, but that's how I felt, and I'm sure it's because of the values my mother taught me despite everything.

'My mother wasn't born into a Ndrangheta family. My father didn't want an arranged marriage, and he chose a woman whose family had no connection with the mafia. She taught me about warmth and did her best to instil certain values. In the end, I also married for love. I was allowed to decide for myself because I had become the head of the family by then. My wife Paola's parents were against the mafia. My family, of course, saw that as a risk, and they were right about that, because where I am today is partly due to my wife.'

It was a long time after Luigi committed his first murder in 1991 before he dared to turn his back on the career thrust upon him as heir to his father's throne. Luigi was the oldest of five children, so expectations were high. 'I have two brothers and two sisters. Usually, the first-born is destined to become the commanding officer. Then, other Ndrangheta children are often purposely shielded from a life of crime because someone with a clean record can efficiently work as a straw man. Or they might become the family's lawyer, doctor or accountant.

'When you are the successor to the throne, however, it's not enough to know your way around weapons; you must know how to use your head. Before I could lead my family, I had to prove my worth by assisting my uncle Gianni, the commander of our clan at the time. He'd gone underground, hiding from the police. Despite my young age – I was just twenty – he made me his right-hand man. I became his confidant and was one of the few people who knew his whereabouts. I brought him news and medicine; in return, he sent me back with a list of orders and assignments. He oversaw the clan's military branch: arms and drug trafficking, extortion and murders. Occasionally, he'd send me to Reggio or other Calabrian cities to handle the PR for my family and arrange joint cocaine deals with other clans.

'We had ties with the De Stefano family based in Reggio Calabria, and in the 1990s, we also started working with a branch of the Sicilian Cosa Nostra. I was privy to this type of information, generally kept from someone as young as I was, because I was my uncle's confidant. At that time, Cosa Nostra oversaw all the mafias, but today, the Ndrangheta has assumed command. Back then, for example, we collaborated on a shipment of cocaine worth one and a quarter billion lire – more than half a million euros – which was a lot of money in those days. Everything would arrive by ship in Calabria. We weren't very close to the cartels back then, so we used intermediaries who travelled to Colombia on the family's behalf; the Colombians welcomed them like royalty. By now, the Colombian and Mexican drug cartels prefer to negotiate directly with the Ndranghetists, because they guarantee money, silence and global distribution channels.'

*

Luigi Bonaventura was a clan member from birth, a 'young man of honour', but he didn't receive his formal Ndrangheta baptism until he was twenty-one. At the time, he was on the run and hiding in a secret lair near Crotone; due to his age and criminal merits, he was immediately inducted into the second rank of *camorrista*. Shortly after his baptism, he was arrested and spent a brief time in jail.

When he was thirty, Luigi rose to the third rank of *sgarrista*, and stepped into his uncle Gianni's shoes as head of the family. He commanded two hundred men. 'In Crotone, they used my name to intimidate people and get things done. I made decisions about trafficking in arms and drugs, but also regarding human lives. When I was younger and still a foot soldier for the clan, I didn't ask myself many questions. In that position, you are expected to obey your commanding officers. But now, everything had changed. If an enemy had to be eliminated, I gave the order. I started asking myself: who am I to decide who can live and who must die?

'Around that time, I married Paola; we had a son and a daughter, and I started contemplating my children's future. I didn't punish them the way my father had beaten me, but I couldn't ignore the fact that they, too, were Ndrangheta children. Somehow, I had to pass on to them the Ndrangheta way of life, for their own survival as well.

'I asked myself: what's honourable about robbing your children of their future? Because my son's fate had already been decided: he would end up in prison, he would be murdered or he would have to kill others. I wondered if I would be able to say "*bravo*" to my son when he killed someone. Maybe it sounds hypocritical or like empty rhetoric, but I would have preferred to see my boy completing his studies or finding a job that puts bread on the table and doesn't hurt anyone. I watched as many of my firmly held beliefs crumbled, and

I started noticing the value in other things. Slowly, I began to consider collaborating with the justice department.

'My wife Paola was the first person I told. I trusted her more than anyone in my circle. I had always wanted to spare my family a confrontation with the Ndrangheta, so I had become adept at hiding certain things. At home, the police carried out sporadic raids, but they never found anything. I was trying to keep the Ndrangheta out. Paola knew my family was different, but she didn't know the precise details. This was back in the early years of the new century; the Ndrangheta wasn't very well known, and almost no one in Italy talked about it. We hardly even used the word Ndrangheta among ourselves. The name only caught on in Italy – and beyond – after that bloodbath in Duisburg in August 2007.

'I felt like I was betraying Paola because I'd only let her see part of who I was. She still believed that our income came from legal sources: we ran a Mexican restaurant, a security company, and an events agency. At the time, there was less awareness than there is now about the mafia's working methods, in which legitimate businesses are combined with illegal deals. Paola had believed me when I said that everything was legit.'

But then, for the first time, Luigi told his wife who he really was. He revealed that he had lived an intensely criminal life from an early age and that, when he had turned thirty, shortly before they were married, he became a boss and had been at the helm for four years. 'I told Paola I wanted to distance myself from the rest of my family. I wanted to give my children a different kind of upbringing and future. She was stunned and couldn't grasp it immediately, but luckily, she decided to stand by me.'

Luigi didn't want to feel like he'd betrayed his father, so he shared some of his deeper motivations with him. 'I knew it was perilous but couldn't stop myself. One day, I said that although the Ndrangheta tradition was supposedly based on honour, I wondered what was honourable about robbing your children and grandchildren of their future. His didn't flinch, and it almost seemed like he hadn't heard me, but he didn't waste any time telling the rest of the family that I wanted out.

'As the head of the family, I had been the engine of a machine driven by money and power. But now that I'd turned against them, I was nothing but a business risk that had to be eliminated. The threats started straight away. Clan members dropped in, saying, "If you don't stay at your post, we'll kill your wife and children." They dragged my name through the mud by saying I was crazy. They tried to poison me. They even sent a priest to tell me that it would be better if I didn't turn my back on my family. Friends who visited us at home were threatened at gunpoint. Clan members told my in-laws that they'd end up with us in a hole in the ground.'

Luigi's family owned two large houses in the centre of Crotone. They'd intentionally neglected the upkeep of the exterior to arouse less police suspicion. 'I lived with my family in one *palazzo*, and my father lived in the other, close by. One night, a car pulled up as I was walking down the stairs outside. My father, an uncle and a few other guys got out. Something wasn't right, so I went back inside, but my father followed me. He opened the front door and started shooting as I ran up the stairs; but he missed. The following morning, I made another attempt to leave the house. It was broad daylight, so I didn't expect they'd try again, but I was armed, just in case. My father was there again, and he started shooting. To defend myself, I shot him in the leg. He ran out of ammunition without hitting me and limped away.

'In other words, my father made two attempts on my life. In the

Ndrangheta, your closest relatives are responsible for regaining the family's honour, so your father or brother usually carries out your assassination. Supposedly because family honour is "sacred". Of course, that's nonsense. Those who give the orders invented those rules to undermine everyone else. For a long time, almost no former members had dared testify against the Calabrian mafia precisely because of those relentless rules surrounding the so-called family honour.

'Among the established Ndrangheta families, I was the first to turn informant. And I was terrified about collaborating with the justice department. I mulled it over carefully before signing on. At the time, there were only a handful of penitent witnesses, and most had started in prison, hoping to reduce their sentence.

'In 2007, I volunteered to cooperate with the judicial authorities, but I wasn't trying to dodge my punishment. I could have taken some money with me and left then and there without saying a word. But Paola and I decided that breaking free of my family wouldn't be enough. I had harmed others, and I hoped to make amends by working with the judicial authorities. In any case, if it's money you're after, you don't want to become an informant in Italy. What you get is a new identity, a house in a secret location and an allowance of around fifteen hundred euros a month.

'Paola and the kids – my son was five and my daughter two – joined me in the witness protection programme. Paola's parents and brother joined us as well, because they were no longer safe in Crotone. It was impossible to imagine beforehand how much our lives would change. It's worse than a funeral because it's not just one person who dies, but your entire universe: your mother and father, your brothers, sisters, aunts and uncles, your cousins, friends and neighbours. All at once, everyone and everything is gone. Or rather, you no longer exist for them.

'It's a traumatic shift, and that means government support is crucial. In such cases, the government must be understanding and empathetic. They have to offer support from psychologists and social workers. You come from a world populated by villains, and you're one, too. You don't know how you will deal with some situations; you might be a danger to yourself or others. The government needs to help you stay on the right path.

'Many public prosecutors I've worked with have shown me the human face of the government. But the institutions charged with protecting me and my family have lacked any sense of warmth. They haven't been there for us. We were lodged in high-risk locations, first in the city of Termoli, in a so-called secret location in a neighbourhood where everyone knew mafia informants were being housed. There were Ndrangheta members who tried to pressure me into giving false testimony on their behalf or withdrawing my testimony in exchange for leniency and an annual salary of a million.

'A few security people would occasionally drop by, but they didn't show much empathy. And it took a year and a half before we received our new IDs. People sent us bullets through the post. Then a large cache of Swiss weapons was discovered nearby in a garage belonging to the former head of my security team. The police found a letter when they confiscated the arsenal: "Soon, Bonaventura will disappear beneath seven metres of soil."

'The authorities transferred us to a different city. There, too, I ran into someone from my clan: an informant who was deemed unreliable and had been kicked out of the witness protection programme. Clearly, the Ndrangheta knows where to find me, but I only get security when I go to court to testify. Other than that, I hardly leave the house. I don't take my kids to school; we rarely go to a restaurant or the cinema. That's to protect them but also to protect others, because if someone kills me on the street, innocent victims might get caught in the crossfire.

'Of course, I wouldn't need to contact the media if the witness protection programme were functioning as it should. Then, it would be in my best interests to keep my head down, adopt a new identity and find an inconspicuous job. But to me, media attention is essential because I feel safer in the spotlight. The Ndrangheta is a criminal organization that doesn't like to kill anyone in the public eye. That could sway public opinion and trigger a government reaction that could jeopardize the power of the clans.'

Luigi Bonaventura senses that the Italian government has little interest in former mafia members who've turned state's witnesses. 'In fact, such a poorly functioning witness protection programme is practically a spanner in the works, meaning the project – in this case, a well-oiled machine to combat the mafia – will never reach completion. The way things stand, a boss, a potential informant with a particular status, will never cooperate with the justice department, and so, they'll never find out what he knows. It's almost as if, in some circles, their information is unwelcome. Some people don't want to eliminate the mafia because it's become essential to their livelihood.

'The consequences are also damaging for the rest of Europe. That's because although the mafia starts here in Italy, it ends up abroad. It's common knowledge that the Ndrangheta imports massive amounts of cocaine through the port of Rotterdam. And that's only possible with the help of local criminals, whether Dutch nationals or people from other countries. Sometimes, these individuals work for multiple organisations, enabling the arrival, unloading and sorting of goods. They're paid for their services either with money or a share of the drugs.

'I was also involved in drug trafficking; some of our people were sent to the Netherlands to organize transit. Then we'd transport the drugs to Italy over the highways. Once, there was a large police operation, and some fifty men were arrested. The police seized cocaine and more than sixty thousand ecstasy pills, which had been produced for us in the Netherlands.

'But the Ndrangheta is involved in more than drugs. It's a multinational at the service of the underworld. We know the motive behind there being so little mafia bloodshed outside Italy: it is to keep the authorities in other countries from becoming alarmed and taking action. The judges I've cooperated with have more courage than all the world's Ndranghetists put together, but they also need international support in their battle against the mafia. I don't want to frighten anyone, but I want to warn people outside Italy: it's not enough to get upset about someone drawing a gun and shooting. The mafia's actual killings take place in the economic and social arenas. The mafia contaminates the economy with dirty money, and they have various ways of undermining a country's freedom and democracy. They infect the fabric of society, the press, politics and different power levels. The Netherlands needs to understand that if it wants to remain the beautiful country it is today, with a healthy social fabric, it must stand up to the mafia now. But if the Netherlands continues to underestimate the problem, the situation will get out of control, like it did in Italy.'

A year after Luigi first contacted me online, N and I met him and his family in a coastal town in central Italy. Luigi was on his guard and seemed nervous. We had a meal together in a modern restaurant, and Luigi sat where he could observe everyone who came and went. Paola turned out to be a charming, warm-hearted woman with a vulnerable look in her eyes. Their son had Paola's dark curls and was the politest 13-year-old I've ever met. Their daughter, a dreamy ten-year-old, resembled her father and couldn't stop cuddling him. They'd just adopted a glossy, curly-haired, long-eared puppy that was waiting patiently under the table. Luigi proudly boasted of his kids' good school grades and urged them and Paola to say more about themselves.

At that time, Luigi Bonaventura had been an informant for almost eight years. He had testified before various courts of law, from Reggio Calabria to Turin, Venice and Stuttgart, Germany. Luigi had contributed to dozens of trials and hundreds of convictions. Although his actions had reduced his sentence, he knew that he would soon be called to spend a few years in prison, although he didn't know exactly when. It could be next week, next month, or the month after that.

Apparently, Luigi's nervousness hadn't diminished his appetite. We ordered plenty of fish, and after the meal, we lingered in the café, which also had a pool table. While we waited for the table to become free, I saw Paola start and freeze up: a short distance away, a young girl was holding up her smartphone. She asked if she could take a picture of the puppy. With a strained smile, Paola agreed, making sure neither she nor her husband and children were in the frame.

In the end, a game of pool helped us all unwind. The kids had never played before, so their father taught them how to hold the cue. He demonstrated various techniques with his arms around theirs. Then he let them try on their own. When they hit one of the balls, he hugged them, and when they missed, he offered encouragement.

Once all the coloured balls had disappeared into the pockets, it was time to leave. On our way out, Luigi pointed to a dartboard on the wall. As I looked at the black and white segments surrounding the red bull's-eye, Luigi winked and said it was a pity there weren't any darts. 'I used to have such good aim.'

13

A MEANINGFUL GESTURE

The last time I saw Luigi Bonaventura, we had played pool. That was before he went to prison. Back then, he smoked cigars and hand-rolled cigarettes. But when we spoke again after he was released, he was trying to quit, so he took an occasional drag from an e-cigarette. Before, he'd brazenly shown his face on television. But these days, he hides his greying curls and beard under a cap and a bandana. During interviews, he used to casually drop the names of former clan mates and their government cronies. Now, he tends to keep those names to himself, only sharing them with the prosecutors he works with.

Luigi's sentence had been reduced to three years and three months. We stayed in touch after his release, but for a while, he stopped giving official interviews. And although he continued to cooperate with tribunals, he'd decided to turn his back on the limelight, maybe forever.

It wasn't long, however, before he changed his mind, prompted by the murder of the brother of a former Ndrangheta member turned informer. The brother was killed in the same region where Luigi's family was housed. The man had been murdered in front of his house on Christmas Day at six-thirty in the evening. The two masked gunmen who showed up at his door couldn't have had much trouble finding the place, because the victim's name was on the letterbox.

As a result, Luigi reached out again to the media, and even though he only appeared with his face covered, his message – calling attention to failures in the witness protection programme – had a renewed urgency. There had been earlier fatalities. In the 1980s, for example, the Sicilian mafia's most famous informer, Tommaso Buscetta, had lost two children, four grandchildren and some of his in-laws to homicidal reprisals carried out by clan mates. In late 2018, the murder of the Ndrangheta informant's brother once again highlighted the shaky security surrounding the families of state's witnesses.

Luigi and Paola are primarily concerned about the children's safety. Their son has finished high school; their daughter speaks fluent English and takes extracurricular Chinese. And while Italian children often continue living with their parents for a long time, there will inevitably come a day when Luigi and Paola's kids will want to leave the nest. Will they decide to step out of the protection programme?

Luigi must live with his doubts, wondering if he made the right choice for his family. According to him, the children of informants fall between the cracks. Their lives are threatened by the mafia, yet society excludes them because they're perceived to be mafia children. 'Some people say you can save your kids by keeping them away from the clan. But it doesn't work that way with the Ndrangheta. You can raise your kids any way you like, but if your son becomes a doctor, and one of your old Ndrangheta buddies has a bullet in his shoulder, where's your buddy going to go? Or if a close friend gets sick while hiding from the police in an old shed in the countryside, which doctor will you call? Once you're inside certain circles, neither you nor your children can ever be completely free. Your kids may go abroad, they can go to university, but your family will always continue to put pressure on them and demand favours.'

*

In Italy, roughly twelve-hundred former criminals have decided to cooperate with the justice department. Many, like Luigi, take their families and in-laws with them when they enter the witness protection programme. A few are housed outside the country – an option Luigi would have preferred. The problem is finding a foreign country willing to assume such a risk.

Luigi Bonaventura decided to fight for a better situation for Italian informants, so he set up a special committee to support informers and their families. In a WhatsApp group for family members, sympathizers, activists and journalists, lively discussions take place from dawn till dusk. However, Luigi sometimes intervenes with fatherly advice when the tone gets too heated. The following day, he might kick off the chat with a light-hearted joke or a weighty dilemma, such as: 'What if the magistrate interrogating you had done favours for your family – would you turn him in?' While such predicaments are almost unimaginable, they're sadly not beyond the realm of possibility. In fact, in recent Italian history, judges have been convicted of precisely that: accepting money from a mafia clan in exchange for acquittal or a drastically reduced sentence.

The intelligence services have also made deals with some of the most high-powered mafia bosses: with Antonio Pelle 'Gambazza', the highest-ranking Ndrangheta boss from San Luca, for example. Luigi Bonaventura did a brief stint in the same prison as Pelle during the early 1990s. It turns out that Pelle had also made deals with national politicians. In 1994, for instance, when the inmates were going to vote in parliamentary elections, Luigi was given clear instructions. Pelle and his associates had promised votes to Forza Italia, Silvio Berlusconi's newly established political party, in exchange for legal favours. 'But later, the leading bosses wised up,' Luigi told me during one of our talks. 'They prevented prisoners from all casting their votes for a single party.'

It wasn't just votes that were spread among Italy's various parties, but also the favours done in return. Shortly before Luigi Bonaventura became a witness for the state, he discovered that the Ndrangheta had close ties with the right-wing Lega Nord party. During a lavish lunch in a restaurant in Crotone, a Ndranghetist boasted to Luigi that they had the Lega Nord party more or less 'in their pocket'. I found that intriguing because, at the time, Lega Nord was still fighting for the independence of rich northern Italy from what it considered the 'backward' south. But the Ndrangheta quickly forgave the party its insults against southerners when, during the elections, Lega Nord allied with Forza Italia, which had already proven its worth to the mafias. Over time, the party shortened its name to Lega, and more and more people in Calabria started voting for them.

When Luigi Bonaventura was a member of the Ndrangheta, he wasn't personally involved in negotiating with officials and politicians, so I asked him how he knew about so many deals. Luigi explained that although he was not yet a member of the Santa, for the duration of his uncle's incarceration, he had remained his right-hand man. As a result, Luigi did have dealings with members of the Santa, despite his lower rank: 'I oversaw what happened on the street, but because I represented my uncle, I also had a seat at the table during meetings between higher-ranking clan members from the entire province. And no one dared contradict me if I said I was expressing my uncle's opinion. I don't know how high my uncle's formal rank was, because in the Ndrangheta you don't have to share your specific rank with the people beneath you. Be that as it may, my uncle urged me to join the Santa and he gave me the names of those I needed to talk to in order to make that happen. But I was in no hurry. I didn't want a higher rank because I already had plenty of influence and responsibilities. And when the time came that I could no longer refuse, I decided to quit and cooperate with judicial authorities.'

In one of his first talks with the public prosecutor, Luigi compared the Ndrangheta to chess pieces: 'You have the pawns – I was one of those – and you have the other, more valuable chess pieces, which are active in business and politics. From time to time, I was allowed to act like one of those more valuable chess pieces. My strategy was limited to arguing for as little bloodshed as possible, because we could get ahead in business using just our last name, without resorting to violence. But this was something the others had already started to figure out a long time ago.'

Luigi discovered how members of the upper echelons used his surname: 'They would tell a judge that despite their last name, they had nothing to do with certain family members. They pretended to be squeaky clean. But in real life, if they wanted to put pressure on someone, they'd say, "If you don't cooperate, my cousin might get angry, and we don't want that, do we?" Whether subtly or in a more obvious way, they made sure the other person knew that they belonged to a Ndrangheta family.'

According to Luigi, those two branches of the Ndrangheta – the one dealing with the street and the other with higher levels of power – were mutually dependent. 'They can't exist without each other. We are all familiar with the military wing of the Ndrangheta, from the smallest extortionist to the biggest narcotics dealers, the ones dealing with the dirty money. They strengthen the criminal brand. And then there's the more intelligent, strategic division, the machine made up of white-collar criminals, which cleverly uses the strength behind that brand name. They create a sort of borderline economy, teetering on the brink between what's legal and what's not. They mix shady business with things you might think are above board. Often, these types of borderline entrepreneurs and borderline politicians aren't official members of the Ndrangheta; they might be distant cousins or straw men, people without a criminal record who receive aid from the military branch to grow and assume posts crucial to the clan. Among their ranks are prominent lawyers and judges.'

Luigi gave an example. 'Once, when my family needed an anti-mafia certificate to bid on a public contract, a certain lawsuit jeopardised the family's clearance. To resolve this, the chief prosecutor, who was elderly, retired and went to work for my family's business so he could vouch for us. Insane. That's how powerful my family is.'

All those valuable contacts make it difficult to win convictions for the 'borderline' members of Luigi's family. 'My witness statements have made life difficult for our clan's military wing, but the strategic and financial arms are still as powerful as in any of the strongest Ndrangheta families. My family's portfolio includes football teams, real estate, construction companies and waste management. They own specialized waste treatment facilities, some of the largest in Europe. To give you an absurd example, our clan earned a lot of cash trafficking cocaine. However, when the police did seize a shipment of cocaine in the port of Gioia Tauro, they packed it into large bales and brought it to be destroyed in one of our special incinerators. That way, the clan kept profiting from it, one way or the other.'

Investing in football clubs is also crucial. 'We wanted to elevate the Crotone team to the Serie A to increase our gambling profits and we happened to own the stadium's security company then, so we used our people there to influence the outcome of the games. The security guards would threaten and bribe members of the opposing team. Furthermore, we arranged for Calabrian players to be hired by teams in northern Italy, making them more valuable. A lot of prestige is associated with owning a football club, and you gain a strong social platform for influencing voter behaviour.'

Those Ndranghetists who are members of the Santa, the Ndrangheta's 'sacred' circle, have a clever way of recognizing each other in public without being detected by outsiders – they touch their chin as if stroking a beard. The gesture is a sly reference to General Garibaldi's beard. In the nineteenth century, Garibaldi used his army to bring about Italian unification. To this day, during their induction, new members of the Santa swear a solemn oath invoking the name of Italy's founding father, Garibaldi, who was also a Freemason.

In the spring of 2014, the carabinieri captured such an initiation on video for the first time. It was in a barn near Calolziocorte, a northern Italian village between the mountains and lakes near the Swiss border. The video shows five men standing in a circle, their heads bowed as if in prayer. A table holds the props needed for such a Ndrangheta ritual – a gun, a knife and a handkerchief. The master of ceremonies begins: 'On this sacred evening, in the silence of the night and under the light of the stars and the moon's glow, I unite the sacred chain.' Then, the others lead in the man awaiting admission into the Santa. The leader orders him to repeat, 'I swear to deny everything until the seventh generation, including the entire criminal society I have known so far, in order to save the honour of my wise brothers.' To keep the group's secrets, a member of the Santa may betray all the clan members below him in rank. If he commits a serious transgression, there are two options: he either drinks cyanide or shoots himself with a bullet from his own gun.

I am reminded of that oath when I find a website belonging to one of Luigi's blood relatives. I had googled the man because I had read in Luigi's statements that this particular kinsman had sent him death threats. The man's homepage shows a black and white portrait of a smiling, grey-haired businessman with an impressive track record: he was the chairman of the board of a major football club, owned several discos, a radio station and a television station, and was vice president of the regional employers' organization. He invested in wind turbines and solar panels, and also owned various transportation companies and processing facilities for residential waste, industrial waste and hazardous toxic substances. What's more, he was the proud owner of a Michelin-starred restaurant.

Beneath the homepage's polished photograph, a few news items were prominently displayed. For example, the businessman had decided to resign from the board of the football club, which had recently climbed to the Serie A, in order to focus more fully on innovative missions in emerging international markets. In addition, his lawyers announced his definitive acquittal on charges of ties with organized crime, corruption and fraud. On appeal, the court had overturned its earlier conviction and rescinded the seizure of the man's businesses and property. Finally, the businessman was delighted to announce that one of Italy's largest daily newspapers had been found guilty of libel. The paper had reported that after retiring, a former chief prosecutor had gone to work for the businessman, who had been erroneously labelled a mafioso.

Before I click away from the site, I look at the image of the man on my screen again. The composition of the photograph highlights the businessman's confidence and approachability. Perhaps he suggested the pose himself. He's bending forward slightly, with his right hand touching his clean-shaven chin. For some, that's just a coincidence. For others, it's an impressive calling card.

14

THE HISTORY OF SILENCE

As life quietly goes on in my village, my head sometimes spins when I think of the criminal net the Ndrangheta has cast, not only throughout Calabria, but all over the world. How could such a seemingly unstoppable criminal multinational have been born in a forgotten corner of Europe? Who or what caused groups of Calabrian bullies to grow into a global power? How can the Ndrangheta be simultaneously archaic and modern, provincial but also globalized? Ostensibly religious and yet boundlessly cruel?

Few can explain the complex history of the Ndrangheta as clearly as Enzo Ciconte, a Calabrian in his early seventies with piercing eyes and snow-white hair. He wrote some of the earliest books about the Ndrangheta; his first was published in 1992, when the Calabrian mafiosi had yet to make a name for themselves as a serious criminal organization. Professor Ciconte advises the parliamentary Antimafia Commission and teaches the history of the mafias at universities in northern Italy. Every summer, he and his wife return to their holiday home in Calabria, a stone's throw from the Tyrrhenian Sea. Sitting at a table on their plant-filled veranda, we review the vast contradictions within the Ndrangheta.

I'm recording the interview for a segment of a Dutch radio

programme designed to highlight the Ndrangheta's most striking features; many of Ciconte's answers will, therefore, be edited out. And while Ciconte is undoubtedly aware that most of what he says will end up on the cutting room floor, he talks patiently and at length.

'The first traces of organized crime in Calabria were found in the 1820s,' he begins. 'Back then, a series of phenomena emerged that we now describe as mafia-related; this included extortion, violence, omertà, protection rackets and exercising control over a particular territory.' Yet the term Ndrangheta, which is generally believed to derive from a Greek word meaning 'bravery', didn't appear in print until the twentieth century. According to Ciconte, journalists began using it to distinguish the Calabrian mafia from Cosa Nostra and the Camorra. 'The organization's members usually spoke of a *picciotteria* or *onorata società*, but later, they adopted the name Ndrangheta. At least, that's when they don't deny the existence of the Ndrangheta altogether, which is typical of mafiosi.'

Like most people, I long assumed that Cosa Nostra was the first Italian mafia, but it seems the Neapolitan Camorra is probably older. 'The name Camorra was already in use in 1735,' Ciconte explains. 'The term Cosa Nostra, like Ndrangheta, appeared somewhat later, in the 1820s, although the word "maffia" didn't show up until 1861, in a text written by a general. The general wrote that the word referred to what the Camorra was called in Sicily. He spelled the word maffia with two f's, which was then common in the Sicilian and Calabrian dialects. Funnily enough, the word still has two f's in Dutch.' After a brief pause, he continues: 'Few people can be bothered digging through the archives, and so, for convenience, people usually say all three Italian mafias emerged around 1860, about the same time as Italy's unification. But they had really been around a lot longer.'

*

Bandits, swindlers, thieves and murderers – there have always been criminals, in all times and places. Ciconte writes in his book *Storia criminale* that what distinguished the mafiosi in southern Italy from other criminals was their relationship with the powers that be. Before Italian unification, the Kingdom of the Two Sicilies, as southern Italy was then known, had a feudal system of government, ruled by barons and other large landowners. But starting from 1800, as feudalism gradually disappeared, the rules of the economic and social game shifted. The bourgeoisie acquired more possessions and increased their political power, and they sometimes seized land illegally. Of course, the members of the aristocracy were eager to hold onto their property and privileges. So, they employed farmers and shepherds with criminal tendencies to guard their estates and intimidate their adversaries. And while the state authorities kept changing, with Spanish, French and Bourbon Kings rapidly succeeding one another, major landowners relied on armed criminals to provide private surveillance, often allowing them to hide on their property. In the meantime, those criminals decided to join forces.

The first written Ndrangheta codes of conduct were discovered in the late nineteenth century, but were likely already in use much earlier. The words rhymed and were set to a catchy rhythm, making them easier to memorize and pass down by word of mouth. You might wonder how the Ndrangheta, which began as a criminal network of illiterate farmers and sheep herders, could develop such an elaborate system of esoteric rituals and metaphoric phrases. According to Enzo Ciconte, it all happened within the walls of nineteenth-century prisons. At the time, criminals from southern Italy shared prison cells with political opponents of the Bourbon regime. Italy was still composed of several states, and the Bourbons were the last to rule in the southern regions. The political opponents of the Bourbons were fighting for more rights for the bourgeoisie and were often members of secret societies or Masonic lodges. Gradually, solidarity developed between the various prisoners, and the would-be members of the mafia picked up tips from their cellmates about how to shape their own secret society, including rituals, rules and a unique coded language.

Prisons remained vital places for exchanging information. While incarcerated, criminals from Sicily, Calabria and Naples came into contact and shared intelligence. As a result, the various mafias started resembling one another. Although all three used initiation rites, the Ndrangheta is more attached to traditional rituals and precepts.

According to Ciconte, a Ndrangheta boss's infant son is subjected to rituals practically from birth: 'The parents place a knife and a key in the baby's crib. The knife represents the Ndrangheta, and the key stands for a police officer who holds the key to a cell. The parents hope to discover if the son is of suitable character to join the mafia. If the baby reaches for the knife, he will become a Ndranghetist. But if the baby reaches for the key, the father will direct the baby's hand to the knife instead, because any son who became a policeman would be a disgrace to the family.'

To officially join the criminal community, every son of a major Ndrangheta boss must first undergo a formal rite of initiation. As Ciconte drily remarks, 'No one can become a Catholic without baptism or catechism. The same applies to Muslims and Islamic rituals. The mafia has created its own religion, and therefore, it also has its own liturgy.'

These rituals and codes of conduct strengthen the members' shared sense of identity and form a protective shield, as it were. Ciconte suggests that the musicality and rhythm of the recited texts are meant to be both calming and reassuring. You can imagine some comfort is welcome when a *picciotto,* for example, holds a burning prayer card in his hand. 'He's let blood drip from his finger, usually the index finger of his shooting hand, onto the saint's image. He then sets the card aflame with a candle or a lighter, and while reciting the oath to be eternally loyal to the Ndrangheta, he tosses the image from one hand to the other, trying not to burn himself. From then on, he can only leave the Ndrangheta unscathed if he manages to reassemble the ashes of that prayer card, or at least that's what he's been told. Impossible.'

As these young men undergo initiations to become members of the Ndrangheta, they can't help but be impressed by the symbolism of the often incomprehensible sentences they must recite. 'Everyone who talks about the ritual says it's intimidating. It's like taking an important exam: even though you've done your homework beforehand, you're still nervous, and your hands shake. The same goes for an aspiring picciotto, surrounded by mafiosi, men he respects. It's no accident that, during the ritual, they stand in a circle. The boy feels simultaneously protected and fenced in: if he betrays anyone, he can expect an attack from all sides. And that's intimidating.'

After the initiation, the picciotto moves from the margins of society to become a member of a group that allows him to gain prestige and make money. 'In the early nineteenth century, a young farmer or agricultural worker would hardly know anyone outside his immediate family. He was excluded from the rest of society and could do little to improve his social standing. But he could change his identity and find new sources of income and social stature by joining a mafia organization', Ciconte says. 'Other people, who had perhaps looked down on him, now viewed him with respect and admiration, or else were intimidated by him or afraid of him. That radical image transformation is still one of the key reasons so many young people choose to undergo an initiation into the mafia.'

The members of the mafias have always been drawn from of a mix of poor and uneducated and well-to-do, highly educated individuals. The clans offered the lower classes a way to climb the social ladder and gain power, contacts and financial wealth. For the upper classes, the mafia provided a way to hold on to their possessions and maintain the status quo. According to Professor Ciconte, the collaboration between the two sets resulted in a 'criminal governance of society', which has unfortunately remained constant throughout Italian history.

Ciconte explains that archival materials are not the only significant source of information for those hoping to understand the mafias. 'Silence is also an important historical document.' Whether they are driven by fear, corruption, convenience or opportunism, there are a lot of possible reasons for people to decide to stay silent. 'Without exception, omertà can be found at all levels of society.'

Silence can also be the result of a lack of understanding. For example, Ciconte's work indicates that, for many years, historians paid little attention to the mafias; they were seen as belonging to the underclass and the margins of society, areas where many intellectuals felt out of their depth. Historians have therefore inadvertently contributed to the failure to recognize the complicit role of the middle classes and governing elite, who have always shared particular interests with the mafias. The middle classes and governing powers co-existed with clan members as harmoniously as possible, enabling all parties to benefit from illegal deals. Government policymakers still paint the mafia as a problem of the lower classes. This misconception guarantees that, for generations, people have failed to see the mafias not just as a criminal problem but also a democratic one. It's important to remember that the mafias influence elections and party programmes and rally votes for their choice of representatives. This happens on all levels, whether the elections are for members of a small-town council or the national parliament. Often, people blame the mafia's dominance on the 'absence of the state'. Ciconte argues, however, that it is a result of the 'presence of parts of the state that promote certain criminal interests'.

Another persistent misconception is that mafia organizations only thrive in poorer regions. 'While it's true that poverty is one of the causes, it's not the most crucial.' After all, the mafias have also taken root in northern Italy, where there's plenty of money and the standard of living is much higher than in the south. According to the professor, myths about the link between poverty and the mafia and the so-called absence of government in southern Italy have helped establish the distorted idea that, in essence, the mafias were a sort of knightly order of benefactors, peacemakers and defenders of honour and tradition. Of course, mafia bosses preferred not to exercise their power exclusively through brute force; they also tried to gain society's approval and support, so they sometimes used their authority to resolve conflicts by assuming the role of informal judge. However, Enzo Ciconte contests the widespread belief that they played a crucial role as peacekeepers, although the mafias promote that idea to legitimize themselves.

In the nineteenth century, the Ndrangheta was still primarily a rural phenomenon in the province of Reggio Calabria, in the southernmost part of the region. Clans, or *ndrine,* had also sprung up in other parts of Calabria, although the majority were centred at the tip of Calabria's boot. As is the case today, a Ndrangheta family would rule over a particular village or urban district and for the most part avoid infringing on someone else's territory. And while some of the main bosses may have known each other, there was not yet a central board like the one that exists today. 'The economic boom in Italy following World War II meant that the mafia partially shifted its focus to the cities, where more money could be made. This led to something one journalist poetically described as *la mafia con le scarpe lucide*: the mafia with shiny shoes. Of course, in the countryside, members' shoes would be muddy with earth, dust and muck, but in the city, those shoes would gleam.'

The transformation to a 'businessman's mafia' was further enhanced when the Ndrangheta created the Santa in the 1970s. Since then, the Calabrian clans, like other mafias, have focused on securing lucrative public contracts. More and more often, they went beyond demanding protection money and instead bought legitimate companies outright.

'Today, the Ndrangheta is the richest of all the Italian mafias, but it's important to remember that not all its members are wealthy,' Professor Ciconte says. 'A few families are extraordinarily affluent, but many are less well-off. It's like a pyramid, resembling the rest of our capitalist society. The poorer Ndranghetists are at the bottom of the pyramid, living off relatively small amounts of protection money. Many members of the Ndrangheta had few resources, especially in the beginning, but there have always been well-heeled exceptions. And those with money make the decisions – that's true everywhere, even in the mafia.'

In terms of contraband, during the 1950s and '60s, all three of the mafias concentrated on trafficking illegal cigarettes. Sicilian, Calabrian and Neapolitan clans joined forces and collaborated with foreign smugglers to have cigarettes shipped to their ports. In the eyes of the public, it seemed innocuous enough, giving smokers a reduced price through petty tax evasion in a Robin Hood-like gesture. Soon after that, however, the clans began trafficking in heroin, and cocaine was not far behind. Many of the contacts and routes the three mafias had developed when running cigarettes remained useful when smuggling hard drugs.

'In the 1970s and '80s, the Ndrangheta became increasingly violent; there were countless vendettas and hundreds died. The clans also started kidnapping people, mainly children. Kidnappings are a particular form of violence: savagely brutal because the children were often locked in chains for long periods. The kidnappers demanded insane amounts of money and then told their victims, "It looks like your father doesn't care whether you're released or not. Otherwise, he would have paid the ransom right away." The victims were hidden for months, sometimes years, deep within the Aspromonte mountains. Those who grew up nearby feel at home in those mountains, having played there as children, and there are places where Ndrangheta families had total control over the territory. Once, a kidnapped engineer from Naples managed to escape. He fled to the nearest village and said, "Help, I've been kidnapped." The villagers replied, "Don't worry, come with us." And they handed him right back to the men of the Ndrangheta!'

In the 1990s, using money acquired through kidnappings, the Calabrian clans were able to invest more heavily in drug trafficking. And just as judicial authorities began clamping down on the Sicilian mafia – who had overplayed their hand with the fatal attacks on Falcone and Borsellino – the Ndrangheta stepped into the breach by taking control of cocaine trafficking. 'At the same time, on an international level, there was a major shift in popularity; heroin fell out of favour, and cocaine became the drug of choice.' And so, the Ndrangheta became a leader in importing cocaine into Europe, and to this day, cocaine remains an essential part of their criminal strategy.

The Italian mafias – the Ndrangheta in particular – would never have experienced such massive growth and development if they hadn't shifted at least part of their operations to northern Italy; it was a crucial step, if only to help launder vast amounts of earnings. Residents of northern Italy have long denied the presence of the mafias, although the Ndrangheta began setting up shop there in the 1950s. Ironically, a 1965 anti-mafia government scheme facilitated their move to the north, when men suspected of membership in the mafias were banished to central or northern Italy for three to five years. There, they remained under police supervision but were allowed to receive visitors, including family. The idea was to render these mafiosi harmless by separating them from other clan members in the south.

That turned out to be extremely naive. Outwardly, the banished mafia members often appeared calm, friendly and inconspicuous. Meanwhile, they gave orders in person or on the phone, held clan meetings and laundered money. To that end, they established bonds with professionals in the business and financial sectors. Ciconte calls these professionals *uomini-cerniera* or 'linkage men' because they form a hinge between the underworld and the realm of local businesses, banks and finance companies. 'The Ndrangheta is successful in the north of Italy and internationally because they have local operatives who can easily manoeuvre in the worlds of tax and finance,' he says. 'They understand how to funnel money through tax havens and can invest in places where many Ndranghetists have little access themselves. There isn't much legal risk for these intermediaries, who are amply rewarded for their services. After all, people don't usually jump to the conclusion that these linkage men have chosen to work for the mafia, and anyway, it's difficult to prove.'

Members of the Sicilian mafia tended to return to their warm island after their enforced stay in the north, but their Calabrian counterparts often chose to remain, inviting their families to join them, either for the longer term or permanently. That's how some northern branches of the Ndrangheta became an extension of existing locali in Calabria, aided by the fact that many Calabrian youths went north looking for work. Once there, they supplied the clans with fresh energy and cheap labour. Ciconte stresses that the Ndrangheta is the only mafia that established itself this way in northern Italy and abroad, always maintaining its indestructible links with Calabria, the Ndrangheta's homeland. The home base doesn't expect such satellite branches to get in touch for every trifle, but the Calabrians do keep an eye on the clans in northern Italy and abroad.

According to Ciconte, Calabrian Ndranghetists sometimes even have the final say about the induction of a picciotto in a northern clan. In any case, before a clan baptizes a young member, they must first check out his family. For example, a young man can't join the Ndrangheta if his family honour has been tarnished and he has failed to restore it by force. Being gay or having an unfaithful wife would also disqualify him. On a more formal level, prison officers and those who work or have worked for the police are also barred from initiation, as are magistrates and members of the military, because the mafia's oath would clash with their sworn allegiance to the state.

Experts often remark that the Ndrangheta is Italy's strongest mafia and the most potent mafia internationally. I asked Ciconte if it was possible that the Calabrian mafia had become more powerful than those of Russia or China. 'Undoubtedly, the Russian and Chinese mafias are larger in terms of numbers. But, in addition to the Ndrangheta's dominance in international cocaine trafficking, the structure of the Calabrian mafia has certain characteristics that increase its power. For instance, the Ndrangheta is the only mafia that has spread beyond Italy to establish roots in every corner of the globe. It is firmly established throughout Europe and from Australia to Canada.'

The Ndrangheta establishes international contacts through, among others, the Freemasons. 'The Ndrangheta has infiltrated Freemasonry, primarily because it's an international organization and the Ndrangheta clans need an international network. For example, an Italian Freemason might contact a British one, saying, "We need a particular permit. Can you lend us a hand?" Another reason is that magistrates, military personnel and intelligence agents are all allowed to become members of a Masonic organization. While such professionals couldn't afford to be seen on the streets with a mafioso, meetings between a magistrate and a mafia member could easily take place inside the Masonic Lodge if both are members. Many lodges have gratefully accepted cash donations from members of the mafia.'

The Ndrangheta also maintains a warm connection with the Catholic Church. 'To understand the bond between the Church and the mafia, we must look back to the time of Italy's unification,' Ciconte says, 'when the mafias were starting. For many years, the Church had two major ideological enemies: the liberals, who had achieved Italian unification and drastically restricted the Vatican's territory, and the communists, who were atheists and had become an important political movement in Italy.'

You could say that the mafia didn't oppose the Church, and the Church didn't take a stand against the mafia. Barring a few exceptions, priests, bishops and popes didn't seem to be against the mafia. 'Members of the mafia called themselves Catholics, christening their children, taking part in first holy communion and confirmation, and marrying in church. A priest was called when they died, and the funeral was held in a church. They lived the life of an ordinary Catholic as well as the life of a member of the mafia. Beyond that, they also footed the bill for the parish, the priest, the processions and village festivals for patron saints. So, the Church found mafiosi useful, and viewed them as friends rather than enemies.'

Even today, Catholic processions sometimes come to a respectful halt in front of the houses of the local mafia bosses, and the saint's statue is carried by low-ranking picciotti. 'Mafiosi call themselves Catholics, but I don't understand how they can reconcile their faith with killing people. They're creating their own God.'

Priests were not formally allowed to join the mafia, but there were certain benefits to having a priest in the family. For example, a family priest could perform a fugitive's secret, consecrated wedding, as was the case for the Sicilian mafia boss Totò Riina. Things changed in 1992, however, when that same Riina ordered the bombings that led to the deaths of two prosecutors, Giovanni Falcone and Paolo Borsellino. 'Then, the Church started distancing itself from the mafia. A year later, in the Valley of the Temples in Sicily's Agrigento, the Pope proclaimed, "Mafiosi, repent!" Shortly after that, two priests who had dared to stand up to the mafia lost their lives.' That raised the level of fear and the Church decided to maintain a more or less open-door policy for mafiosi. 'Unfortunately, there are still priests who maintain close ties with members of the mafia.'

Mafia organizations have been around for almost two centuries, but the legal definition of the term 'mafia' only recently entered the Italian criminal code. Since 1982, Italy has had an internationally unique anti-mafia law: article 416 of the Italian organized crime law was expanded to include a definition of mafia-related crime, 416bis. This extension to the law meant that proving someone was a member of a mafia-type organization was enough to convict them and seize their property. As a result, an individual could be prosecuted on suspicion of being a member of a mafia organization, even without proof of their having committed any specific other crime.

Implementation of 416bis did not occur without bloodshed. The Sicilian politician Pio La Torre and police prefect Alberto dalla Chiesa, both passionate champions of the law, were murdered by Cosa Nostra. The anti-mafia law first proved its value in Sicily, but soon also in other parts of Italy. To this day, extensive trials continue to convict dozens and even hundreds of members of mafia organizations simultaneously. But the law also made countries outside of Italy more attractive to mafia organizations; beyond Italy's borders, money, businesses and real estate could be hidden from the Italian judicial system. Moreover, sentences in the rest of Europe are often much lighter and those suspected of participating in a mafia organization can only be arrested if there is evidence of their having committed an additional crime.

According to the definition of 416bis, people who belong to or cooperate with a mafia-type association use the power of intimidation and the resulting conditions of subjugation and silence (or omertà) to commit criminal offences or to manage and control, directly or indirectly, economic activities, public contracts and public services, or to obtain unlawful profits or other advantages illegally. They also restrict the right to vote freely in elections by securing votes for themselves and others.

It is important to note that the law doesn't focus on violence but on intimidation. That's because members of a mafia organization don't necessarily have to use violence to appear intimidating. The fear of violence they generate stems from the violent reputation they have built. Ciconte explains, 'Suppose someone approaches you, saying, "Don Peppino sent me." If you know Peppino's the boss of the local Ndrangheta clan, you'll pay the protection money, the pizzo, right away. Because you're afraid that if you don't hand over the money, something bad will happen to you, your family or your business.'

Outside Italy, this implicit violence often makes it extremely difficult to prove mafia activity. As a rule, the Ndrangheta prefers to let sleeping dogs lie. The murder of six men in Duisburg, Germany, was a resounding exception. 'In Europe, people don't want to admit that mafia-type practices are occurring under their noses', says Ciconte. 'Look, I'm Calabrian, and I don't enjoy hammering on about the dangers of the Calabrian clans. But I wouldn't do my native soil any favours if I stopped. I want to drive this phenomenon out of my region, and I can only do that by explaining what the Ndrangheta does and convincing people that they do not have to live with it.'

15

A PERFECTLY NORMAL FAMILY

Journalists outside Italy aren't usually inclined to go looking for the Ndrangheta in their own back yard. Instead, they generally pay a quick visit to Calabria, sometimes going to great lengths to interview Ndrangheta families. These journalists all come face to face with the omertà, the Ndrangheta's iron-clad law that enforces silence under penalty of death, and therefore rules out the chance of obtaining any meaningful or reliable quotes.

Calabrian journalists, on the other hand, know better than to turn to Ndrangheta suspects when they want answers to their questions. Instead, they ask the suspects' lawyers, hoping to hear arguments for the defence. Although in the past, *capi*, or mafia bosses, including Mommo Piromalli, would occasionally give brief interviews, the current generation usually avoids journalists.

I was intrigued by a 2013 episode of the Dutch television programme *Brandpunt* containing an in-depth piece about the Ndrangheta in Calabria. In the segment, Dutch journalists visited a priest named Pino Strangio in San Luca on a grey December day. They asked the priest to introduce them to the family of Francesco Nirta, who had recently been arrested in a Dutch snack bar.

Francesco Nirta, a member of the Nirta–Strangio clan, had been listed as one of Italy's most dangerous fugitives for six years. He was facing a lifelong prison sentence for committing one of the honour killings in the San Luca clan war. When Nirta was arrested, he was eating French fries with a Moroccan and two Dutch companions. They were sitting at the window of a snack bar near Nirta's flat in the Utrecht suburb of Nieuwegein. In Nirta's home, police found forty kilos of cocaine, and in a car belonging to one of the other men, eighteen thousand euros in cash.

The camera crew from *Brandpunt* had started filming their segment in Nieuwegein. There, they showed a picture of Nirta, a balding forty-year-old with a hollow, slightly squinting gaze, to a woman who lived on the same floor. Her exact words were, 'We couldn't never have had a better and quieter neighbour than him.' The camera crew then shot footage of the kitchen in Francesco's sealed flat through a gap in the cream-coloured blinds. There was nothing unusual to be seen: some pans on the stove, a few white plates in a plastic dish rack and bottles of olive oil, red wine and tomato sauce on the kitchen counter. A tin of Illy coffee stood on the table, which was covered with the same rose-patterned tablecloth I have at home, a type sold at almost every Calabrian market. Might his mother have packed it for him when he left San Luca years ago?

The crew from the KRO, the Dutch Catholic broadcasting network, then travelled to San Luca, to peek inside Francesco Nirta's childhood home. And they were in luck, because the local priest, Don Pino Strangio, was prepared to put in a good word for his fellow Catholics with the family, and a police escort accompanied the Dutch film crew to the house. Francesco Nirta's mother and youngest brother were the only ones who still lived there. Like many Calabrian homes, it had marble floors and was furnished with dark leather sofas, glass display cases and a profusion of wood. Francesco

Nirta's mother, Palma, was a petite, wizened woman in black, who looked like she had been in mourning for decades. As they sat at the kitchen table, covered with a clean white hand-crocheted tablecloth, the Dutch visitors showed Palma a photograph of Francesco on letter-sized paper. Francesco's mother tearfully kissed the print. 'I see an angel. My son is an angel.'

Stefano Nirta, Palma's youngest son, looked on patiently and then came to his brother's defence. According to Stefano, Francesco had fled to the Netherlands because of a wrongful conviction in Italy: 'The police and the judges see us all as criminals as soon as we're born. There are many families here in San Luca named Nirta. The authorities don't even know who's who. At first, they didn't care about us, but since 2007, suddenly we're all bosses or members of the Ndrangheta.'

'We have nothing to do with the Ndrangheta,' Palma proclaimed, wagging her finger while the corners of her mouth drooped in disapproval. 'And nothing to do with what they call the mafia, either,' she added.

'We're just *una famiglia normalissima*,' Stefano emphasized.

A perfectly normal family. In San Luca, the television crew didn't mention the forty kilos of coke with a market value of millions found in Francesco Nirta's flat in Nieuwegein. And no one said a word about Palma's husband Giuseppe Nirta, the father of her eight children. A few years earlier, he'd been arrested in a bunker near their home and sentenced to life in prison for the same murder for which their son Francesco had been charged. That murder of a shepherd was one of the last in the infamous San Luca vendetta, which culminated in the six deaths in Duisburg in the summer of 2007.

The feud had begun back in 1991 during a tragic carnival night.

Francesco Nirta, just seventeen at the time, was the one who angered the Vottari family by initiating an egg fight. The Vottaris beat up Francesco, prompting him to drag his three older brothers into the fray. Later that same night, the brothers' car was targeted by gunfire. Two of them, Gianluca and Sebastiano Nirta, were severely injured. Domenico, the third brother, died, as did one of the Strangio boys, who had come with them.

After that, the Nirta–Strangio clan and the Pelle–Vottari clan carried out a series of honour killings and reprisals. In the meantime, Palma's boys were growing up and intermarrying with the Strangio family. On Christmas Day in 2006, almost everyone was gathered at the home of Palma and her husband when the festivities were brutally interrupted. Members of the Pelle–Vottari clan burst in and began firing with pistols, a Kalashnikov and a hunting rifle. Palma's son Francesco was shot in the heel, and her five-year-old grandson in the foot. Her oldest son, Gianluca, had been the intended target, but it was his wife, Maria, who was hit in the chest in the presence of her three young children. The following Assumption Day, the family avenged the death of their beautiful Maria by leaving six bodies on the doorstep of the Da Bruno restaurant in Duisburg. Palma's son Sebastiano later stood trial for the six counts of murder. Would he become the fourth of Palma's sons to be sentenced to life in prison, following in their father's footsteps?

The Dutch television programme didn't mention this bleak family saga. Instead, footage of San Luca's rundown streets and the stares of hostile bystanders accompanied the visit to the home of the Ndrangheta family. Finally, the same Italian police officers who had earlier escorted the TV crew to the church and the Nirta family's home were shown urging the crew to leave town before the locals became unruly. For viewers, these images reaffirmed San Luca's international reputation as a deplorable village, doomed to remain a Ndrangheta ghetto for all time.

More revealing was the interview the Dutch recorded with the priest, Don Pino Strangio. He calmly described the time local criminals had threatened him by setting fire to his car. How had Don Pino reacted to the violence? During mass the following Sunday, he had 'thanked' his 'brothers' for not killing him.

When Don Pino Strangio spoke to the Dutch television crew among the church pews, dressed in his black suit and white clerical collar, he had been San Luca's priest for over thirty years. It's anyone's guess how many marriages and baptisms Don Pino might have blessed during that time, strengthening ties between Ndrangheta families. How many fallen men and boys would he have buried? How many secrets had he seen, heard and kept to himself? 'They say there is a lot of money in San Luca,' the priest told his Dutch visitors. 'To be honest, all I see is poverty. And prisoners who are not allowed a visit from their wives.'

As a clergyman, Don Pino offered solace to many widows, and to women whose husbands, sons and brothers were imprisoned. But he had other important responsibilities in the area too. One was looking after the Sanctuary of the Madonna of Polsi, the pilgrimage site where the Ndrangheta's leaders hold annual meetings and where, one month after the Duisburg massacre, peace was restored between the San Luca clans.

For centuries, the Catholic Church has maintained a code of silence, or omertà, at its highest levels. The first pope who dared to utter the word Ndrangheta in Calabria was the Argentinian Jorge Mario Bergoglio, Pope Francis. His predecessor, Joseph Ratzinger, Pope Benedict the Sixteenth, had also visited Calabria, shuffling through the quiet halls of the Carthusian monks' monastery in the remote mountain village of Serra San Bruno. In his sermon there, Ratzinger stressed the value of silence. That visit occurred shortly before Ratzinger became the first pope in six centuries to step down. He was replaced by Bergoglio soon after.

Expectations were high when, in June 2014, the newly elected Pope Francis decided to visit the Calabrian town of Cassano allo Ionio. At the time, Cassano was mourning the death of a three-year-old child caught in Ndrangheta crossfire. The boy's name was Cocò, and both his parents were in prison. He'd been left in the care of his 52-year-old grandfather Giuseppe, who'd also been jailed for drug trafficking on various occasions. Despite his responsibilities, Grandpa Giuseppe continued making deals so conspicuously that his competitors became angry. He knew his life was in danger, but he felt safe in his car with his grandson in the back seat and his girlfriend beside him. He was wrong. One dreary January day, the grandfather's burned-out Fiat Punto was found with a fifty-cent coin on the roof, signalling that the hit was payback. Three charred bodies were found inside the car.

Little Cocò's tragic fate drew the hugely popular pope to Cassano, and nothing could keep me from being there. Bergoglio had only recently taken office, but his statements had already aroused much controversy. Shortly after his appointment, he decided to clean house at the Vatican's bank, widely known as a place where members of the mafia could store their dirty money. On his watch, the Vatican would no longer provide a tax haven, and the pope appointed new bankers to ensure that all transactions from then on would be above board. It was a major shake-up. In Italy, people speculated that the ambitious pope had made mortal enemies among the mafias. Since then, Bergoglio seemed to have toned down his message, but his visit to Calabria held the promise of a fresh provocation.

Armed with a new video camera, N and I took our chances and drove to Cassano. We arrived in good time, but a seemingly endless crowd had already gathered in the massive field where the pope was scheduled to speak. People had arrived by bus from all over Calabria; the media would later estimate the size of the crowd at 250,000, enough to fill five football stadiums. The audience was herded into various areas cordoned off with crowd-control barriers. Many groups had come prepared with guitars, tambourines, picnic baskets, sun hats and specially printed T-shirts. Here and there, people danced and sang hallelujah, their faces radiant.

With my new camera in my hand, I didn't see much point in finding a place at the back of one of the already over-full audience areas, so I pinned my hopes on my press card. With it, N and I sailed through the various checkpoints until we were close to the stage and could speak to someone from the organization. And although I had no idea if or when our footage would ever be used, I bluffed and said the Dutch Catholic broadcasting network had sent us. That turned out to be the right move. We ended up, blessedly, sitting with about fifteen others on the covered and elevated press gallery. The stage was to one side and a sea of believers to the other. For many, the only clear glimpse they'd get of their idol would be projected onto a large screen.

The altar, ready for mass on the sun-drenched stage, was reminiscent of the setting of Pope John Paul the Second's emotional 1993 homily in Agrigento against the violence carried out by members of the Sicilian mafia. While there were no impressive Greek temples here among the Calabrian citrus trees and rice fields, the size of the stage and the number of spectators were much more significant. How far would Bergoglio dare to go?

Whatever your views on the Catholic Church, those in charge of God's earthly representative gave the audience a jaw-dropping curtain opener, when Pope Francis arrived in a white helicopter floating through the clear blue sky. The popemobile, making its rounds through the ecstatic crowd before the service began, was only slightly less spectacular. As is the custom, the pope was handed dozens of children through a thicket of waving arms and picture-snapping cell phones. He patiently kissed each baby, one by one, on their forehead. Some grim-looking bodyguards surrounded Bergoglio, but he towered above them, beaming.

Then, the pope strode onstage and began the service in the presence of rows of mitred bishops. That day, the hymns and prayers revolved around Corpus Christi, the sacrament day devoted to the body of Jesus Christ, reflected in the distribution of communion wafers during every Catholic mass. From the gloria to the amen, everything went according to the liturgy booklet that had been handed out in advance – everything, that is, except for the long-awaited sermon.

The audience snapped to attention when the pope began to speak in his own words. 'When one does not adore God, one can become an adorer of evil, like those who live lives of crime and violence. Your beautiful region is scarred by the consequences of that sin,' he said. 'The Ndrangheta is this: the worship of evil and contempt for the common good.'

Bergoglio's harsh words were softened by his almost child-like voice. After a brief silence, the crowd erupted in loud, liberating applause, and the pope continued with increasing emphasis: 'We must fight this evil and drive it away! We must say no to it! Those who in their lives follow the path of evil, as mafiosi do, are not in communion with God: they are excommunicated!'

We'd left the press box to shoot some footage among the crowd, closer to the stage. In reaction to the pope's statements, the mood was slightly euphoric. His idea of excommunicating members of the mafia and banning them from the religious community seemed so simple and obvious it was hard to understand why the Church had not announced something similar much earlier. And although the pope's message was directed primarily at the priests and bishops, it made me think. How literally could you take such an excommunication? Would it ever be possible, in a Calabrian village, to bar members of the Ndrangheta from the church community? For goodness' sake, how would priests in Calabria ever enforce such a ban? Were they to exclude all suspected Ndranghetists from attending mass from that day forward? Easier said than done.

Yet a cultural shift soon became noticeable. Unusual reports about processions appeared in the newspaper. For example, two weeks after the pope's sermon, there was a procession in the Calabrian village of Oppido Mamertina. It was a major annual event – the statue of the Virgin Mary was carried on dozens of shoulders, accompanied by a brass band trailing a long parade of followers. As in previous years, the statue bearers halted for thirty seconds in front of the home of the local Ndrangheta boss. It was a deeply rooted tribute to the now 82-year-old clan leader, who because of his advanced age had been allowed to serve his life sentence for murder and other crimes under house arrest. At first, it seemed as if everyone would play along. But then, a lieutenant from the carabinieri stepped out of the procession, clearly demonstrating his dissent. His officers filmed the priest and those carrying the statue of Mary, so that their video could later be used as evidence.

It wasn't until I first visited the Sanctuary of the Madonna of Polsi, a few years after the pope's appearance, that I fully grasped how complex life could be for a priest in Calabria and how difficult excommunication could be to put into practice. It was the day of the procession of the Madonna of the Mountain, the annual religious ceremony that takes place deep within the Aspromonte mountains. For more than a century, it has attracted streams of pilgrims and brought together the most important members of the Ndrangheta. Before I left home, I'd asked the priest in charge of the sanctuary, Tonino Saraco, for an interview. Tonino Saraco had recently taken over from Don Pino Strangio, the helpful priest in San Luca who had been filmed for Dutch television. Don Pino had subsequently faced charges of collaborating with the Ndrangheta. He was still active in the church in San Luca, but because of the criminal charges, he had stepped down from his post in Polsi.

Don Tonino Saraco, the new head of the sanctuary of Polsi, had been a priest on the Ionian coast of Calabria for fifteen years – one who seemed to have no intention of bowing down to the clans. Long before Pope Francis visited Calabria, Tonino Saraco had exercised the right of excommunication by refusing a Ndranghetist in the coastal town of Siderno access to the ritual of the *cresima*, or confirmation. Shortly after that, the young priest discovered that someone had left five bullets on his car, with a note saying, 'If you continue on this path, we'll shoot these through your head.' The words on his WhatsApp profile were a poignant reminder: 'Living is the greatest asset.'

If you hope to take part in the annual procession of the Madonna of Polsi during the first weekend of September, you have to get up early. Because no matter what corner of Calabria you come from, the road to the sanctuary at the heart of the Aspromonte mountains is long and arduous. Devoted pilgrims journey on foot a day in advance, spending the night in the church's guesthouse. I drove, making sure to leave home before sunrise. Most of the mountain road leading to Polsi was unpaved, full of potholes and covered with stones. The area had no cell phone coverage, but luckily, crowds of people were heading to the same destination. It was so busy that even driving to Polsi became a minor pilgrimage: I fell into step with the other relative latecomers and walked the last few kilometres past parked cars. First, we climbed for an hour and a half up the mountain; then, we descended another hour to the valley of Polsi.

The weather was sunny and mild. Extended families, from young to old, were walking together. Fathers pushed prams, and mothers carried flowers and candles for the Madonna. On the side of the road, groups of musicians with accordions, tambourines and Calabrian bagpipes were playing tarantella songs, and along the hairpin turns, people were having breakfast beside their camper vans and tents. As we approached Polsi, more and more dust clouds were kicked up by dirt bikes racing back and forth. The youths who rode them weren't wearing helmets because, as someone explained, if you wore a helmet around San Luca, you might get mistaken for a masked killer.

Historically, visitors to the Sanctuary of the Madonna of Polsi arrived well-armed, because anything could happen in that remote mountain valley. Sinners might visit the Madonna to ask for forgiveness. Some transgressions were settled on the spot, and not all visitors returned from the pilgrimage alive.

That morning, as we passed through the notorious village of San Luca on our way to Polsi, it looked surprisingly ordinary and serene. Bougainvillea and other flowers brought the empty streets to life, and the blush of dawn made the bare cement walls seem a little less grey. Beyond the village, the road passed olive groves with grazing sheep and goats before entering the quiet forests of the Aspromonte. Soon, the Pietra Cappa, a massive white rock, came into view. Some of the Ndrangheta's kidnap victims had used that huge, barren rock as a reference point in the otherwise densely forested mountain area, where it was almost impossible to get your bearings.

Police in cars or on horseback were stationed along the road. After the carabinieri had used hidden cameras to film the annual gathering of the Ndrangheta's leaders during this religious festival, it seemed obvious that the clans would choose to hold their board meeting elsewhere. And yet the Madonna of Polsi remained the predominant patron saint for the Calabrian mafia members, and they were unlikely to keep their distance completely.

Most of the police officers were in Polsi, where an unsettling mix of devotion and bustling commerce filled the air. Wooden kiosks displayed souvenir images of the Madonna of the Mountain adorned with gold chains, or of the Archangel Michael – another of the Ndrangheta's patron saints – as well as posters of Jesus holding a radiant heart. Scarves, bibs, prayer beads, tambourines and fridge magnets were all on sale. At other stalls, smoke billowed. There were grilled sausages, hamburgers, fries and beer.

As I walked on, I spotted a weapon on a bench beside the church. A child picked it up, but thank goodness, it was just a water pistol. The church smelled of sweaty pilgrims. Some of them had spent the night in there. A young man standing in the doorway asked me where I was from. He told me he was from Scido, a village near the Tyrrhenian coast. He was eighteen, and every year for the past five years, he had walked the thirty kilometres to the festival of the Madonna. He had noticed that the number of pilgrims had dwindled recently, although he didn't know why. 'Might it have something to do with the recent operations targeting the Ndrangheta?' I asked. He shook his head. 'I don't know anything about that.'

The statue of the Madonna was carried around the church, and the procession looked much like any other. I left and searched the sanctuary for the white column displaying a smaller stone version of the Madonna; that's where Domenico Oppedisano had been sworn in as head of the Ndrangheta. But the column was gone. In its place, where police had filmed the Ndrangheta bosses standing in a circle, was a bust of a bespectacled priest who had been shot dead near Polsi in the late 1980s after he had pleaded for the release of a kidnapped boy.

After the procession, as the crowd pressed into the church to kiss the feet of the Madonna statue, I climbed the stairs of the old monastery. Don Tonino Saraco had cordially replied to my request for an interview and had invited me to his office high in the monastery. On the top floor, portraits of his predecessors lined the walls of a covered gallery. How often, I wondered, had those men looked the other way?

At the far end of the gallery, the door to Don Tonino's office stood open. He had removed his cream-white cassock and sat at his desk, smoking a hand-rolled cigarette. In his short-sleeved black shirt, with his white clerical collar dangling loosely from his neck, he looked more approachable. I imagined his relief at having his most important appearance of the year behind him. The procession and service had been attended not only by hundreds of worshippers but also by the bishop, many bigshots from the police and a film crew from RAI, the Italian public broadcasting network. Everything had gone according to plan; there had been no mishaps or unexpected blunders.

I asked him what had changed in Polsi since his appointment.

'There are security cameras everywhere, inside the church as well as on the outside, and we now keep records of the pilgrims. In other places, that might seem trivial, but here it has more impact.' He didn't dodge the issue, instead admitting, 'I'm an outsider, and I was afraid the people of San Luca wouldn't accept me, but the opposite has proved true. They welcomed me with open arms. The San Luca women who help me organize the mass are remarkable people. The media gives people the wrong idea. There are certainly a few rotten apples, but it's wrong to say everyone in San Luca is bad. When you do that, you're feeding evil. There are a few wicked people and very many good ones.'

I asked if the priest from San Luca had also supported him. He didn't answer my question but pressed his lips together and gave me a helpless, apologetic look.

I told him I knew what had happened in Siderno and asked, 'Do you follow Pope Francis' lead in saying that members of the mafia don't belong in the church?'

'I think it's a good guideline,' Don Tonino said. 'But the problem is that I often don't know if someone belongs to the mafia or not around here. And it's almost impossible to find out. To me, everyone who comes to Polsi is a pilgrim. I can only point out that the Madonna isn't open to anything besides love and compassion. If a Ndranghetist comes to Polsi to repent, he is welcome. But if he comes to Polsi for another reason, the Madonna won't listen to him.'

I thought it clever of Don Tonino to let the Madonna have the final say about excommunicating members of the Ndrangheta. During the service, when the bearers briefly placed the statue of the Madonna of Polsi on the ground, I had been able to examine her more closely. She was sitting upright in a chair, dressed in her robe of sky blue and pale pink. Her legs were slightly apart, perhaps to help her balance the weight of both the massive silver and gold crown perched on her head and the naked baby Jesus on her arm. He also wore a disproportionately large crown, and was holding a heart in one hand and a golden orb in the other.

While pondering the possible meaning of the heart and the golden orb to members of the Ndrangheta, I scanned the crowd for grumpy-looking men. But I didn't see any. Instead, my eyes came to rest on two gruff-looking women sitting at the top of the stone tribune. They were Aurelia and Teresa Strangio, two of Giovanni Strangio's sisters. Strangio was the 'killer of Duisburg' who'd been sentenced to life in prison after his arrest in an unassuming Dutch terraced house in Diemen.

Aurelia's mass of dark blonde curls was what drew my attention. I remembered seeing pictures of her during her brother's trial: she, together with her mother and other female family members, had chained themselves to the pews of Reggio Calabria's cathedral. Their message? Giovanni Strangio was innocent and was only facing prosecution because of his last name. They wore a picture of him emblazoned on their T-shirts and, in San Luca, they'd hung a banner showing the blue-eyed Giovanni beside an image of Jesus on the cross.

The supreme court of cassation, Italy's highest court of appeal, upheld Giovanni's life sentence. From prison, he sent word that he wanted to speak to the pope. 'He will be able to read my innocence in the eyes God gave me.' Giovanni said he had only gone to Germany to bake pizzas and escape the poverty of San Luca.

One of Giovanni Strangio's restaurants was called San Michele, after the Archangel Michael. The getaway car that had been captured on security cameras the night of the massacre at the Da Bruno restaurant in Duisburg was later recovered in Ghent, Belgium. It contained DNA traces from Giovanni and his brother-in-law Sebastiano Nirta, the older brother of Francesco Nirta, who had been arrested in a snack bar in the Dutch city of Nieuwegein. Several years after the Italian supreme court upheld Giovanni's conviction, it would confirm Sebastiano Nirta's sentence to serve life in prison for his role as the second gunman in the Duisburg massacre.

Ironically, Giovanni Strangio's sisters had given prosecutors valuable information during the criminal proceedings surrounding the San Luca vendetta. The judge later sentenced the sisters to several years of house arrest for mafia-related crimes, including storing weapons and delivering messages for the clan: they had travelled to meet their husbands and brother in the Netherlands with bags full of food, cash and guns. It was that trip, undertaken at the end of 2008, that led police to the Amsterdam hideout of Aurelia's fugitive husband, Giuseppe Nirta. Six months later, police tracked down Teresa's husband, Francesco Romeo, in Diemen, near Amsterdam, along with the family of her brother, Giovanni Strangio.

During the celebration of the Madonna of Polsi, Aurelia and Teresa appeared noticeably bored as they sat in the upper reaches of the public gallery next to the church, listening to the service. Both were dressed in black T-shirts and jeans, setting them apart from the rest of the festively attired crowd. They looked isolated, surrounded by a circle of empty seats. A younger woman bearing a striking family resemblance was squeezed between the sisters, perhaps one of their daughters. She'd gone beyond a simple black T-shirt, maybe to honour the feast day of the Madonna; her T-shirt, covered in rhinestones, displayed a new-fangled icon: a skull with red, heart-shaped eyes.

The communion rite began and the priest announced that alternatives were available for gluten-intolerant participants. While many people descended the stands to form a long line before the altar, I kept my eye on the three women. They didn't go down for a communion wafer. Not even one that was gluten free.

16

EVERYTHING'S UNDER CONTROL

O ver time, the number of connections between the Netherlands and the Ndrangheta was becoming more noticeable, as was the frequency with which mafia prosecutors in Calabria linked Ndrangheta clans to drugs imported through the Netherlands. And it was hard to ignore the disproportionate number of dangerous Italian fugitives being arrested in the Netherlands after living and working there peacefully for years. Experts pointed to the likelihood of Ndrangheta investments in Dutch businesses and real estate. There were indications of money laundering and infiltration in the legal economy, but Dutch judicial authorities hadn't yet investigated them.

Despite worrying signals that Europe's most powerful mafia was operating within the geographical borders of the Netherlands, hardly a word was written or spoken about the Ndrangheta. In the Dutch media, any mentions of the Ndrangheta were still detached and superficial, as if the Ndrangheta only involved criminals in southern Italy and had no real bearing on our country. Did the Netherlands believe, as northern Italy had long done, that it was resistant to the mafia?

On 31 July 2014, Dutch police arrested Marc B., a man from Rome who ran an upscale, bustling Italian restaurant in the historic heart of Amsterdam. According to Italian police, he supplied cocaine to the Ndrangheta, more specifically to the Cacciola clan from Rosarno – relatives of Maria Concetta Cacciola, the state's witness who had died after being forced to drink hydrochloric acid. Authorities timed the arrest of Marc B. to coincide with the arrests of fifteen other suspects detained in Germany and Calabria. Most of the suspects were held in pre-trial detention, but an Amsterdam court decided Marc B. wasn't a flight risk, so he was released. He promptly left the country.

Behind those arrests was the testimony of another young woman from Rosarno, Giuseppina Multari, who was related by marriage to Maria Concetta Cacciola. Giuseppina's husband was Antonio Cacciola. He suffered from depression and alcoholism, making him a potential liability to the family. One night, he committed suicide, or at least that's what Giuseppina was told. From then on, she was held captive at her in-laws' house. Eventually, she summoned up the courage to ask her father to deliver a letter to the police, telling them she was ready to testify against her in-laws. She'd been paying attention while being held hostage at the Cacciola home. For example, she noticed that a Calabrian woman who lived in Germany regularly delivered cocaine and weapons to Rosarno. Giuseppina's brothers-in-law then used her food processor to cut the drugs before selling them. She also observed who arrived to do business with her in-laws. She recognized one San Luca man who sold not only drugs but also religious souvenirs in Polsi – she and her late husband had once seen him at the Madonna sanctuary.

Giuseppina's inside information helped the police locate a weapons cache and a hidden Cacciola bunker; it also assisted them in piecing together the cocaine-trafficking route between Amsterdam and Rosarno. The woman who brought cocaine and weapons to Rosarno owned two restaurants and an ice cream parlour in Düsseldorf.

According to court records from Reggio, for two years she had been making monthly trips to Calabria via Germany by rental car, after first picking up fifteen to twenty kilos of cocaine at Marc B.'s home in Amsterdam. The Italian police tracked her cell-phone signal and caught her red-handed in Rosarno.

Today, Giuseppina Multari lives in hiding with her parents and children. Marc B. absconded, while criminal proceedings against him continued in Calabria. He wasn't accused of being a clan member, but he was suspected of systematically collaborating with the Ndrangheta by supplying drugs. The court in Reggio Calabria sentenced the other fifteen suspects to between eight and thirteen years for drugs and arms trafficking and membership of a mafia organization. In March 2021, Marc B. was arrested in the Dominican Republic and extradited to Italy.

A few weeks after police apprehended Marc B. in Amsterdam in 2014, I was surprised by some arrests in my village in Calabria. August had been sweltering, and clouds of smoke from nearby forest fires regularly gathered over the hills. In dismal contrast with the usual carefree summer vibe, the trees had turned into scorched matchsticks and flakes of ash drifted through the windows. Helicopters were being used to extinguish the fires. Firefighters filled huge buckets with seawater and flew back and forth between the sea and the hills, trying to control the flames. Whenever I heard a helicopter, like I did that late afternoon in August, I rushed to my balcony to see where it was heading. Sometimes, the fires crept terrifyingly close to the houses, but this time, I couldn't spot any smoke or fire. Instead, a police helicopter was hovering above the village, with a marksman visible in the opening of the hold. He'd aimed the barrel of his rifle at the street, for cover.

The following day, I read that eighteen people had been arrested, including some from neighbouring villages. I recognized three faces among the photos of those arrested. One worked as a shepherd, and I always said hello when I saw him in town. I liked buying his goat's cheese and fresh ricotta, and his son had mixed cement for the renovation work on my house.

I couldn't really talk to anyone in town about what had happened, but I could read about the investigation, and it gave me a sick feeling in my stomach. The police investigation still revolved around the Ndrangheta foreman from my village who'd been arrested four years earlier in a restaurant at a seaside resort. And, although he had been behind bars since then, like every self-respecting member of the Ndrangheta, he didn't exactly take his defeat lying down. His family's visits to the prison turned into informal clan gatherings. He'd instructed one of his brothers to maintain control of the area and used his family to convey messages to other clan members who were still at large. That way, the extortion could carry on, not just of entrepreneurs but also of the municipality, where his men insisted on being granted a contract to expand the cemetery.

While incarcerated, the boss used an intermediary to command his brother-in-law, the shepherd, to hide weapons in the hut where he housed his sheep and goats. The guns may have been used in an attack, and the boss wanted to keep the police from finding them in his home.

Furthermore, the boss had been upset about the audacity of a local journalist who had written about his legal woes. He couldn't condone that. One of the boss's daughters took it upon herself to go to the journalist's home to convey her father's displeasure. The daughter subsequently faced charges of mafia-type intimidation in juvenile court. But by then the message had become loud and clear, even to me.

How foolish had I been, moving to Calabria and feeling the need to write about the Ndrangheta? I had never felt unsafe in this village – after all, it wasn't San Luca or Rosarno, where you could read the clans' oppressive social control on the faces of passers-by. Or had I been deluding myself?

The mood seemed more strained than usual in the weeks following the arrests. I often saw cars parked along the steep roads leading to the village, their occupants standing some distance away, huddled in whispers. Had they agreed to meet to discuss their next moves, out of the reach of bugging devices?

Maybe it was time I changed my tune and wrote about things that make Calabrians proud, subjects they were happy to discuss. Calabria could undoubtedly use some extra PR – the history and beauty of the region were practically unknown among foreign tourists. And a lack of appreciation for the beauty of the surroundings seemed to give the Ndrangheta's ugliness more room to grow.

I cast my mind back to when I was learning Italian geography at school: I had asked myself who lived in this quirkily shaped toe of the boot, completely lacking in notable cities. Nocturnal satellite photos still show Calabria in virtual darkness, yet the region is home to the ancient foundations of Italian civilisation. Almost three thousand years ago, during the Magna Graecia, or Greater Greece, period, Greek colonists set sail in search of farmland. The name Calabria is derived from the Greek *kalon brion*, meaning fertile land.

The Greeks established their city-states here, and their legacy includes olive trees and temples, philosophical concepts and recipes for wine. Scilla, a glittering fishing village, still bears the name of a sea nymph from Homer's *Odyssey*. There are plenty of other traces of Odysseus, the mythical hero, whose route would have taken him along the Calabrian coast. In any event, there's clear evidence that Plato mentored legal practitioners in Locri. And Pythagoras taught mathematics and ethics in Crotone, which was a powerful city-state at that time and produced many Olympic champions. Crotone is also the location of a Greek sanctuary dedicated to Hera, of which only a single column remains, maternally watching over the Ionian Sea. But sadly, there's little money for preserving Calabria's cultural heritage, and an incredible amount of history remains buried beneath the ground.

So my boyfriend N and I temporarily shifted our focus to Calabria's beauty, in part to distract ourselves from the suddenly oppressive silence in my village. On one of our tourist expeditions we visited Musaba, a museum park belonging to a tireless Calabrian artist named Nik Spatari, who was then in his eighties. I felt heartened by his modern, brightly coloured monumental mosaics and oversized paintings. We were enjoying a cup of coffee in the sun when a film crew turned up – a regional TV station was going to film a piece about the museum. The director wasn't one for small talk and seemingly out of the blue, he told us that they had recently had a dramatic experience. The network had filmed the controversial transhipment of Syria's eighty chemical weapons containers in the port of Gioia Tauro from start to finish. A brief clip had been used for a news programme, but the rest of the footage had unexpectedly been destroyed. Shortly after filming, there had been a break-in at the offices of the TV station and hackers had wiped the computers. Although he was visibly angry, the director said he had resigned himself to the fact that that some of the powers that be in Calabria would not tolerate journalistic watchdogs. Going forward, life would be more peaceful if they focused on making programmes about art and culture.

17

SAY IT WITH FLOWERS

Vincenzo Crupi lives in a semi-detached house on the Willem Alexanderstraat in the Dutch town of Aalsmeer, near Amsterdam. His neighbourhood, the Oranjewijk, is rather ordinary, but the location is ideal for an international entrepreneur like Crupi: Schiphol airport is a fifteen-minute drive from his door, and his office at Royal FloraHolland, the world's largest flower auction, is just five minutes away. Work in the flower trade drew Crupi's parents to the Netherlands, although they never left their home in sunny Siderno, a small town on Calabria's Ionian coast. Vincenzo's approach to the family business was more efficient, and he relocated to the Netherlands in the late 1980s. These days, with his younger brothers Rocco and Giuseppe, he has a well-established transport chain running between the Netherlands and Italy. The flowers travel via Fresh Export, Vincenzo's company based in Aalsmeer, to his brother Rocco's distribution point in Latina, near Rome, and then on to Giuseppe's wholesaler in Calabria.

On its website, Fresh BV, a private limited company, touts itself as the ideal business intermediary for trade between the Netherlands and Italy. It says 'ReF.R.E.S.H the world' at the top of the grainy homepage, alongside a picture of a pink tulip. It sounds like a slightly

175

clumsy slogan for a company that exports flowers. Or is it an inside joke?

The Dutch wouldn't think twice about Vincenzo Crupi's origins in the infamous Italian town of Siderno. Most of Aalsmeer's residents have never heard of the Ndrangheta. So Vincenzo's marriage to Concetta Macrì, the daughter of a powerful boss in the Calabrian mafia, wouldn't set off alarm bells, either. Moreover, he isn't a stereotypical mafioso: he dresses modestly, looks harmless and is reliable.

The Dutch police don't bother him, meaning he can go about his business unhampered. He can tuck cocaine into shipments of flowers heading for Italy, but no more than ten kilos or so at a time to keep the risks to a minimum. Still, each consignment is worth approximately five hundred thousand euros. Vincenzo Crupi uses the cash his family sends back in the empty flower carts to pay his Dutch flower suppliers. After all, who wants to report everything to the tax authorities?

To increase the Crupis' tax benefits, he even has a few Dutch associates who manage shell companies for him, including one in Madeira. In short, he enjoys ample professional support and plenty of breathing space. He does his own thing at Royal FloraHolland and continues to do so even after his people defrauded flower merchants out of millions of euros. The Dutch National Police Force has long been aware of the scam. It's mentioned in their first handbook about the Ndrangheta in the Netherlands, from 2011: 'The business used by the member of the Ndrangheta to bring Dutch companies in the flower sector into contact with Italy always paid for the initial delivery. Subsequently, a large order arrived from Italy, which the Dutch delivered but were never paid for. Once in Italy, the flowers were resold to other companies. The three Dutch companies involved in the scam suffered approximately two million euros in losses. A representative of one of the defrauded companies travelled to Italy to ask about the unpaid bill. He was warned never to show his face there again, or his life would be in danger.'

However, the 'member of the Ndrangheta' mentioned in the police handbook wasn't Vincenzo Crupi, but his fixer, Gianluca. Although Gianluca had been convicted in Italy of drug trafficking and murder, he had been living in the Dutch municipality of Hoofddorp under a fake passport since 2000. He had no problem working for Vincenzo Crupi and recruited unsuspecting Dutch flower producers as clients for Fresh until the summer of 2009, when he was apprehended by police. According to the police handbook, Gianluca then entered the procedure for extradition to Italy without being further questioned in the Netherlands. The report described the fraudulent practices: 'According to detectives, although there is no "hard evidence", it's assumed that additional members of the Ndrangheta are involved. The detectives believe they only uncovered the tip of the iceberg. At the Dutch flower auction alone, dozens of Dutch companies are said to have fallen prey to such Italian scams. However, many had no plans to press charges "because they'd never recover a penny of what they'd lost".'

Why wouldn't the defrauded flower merchants expect to get their money back? It seems the Crupi brothers knew how to run their business. They used bankruptcy fraud and shell companies to lead creditors astray and prevent investigators from finding a way to their door.

Four more years passed and several more flower suppliers went bankrupt before the Dutch police began investigating the scam. A warning arrived from Italy – Vincenzo Crupi's brother-in-law Domenico, a strapping forty-year-old from Siderno who was then living near Aalsmeer, was planning to murder someone at Royal FloraHolland. Domenico had succeeded the fixer Gianluca and maintained close ties with Francesco Nirta, the fugitive from San Luca who had been arrested in a snack bar in Nieuwegein. Recently, two men had beaten up Domenico, and he suspected that one of the flower merchants he had swindled was behind the attack. At Fresh, Domenico didn't hide his urge to use his gun but his brother-in-law Vincenzo Crupi tried to talk him out of it, because bloodshed doesn't go with successful Ndrangheta entrepreneurship, especially abroad. After all, newspaper stories about embezzlement, fraud or cocaine trafficking are far less shocking than reports of murders. The Dutch police were also aware of the situation and at the end of 2013, they visited Domenico to tell him they were keeping an eye on him.

Things remained quiet around Fresh until the summer of 2014. At that time, an Albanian lorry driver named Arben was making regular trips for the Crupis between Italy and the Netherlands. He was unaware that the police were reading his text messages and had bugged the cab of his lorry. During his journeys for the Crupis, Arben often arranged nocturnal meetings with men he referred to as 'amore' at petrol stations in the vicinity of Milan and Rome. The Italian authorities strongly suspected that instead of lovers, Arben was meeting people who'd come to pick up cocaine. After one such quickie date with Arben, the driver of a car carrying six kilos of coke and four cell phones was detained.

Although the police didn't arrest Arben, the Crupis switched lorry drivers before the next trip to Italy. The Dutch police followed this new Italian lorry driver, who first drove his shipment of flowers to Rotterdam, where a man of Moroccan origin handed him a bag. When the lorry reached the Italian city of Bergamo, the vehicle was stopped and found to be carrying eleven kilograms of cocaine.

Vincenzo Crupi, who used a special encrypted smartphone that could not be tapped, suspected that someone in Italy had been telling on them. He naively believed he was safe in his office in Aalsmeer, but Dutch investigators had hidden video cameras and microphones there in the autumn of 2014, at the request of their Italian associates. They were about to overhear some fascinating conversations between Vincenzo Crupi and his brother-in-law, Vincenzo Macrì.

Vincenzo Macrì was the son of a legendary Capocrimine, or elected commander, of the Ndrangheta. After spending thirteen years in an American prison for drug trafficking, he temporarily moved to Aalsmeer. He was staying in a house owned by his brother-in-law, and they were working together. In the offices of Fresh, the men used the Calabrian dialect to talk about places in South America where Macrì might settle to buy drugs. Macrì said he would like to move to Venezuela, where he knew a lovely woman and felt at home. But Crupi believed an office in Colombia would be more convenient, because that would give Macrì a perfect excuse to fly there regularly. He also wanted to use Macrì as a trusted representative in Bulgaria and Serbia because, he said, 'We still need to raise a whole lot of money in Europe.'

Crupi and Macrì also chatted about their network in Calabria and Canada. They used nicknames like 'the chosen one' and 'Chubby'. They gossiped about who they liked and who they didn't, about who was skimming off the top and who was trying to give some other guy a bad name. One recurring theme was the chaos in Toronto following the murder of Carmine Verduci, a prominent elderly Ndrangheta figure they had both known well. The brothers-in-law Crupi and Macrì not only wondered about the perpetrators of Verduci's murder and their motives, but they also decided that one of them had to go to Toronto to calm things down. Ultimately, they agreed that Vincenzo Crupi should go to Canada to prevent a war between the families.

While discussing a massive shipment of stolen Lindt chocolates, Crupi and Macrì let slip even more details about their international network. Over several months, 7.5 million euros worth of milk chocolates had been stolen from a warehouse in Italy, representing 250 tonnes of creamy truffles wrapped in red and white cellophane. The Crupis had most of the spoils, but they were finding it difficult to find buyers for the undocumented bonbons. They'd sent a large shipment to Canada, where Vincenzo Crupi's sons tried to sell them off. A portion remained in the Calabrian city of Siderno and the rest was stuck in Aalsmeer.

The longer the chocolates remained on the premises of Fresh, the more pressure Crupi and Macrì exerted on their contacts to find buyers. In December 2014, they finally found an interested party in Hungary. Macrì hired a Dutch transport company to make the delivery, because a Dutch lorry wouldn't attract much police attention while driving through Germany. He was all the more surprised when he heard that the vehicle, containing 15,040 kilos of chocolate, was stopped on the A2 near Utrecht, before it had even left the Netherlands. At the time of the arrest, officers told the driver they knew what the lorry was carrying, and that they also knew the stolen chocolates had been loaded on the premises of a flower company. Now Macrì was certain: someone was tapping his phone. But why hadn't the chocolates been seized at Fresh? Vincenzo Crupi thought he knew the answer: 'This is Royal FloraHolland, the world's largest flower auction! Of course they wouldn't want the news to get out that they found so much stolen chocolate here. So, they waited until it was off the premises and intervened when it was on the road.'

It wasn't until March 2015 that the Dutch police and Fiscal Information and Investigation Service raided Fresh's office and Crupi and Macrì's homes on suspicion of embezzlement, bankruptcy and

VAT fraud, money laundering, and receiving and handling stolen goods. At Fresh, the police also found a few remaining boxes of stolen Lindt chocolates.

The police also visited Crupi's other brother-in-law, Domenico, for the second time in eighteen months, in the neighbouring municipality of Kudelstaart. They found a gun in his home and handcuffed him for firearms possession.

The fourth person the police paid a visit that day was Massimo Dalla Valle, a businessman working for Vincenzo Crupi. For some time, Dalla Valle had been focusing on managing the sale of cold-storage goods, particularly in Eastern Europe. Before working for the Crupis, he had gained experience shipping products like Dole bananas and pineapples in Antwerp, Belgium. Della Valle wasn't Calabrian; he was part of a wealthy family from Padua, and his mother held a prominent political position in the Lega Nord party. In a wiretapped conversation, Della Valle boasted that he'd 'spoken the language of the Ndrangheta for twenty-five years'. For the time being, Dalla Valle was released in the Netherlands, as were the brothers-in-law Macrì and Crupi, who got together that same afternoon in the offices of Fresh.

Six months after the Dutch raids, in September 2015, the Crupi brothers were arrested in Italy, together with Massimo Dalla Valle and forty other suspects. In 2017, the court of first instance in Reggio Calabria convicted the Crupis of being members of the Ndrangheta. The case against Vincenzo Macrì faced delays, because shortly after the raids in Aalsmeer, he fled to South America on a fake passport. He was subsequently arrested in Brazil, extradited to Italy and, in 2019, convicted of Ndrangheta membership. All the men appealed the court's decision.

The arrests in Italy alerted the Dutch to the unwelcome news that members of the Ndrangheta had been making themselves at home at Royal FloraHolland, in the logistical heart of the Dutch economy. A single bankrupt flower grower appeared on camera, angry and heartbroken that the underhanded Calabrian mob had destroyed his flourishing business. However, one Dutch business associate, John van Tol, came to Vincenzo Crupi's defence. Van Tol heads a large flower company that also imports vases and baskets from China and puts together gift packages. During the raids in March 2015, the police found a few boxes of stolen Lindt chocolates on his business premises.

I met John van Tol while recording a podcast about the Crupi case, just after the brothers were convicted in the court of first instance in Reggio Calabria. It was a bitterly cold evening in December, so we kept our coats on for warmth while we sat in the kitchen of his company in the Dutch polder. John, a sturdy-looking man in his fifties with close-cropped hair, wore a dark blue bomber jacket. He was cheerful and eager to tell his side of the story.

'I met Vincenzo Crupi in 2013, and for over two years, I supplied flowers to Fresh on a commission basis. He exported primarily roses to Italy – a massive number of roses, plus many chrysanthemums and orchids. I think I supplied as much as eighty per cent of his flowers.'

When John first met Vincenzo, he had been active in the flower and plant trade for quite some time: 'First, Vincenzo worked for someone else for more than twenty years. Then, about ten years ago, he started Fresh. Fresh was a major player at the auction for a while, especially regarding flowers. It wouldn't surprise me if their turnover was in the range of twenty or thirty million.'

The two communicated in English, because Vincenzo didn't speak Dutch and John didn't speak Italian. 'But we clicked. I still think he's a nice guy. It's a shame he's locked up,' John said. 'And I don't believe everything they say about him in Italy. To me, he's an amiable, down-to-earth guy.'

John and Vincenzo didn't limit their contact to the office; John was also a guest at Vincenzo's home. 'I regularly had dinner with him. He'd hired a chef to work at his house in Aalsmeer.'

How did John reconcile Vincenzo's private chef with his otherwise 'down-to-earth' image? 'I think you mustn't forget about the cultural differences between the Netherlands and southern European countries. Besides, his wife didn't live with him here – she was still in Latina, near Rome, and Vincenzo saw her on weekends. He flew to Rome every Friday, and on Sunday evening or Monday morning, he'd fly back to Schiphol. Apart from that, he drove an older-model car, didn't wear expensive clothes and lived in a sparsely furnished house.'

Vincenzo Crupi also introduced John to his brother-in-law, Vincenzo Macrì, who lived on the same street. 'We called him Enzo. Enzo is the brother of Vincenzo Crupi's wife, Concetta. As I understand from the newspapers, the father of Concetta and Enzo was a big shot in the mafia. The Crupis told me that the man had been shot because he didn't want the Ndrangheta to get involved in trafficking drugs.'

I asked John if he knew that Enzo had gone to prison for drug trafficking. 'Yes, he'd told me about that. Enzo spoke fluent Spanish, which he'd learned while doing time in America. He said he never wanted to go to prison again, and that he'd sworn off doing stupid things.'

Over time, Vincenzo Crupi ran up huge debts with John van Tol. 'Of course, people in Italy have a different way of dealing with debts than we do here in the Netherlands, but the flower auction carries on every day. We had to suspend him once and then he wasn't allowed to buy any flowers for a while. Maybe there was a bit of a head-to-head, but I've dealt with that from other clients, as well. At one point, as collateral, I got my hands on the mortgage papers for one of the two houses Vincenzo owned in Aalsmeer. Just in case he defaulted on the amount he owed.'

By the time of our conversation, John had become the owner of that house. He rented it to his Polish employees. The Crupi family still owned the other property on the same street and John acted as its letting agent.

To John, Vincenzo Crupi's indebtedness to him made it seem highly improbable that he was smuggling cocaine: 'If you're genuinely in that line of work, money's not a problem, right? So why would you want all that hassle? The first time the police raided him, he told me he hadn't done anything. After that, a lot of stories did the rounds and sometimes I wonder what's true. But no one's shown me any cocaine they found among the flowers. They did find some stuff in or near his lorries twice. I'm not saying Vincenzo knew nothing about it, but it also doesn't prove he arranged it. They certainly didn't load a single gram of coke into the cargo on my premises; otherwise, I would have seen it on the security cameras.'

As John reiterated, Vincenzo was not a big shot: 'If he was in the drug trade, he could have worn the most expensive clothes, but Vincenzo and his wife were very casual. My clothes cost much more, but his looked like they were from Zeeman, the Dutch discounter. I cleared out his house. Let me put it this way: I don't think that guy cares about money.'

When John and his girlfriend were in Calabria to visit the Crupi family in 2014, between Christmas and New Year, they didn't see much extravagance either: 'At the time, Vincenzo Crupi was in Canada, but Giuseppe and his mother were there. We celebrated Christmas Eve with them. And New Year's Eve, nothing much, we left shortly after midnight. While we were there, we ate well, but no bottles of Moët were cracked open or anything like that.'

All in all, John thought the stories about the Crupis were greatly exaggerated. Moreover, he was highly critical of how the Dutch authorities dealt with the case. 'During the raid, they came here too, with twenty-five men, turning the entire place upside down. They took my bookkeeping records and didn't return them until a year later, with nothing but a "sorry". In the end, all they did is send the case files to Italy. Why hasn't the Dutch justice system taken any action?'

When I asked about the stolen chocolate truffles that the police had found on the premises of John's company, he replied: 'I used that chocolate for gift baskets during the holidays – Vincenzo gave them to his business associates. That's why I kept those boxes here. Later, I read in the paper that someone had stolen an enormous supply of chocolate. But what was I supposed to do with those ten boxes I happened to have?'

John explained that he's mainly in touch with one of Vincenzo Crupi's sons in Canada. 'If anything happens, I call him, like when there's a problem with a tenant at Vincenzo's house. I'm still a friend of the family. Does that make me a friend of the Ndrangheta? I don't know anything about that, and maybe I don't want to know, either.'

I still wondered if John knew that the young man he sometimes phoned in Canada was technically living as a fugitive. The court of first instance in Reggio Calabria had convicted him in absentia for collaborating with the Ndrangheta and receiving stolen goods. That got John's attention. 'I can't read Italian. I only know what I see on television and what they tell me.' He chuckled and concluded: 'But, of course, they don't tell me everything.'

18

WARFARE IN THE LAW COURTS

'The Ndrangheta is powerful precisely because it can convince others it is completely ordinary and not dangerous,' says Antonio De Bernardo, the public prosecutor who brought charges against the Crupis in Reggio Calabria. He is in his forties, with chiselled features and a determined look. His long sideburns are reminiscent of a gladiator's helmet. De Bernardo joined Reggio Calabria's public prosecution service in 2006 and almost immediately set to work on the most critical criminal cases ever brought against the Ndrangheta. During the Crimine maxi-investigation, he and his colleagues uncovered the Ndrangheta's provincial leaders and various national and international branches. Because of death threats, De Bernardo is permanently protected by four bodyguards.

In 2017, I met De Bernardo at his offices in Reggio Calabria's Palace of Justice. He told me I was the first Dutch journalist to visit him in person. I was trying to learn more about the Crupi family and their position within the Ndrangheta. Was the Crupi surname linked to a clan here in Calabria? 'Perhaps less than other names,' De Bernardo said. 'But alarm bells certainly started to ring for those who knew the families the Crupis were related to. Not only was Vincenzo Crupi married to the daughter of Antonio Macrì, who was once

Capocrimine, its most prominent leader, but Crupi's uncle was also an important figure within the Canadian Ndrangheta.'

When they were arrested in 2015, the Crupis had no convictions on record. And yet they had figured in legal investigations fifteen years earlier because weapons had been found in their possession in Siderno. Anyone who investigated their associates would immediately have been concerned. So how could the Crupis have gone about their business for so long in the Netherlands? 'I believe no one was watching them,' said De Bernardo. 'In 2013, the Crupi brothers attracted the attention of my judicial associates in Latina, Italy, who began sharing that information with the Dutch. When the Crupis turned up in a broader investigation into Ndrangheta clans in Siderno and Toronto, the office in Reggio joined in.'

As part of his investigation, De Bernardo asked two former Ndrangheta members who had turned state's witnesses if they knew anything about the Crupi family from Siderno. Both informers said that the Crupis had been known as successful cocaine smugglers since the 1980s, using their flower business as a cover. The family had established this reputation among clans in Siderno and along other parts of the Ionian coast.

To understand the Crupi family's position within the Ndrangheta, we must go back to the 1960s, when Vincenzo Crupi's father-in-law, Antonio Macrì, was not only the boss of the Ndrangheta in Siderno but also Capocrimine, the president of their top council. Back then, the council included Mommo Piromalli from the port city of Gioia Tauro, who later had Antonio Macrì killed. Macrì had been on good terms with the Sicilian mafia and knew Totò Riina personally. He was known as the 'boss of two worlds' because he established criminal outposts in North America for smuggling cigarettes, among other things. Antonio Macrì was an 'old school' Ndranghetist: he didn't shy away from extortion and murder, but he drew the line at drug trafficking. He was in his seventies in 1975 when he was shot and killed by Mommo Piromalli's henchmen. Thousands attended Macrì's funeral, including business associates from the United States, Canada and Australia.

Antonio Macrì fathered children into old age: seven daughters and two sons. At the time of his murder, his oldest son was only sixteen and the youngest, Vincenzo Macrì – who would later work with the Crupis – just ten. Both were too young to defend the family's honour. And so, Francesco Commisso, Antonio Macrì's former right-hand man, assumed control, making the Commissos the most prominent Ndrangheta family in Sidorno. The family strengthened its bonds with Canada and Australia and began investing in drug trafficking.

As an adult, Vincenzo Macrì, who has a ruddy complexion, was known as 'Pumadoru', which means tomato in the Calabrian dialect. He was seen as an asset to the Commisso family because he was a Macrì, and his surname still commanded respect and trust within international criminal circles.

In Toronto, Vincenzo Crupi's uncle became the head of all those Ndrangheta families that had originally come from Siderno. Perhaps that made Vincenzo Crupi an interesting matrimonial match for Concetta Macrì, the former Capocrimine's daughter and Pumadoru's sister. Vincenzo's brothers Giuseppe and Rocco married girls from two other prominent Ndrangheta families from Siderno and Toronto.

It seems that not all Ndranghetists can cope equally well with an arranged marriage. Wiretapped conversations revealed that Giuseppe Crupi, the tallest and most athletically good-looking of the three Crupi brothers, was destined to strain the relationship between the Commissos and the Crupis. In overheard exchanges, a somewhat enigmatic phrase caught the attention of the police: 'Peppe is no longer Peppe's Peppe; now he's Sandro's Peppe.'

'It was a while before we figured out what that meant,' Antonio De Bernardo told me. 'It turned out that Giuseppe Crupi – Peppe for short – was married to the sister of boss Giuseppe Commisso, another important Peppe. But Peppe Crupi was having an affair with the daughter of Alessandro Figliomeni, or Sandro for short.' Sandro Figliomeni was a member of the Santa, making him a leading Ndrangheta figure; at the time, he was also the mayor of Siderno. So because of the affair, Giuseppe Crupi had, in effect, aligned himself with a different Ndrangheta family: Peppe (Crupi) was no longer aligned with Peppe (Commisso) but with Sandro (Figliomeni). It didn't matter that Giuseppe Crupi was in the process of getting divorced; he had exposed the Commissos to ridicule and, as punishment, he was temporarily kicked out of the clan. The Commissos withdrew their backing from mayor Sandro Figliomeni, and it wasn't long before Figliomeni was forced to step down. Figliomeni's daughter later broke up with Giuseppe Crupi and moved to the Ivory Coast.

Another wiretapped conversation revealed how Vincenzo Crupi apologized to clan leaders for his brother's behaviour and said that they wanted to continue collaborating with the Commissos. Luckily, the Crupis and their business were too important for the Commissos to drop them permanently and the familial bonds were soon restored.

Years later, in Aalsmeer, Crupi could still be overheard complaining to his brother-in-law Macrì about how his brother's actions had forced him to grovel before the leaders of the clan. 'In their conversations, members of the Ndrangheta often revisit internal conflicts,' De Bernardo explained. 'That's relevant for our investigations because such rehashed stories reveal much about the pecking order within the families.' The discussions held at the offices of Fresh, captured on video by Dutch police, proved invaluable to Reggio's Public Prosecutor's Office. 'As a bonus, we could explain to our Dutch associates what was actually being said. Because without some essential background information, a grasp of the Calabrian dialect and an explanation of the nicknames, those recordings were incomprehensible to them. To get to the bottom of who they're talking about, you need to know who holds the cards within the clans and who's up and coming; you also have to understand how history has shaped family dynamics. For us, contextualizing this kind of material is part of the job. It's extremely satisfying when you find a new piece of the mosaic and can create a more complete picture.'

The interpretation of conversations by mafia prosecutors is not only crucial to proving an individual's involvement in a specific crime, it can also help prevent potential crimes – such as when Crupi's accomplice in Aalsmeer wanted to shoot someone out of revenge. But Italian prosecutors can also use their powers of interpretation to decipher a suspect's position within the mafia organization. 'The Ndrangheta is based on secrecy, on omertà, on not sharing information,' De Bernardo said. 'If a suspect has specific information about a particular Ndrangheta clan, that tells us he's part of it. And the more information he has, the higher his position within the organization. And if he also goes into action to respond to problems of his own accord, it indicates to us that his status is even more lofty.'

According to De Bernardo, Vincenzo Crupi's status was made apparent, for example, when he took it upon himself to go to Canada to smooth ruffled feathers and prevent more bloodshed after an elderly clan member was murdered. 'He was a manager, an organizer within the Commisso clan.'

In Reggio Calabria, Vincenzo Crupi was solely charged with and convicted of mafia membership. 'You can convict someone by proving they formally joined the Ndrangheta, for example, if several witnesses can attest to an individual's membership, and you have evidence that he has attended rituals or meetings and has made a career within the clan. Even if you can't prove he has committed other crimes,' De Bernardo explained. 'This approach is extremely effective because the punishment for mafia membership is harsh in Italy. During the trial, crimes that had taken place in the Netherlands – such as drug trafficking, embezzlement, money laundering and bankruptcy fraud – were mentioned in court only to prove that the suspects were members of the same group and had been conspiring together.'

The Italian prosecutors are primarily interested in mapping the Ndrangheta's structure. 'When I began working as a public prosecutor, I noticed many Ndrangheta trials ended in an acquittal,' De Bernardo said. 'There was hardly any legal basis on which to build.' The goal of investigations is to build this foundation and expand on it. That makes sense because it's only when you convict members of a group and identify their position within the organization that you can prove the position of others.

When Antonio De Bernardo began his career at the public prosecution service in Reggio, the Commissos had faced few legal proceedings. One case involved a bloody vendetta in Siderno in the late 1980s and traced clan members who had fled to Canada, but beyond that they'd drawn a blank. 'But now, after a few thorough investigations, our understanding has grown,' De Bernardo said. 'We know who the boss is in Siderno; we know which clan members live here and who lives abroad. Without that knowledge, we would never have understood the position of the Crupis within this organization, and we wouldn't have been able to prosecute them.'

*

The mafia prosecutor clearly loved talking about his work, but he shied away from answering some of my questions. Understandably – the case in question was being appealed at the time of our interview, so the convictions were not yet definitive. More than anything, De Bernardo gave me a deeper insight into Italy's legal approach to prosecuting the Ndrangheta. And, because I had a copy of the two-thousand-plus-page criminal file about the case against the Crupis and forty-six other suspects, I could fill in the blanks about what he'd managed to piece together regarding the Siderno clans.

My head was spinning from the number of people and events linked in this investigation. Some of the evidence pertained to the discovery of drugs and various weapons. Another, more extensive section of the file focused on interpersonal relationships. The significance of meetings and conversations, some of which took place in Aalsmeer or on the phone between Italy, the Netherlands and Canada, and many of which took place in Siderno, was explained in light of the traditional rules to which members of the Ndrangheta must adhere. It dealt with their obligations to other clan members, the favours they are obliged to grant one another and the respect they must bestow upon higher-ranking Ndranghetists.

Exchanging favours and greetings is also de rigueur outside of the individual clans, and the file described the Commissos' ties with other families, including the Strangios from San Luca. What's more, the investigation also illustrated the Ndrangheta's role in supplying cocaine to other Italian mafias: it mentioned both a Camorra clan and Sicilian criminals alleged to have received drugs from the Ndrangheta.

I was amazed by how influential some of the contacts of the Crupis and Commissos were – they included Ndranghetists who secured contracts to build the 2015 World Expo in Milan. Other members of the Crupis' direct network had invested dirty money in cramped summer houses or glitzy hotels after first taking the necessary detours through straw men and tax havens. I can still clearly remember the long, palm-lined drive of one such hotel and the pink fountains in its restaurant. I'd once been there as a wedding guest, just before the Italian justice department seized the place.

One section of the investigation in particular sparked my imagination: it was about a suspect who seemed to know Vincenzo Crupi well. According to prosecutors, this man was the head of a related Ndrangheta family. The file stated that he'd asked a senator from Berlusconi's party to bribe a judge in Reggio Calabria. The favour, however, wasn't on his own behalf; he was hoping for a lighter sentence on appeal for one of his close criminal friends. The matter was even more intriguing because the senator in question was working in a supervisory role for Europol, the European Union's agency for law enforcement cooperation. In addition, the senator was also on the board of directors of a Calabrian airport, and he owned construction and cement companies. According to the wiretapped Ndranghetist, the senator owed a considerable debt of gratitude to the Calabrian mafia, making it almost impossible for him to turn down such a request. The prosecutors had assembled detailed evidence proving that someone from the clan had spoken with the senator. But it was unclear if the senator had ever followed through on approaching the judge from Reggio Calabria's court of appeal.

An impressive stack of papers covered Antonio De Bernardo's desk. There was also a black globe on display, and his computer screen showed the gaping jaws of a shark. My eye was drawn, however, to a poster hanging on the wall behind him. It showed a surreal swarm of dozens of identical men dressed in respectable hats and dark raincoats, drifting among tall buildings and a light blue sky.

The work, from 1953, was made by René Magritte, the Belgian artist who also painted a pipe accompanied by the words *Ceci n'est pas une pipe*, or 'This is not a pipe'. As I listened to the mafia prosecutor, the distinguished, well-dressed gentlemen in the painting assumed a variety of identities: I imagined them as judges, civil servants, lawyers, businessmen, doctors, professors, accountants, politicians and members of the mafia.

De Bernardo's bodyguards were waiting in the corridor. Almost from the start, De Bernardo's career has been accompanied by death threats, so he's always been under police protection. 'The first few years, I had a little more freedom of movement,' he told me. 'Then, I started receiving bullets in the mail, and they had to tighten my security.' The bodyguards stay with him all day. They drive him to the courthouse in one of two cars with tinted windows, follow him down the aisles of the supermarket and wait for him at the gym, the dentist's office and when he meets his friends. After that, they bring him home again, waiting until he's safely behind his armoured front door. In a city like Reggio Calabria, where the Ndrangheta has the upper hand, he must constantly take his safety and that of others into consideration when going about his daily life. De Bernardo can only leave his bodyguards behind when he goes on holiday abroad. A few months before the Crupis' arrests, he enjoyed strolling along the canals in Amsterdam. 'A lovely city,' he commented politely.

Oddly, many suspects who receive lengthy sentences in preliminary trials are allowed to roam free before a decision is handed down in their final appeal. Giuseppe Crupi is one example. The supervisory judge in Reggio Calabria did not deem him a flight risk. 'Although we appealed that decision, it didn't help,' De Bernardo said. In this case, someone with a preliminary conviction for mafia membership can enjoy more freedom of movement than his prosecutor.

De Bernardo stressed how much he loves his work. He's not originally from Calabria and was born in Santa Maria Capua Vetere, just north of Naples. It's a small city with an amphitheatre almost as big as Rome's celebrated Colosseum. Spartacus, the rebel gladiator, is said to have fought there. Scenes from gladiator films flash through my mind, showing ancient battles with wild animals and criminals, surrounded by a cheering crowd. However, when De Bernardo appears in Calabrian courtrooms, he can count on little support or appreciation from the audience. That's because in Calabria, few outsiders attend Ndrangheta trials. The public know they would be frowned upon as intruders. As De Bernardo explained, 'Here, mafia trials seem to be exclusively for clan members and their families. And I use that to my advantage by keeping an eye on who's friendly with whom.'

In Italy, the public prosecutor sits in the same area as the suspects and their lawyers, sometimes side by side. All of them face the panel of judges. There are reserved spaces for family members and the suspects' entourage at the back of the courtroom. Courtrooms are usually packed during Italian maxi-trials, like the one surrounding Operation Crimine, in which more than a hundred suspects were tried. Detained suspects attend the trial in cages; in some courtrooms, they're so close to the observers that they could reach out and touch someone through the bars. And even if they keep their hands to themselves, the suspects usually find ways of making their presence known. As the prosecutor explained, 'Whenever I interrogate a state's witness, there's usually another suspect, or a member of the suspect's family, who loudly interrupts, shouting that it's all nonsense.' But that doesn't spoil De Bernardo's fun. 'I love the debate. And I find the feeling of being alone in that arena stimulating – just me against the rest.'

I've attended various hearings of Ndrangheta criminal cases in person, and I was always relieved when the session was over and I could go back outdoors. I began to wonder if an outsider who follows a Ndrangheta trial could trigger repercussions. De Bernardo warned, 'If there's no clear reason for a particular person to be there, they stand out and that can cause problems. For example, during the Crimine trial, the same two local journalists attended all the hearings. But one day, a journalist from Rome turned up. A Canadian television network had asked him to film some of the trial. Subsequently, his home was broken into and his equipment and computers were stolen.'

How does De Bernardo keep from feeling intimidated in court? 'To me, the suspects are people with many shortcomings. You have to view them as individuals and not as part of the group. When conversing with a mafia member, you can't help noticing that these people have some major limitations. And that increases my fascination because you can't help wondering how some have accrued so much power.'

His remarks bring to mind Domenico Oppedisano, the man De Bernardo and his colleagues charged with being the Capocrimine of the Ndrangheta. According to De Bernardo, the strength of the Calabrian clans lies not so much in the leaders themselves but in the way the leader is chosen. De Bernardo was able to more or less follow Oppedisano's election live while investigating Operation Crimine. The new commander of the Calabrian mafia was elected in Siderno, in a launderette of all places. It was owned by the Commissos, the same clan the Crupis belong to. There was a lot of arguing because all the other powerful Ndrangheta clans wanted the Capocrimine to be chosen from their ranks. But in the end, everyone agreed on Oppedisano.

'When you compare someone like Oppedisano with Totò Riina, the vicious leader of the Sicilian mafia, then Riina instinctively instils more fear,' De Bernardo said. 'But I'm more worried about what Oppedisano represents. Riina seized control of Cosa Nostra by force, in an almost military way. But his rise meant the beginning of the decline of the Sicilian mafia, and with good reason. Such a warlike stance leads to deaths, police investigations, organizational unrest and discord, and it pushes members to become informants. The Ndrangheta, on the other hand, absorbs all shocks and finds the best solutions in an almost democratic way. They elected Oppedisano to maintain unity and if they need to, they'll choose someone else for the same reason another day. That makes the organization stable, sophisticated, rock solid – and ominous.'

De Bernardo sees his mission as spreading the word about how insidiously inconspicuous the Ndrangheta can appear, and to encourage better and faster action against them. International collaborations like the one between Italy and the Netherlands create that opportunity. Many operational bases or locali of the Ndrangheta have turned up in Germany and Switzerland. I asked De Bernardo if he thinks a branch of the Ndrangheta might be permanently based in the Netherlands. 'There's no evidence of that yet. The Ndrangheta has a presence in the Netherlands because of the opportunities for drug trafficking and economic profit. But unlike other countries, where Calabrians have been settling for generations, they have no historical roots in the Netherlands. However, it would be best to remain on high alert: the Ndrangheta is developing rapidly, and the mere presence of Ndrangheta-related entrepreneurs can have a huge impact. A mafioso entrepreneur isn't just a businessperson capable of committing mafia-related crimes; they may also use little or no scruples to manage their company. Sadly, many Dutch citizens fell prey to the Crupis' criminal business practices, their scams and fraud. They may not have dealt directly with Vincenzo Crupi, who rarely operated openly through his company, Fresh, and rarely used his own name. Moreover, his victims could not have known how crooked he was because he had not yet been convicted in Italy. Crupi could just as easily have been a regular businessman.'

I asked if it was conceivable that a Dutch entrepreneur, perhaps one with a transport company, could ever be prosecuted in Calabria for collaborating with the Ndrangheta. 'That would be complicated but not impossible. You must first prove that the foreign company knew they were serving the mafia.'

Here, we've touched on a complicated grey area, what De Bernardo calls 'the power of all mafias'. 'It's much easier to attack a dangerous gang of armed robbers, because they are outsiders to the community. With the mafia, there is, as it were, a black core of members – the organization's insiders – who are surrounded by a grey cloud that can be so vast in some areas that there's no room for clear, uncontaminated space. This grey zone can also be inhabited by Dutch or other foreign businesspeople willing to make certain concessions, politicians who grant favours to a clan member in exchange for votes, or a municipal civil servant who looks the other way. The list goes on. The mafia is like a cancerous growth that develops inside the body; it can't live independently and needs healthy cells to grow. The mafia lives and thrives because it is part of society, and that's the reality we must crack down on and eradicate.'

The ambition to crack down on the Ndrangheta is complicated because the Ndrangheta manages to blend in perfectly in an increasing number of sectors. Especially in the international business world, distinguishing members of the mafia's younger generation from other highflyers is often tricky. For example, if you google the names of children whose fathers are bosses in Siderno, you'll find some impressive LinkedIn pages. Many have graduated with MBAs from prestigious universities, some live in Hong Kong or West Africa, one has become a cybersecurity consultant, another has specialized in international law.

'The university educated, up-and-coming generation is very different from their predecessors,' De Bernardo pointed out. 'They elevate the mafias to a new level, which may call for a different form of intimidation. At the same time, it's interesting to note that today, it's hard to find any children from Ndrangheta families who are not on Facebook or Instagram. Trivial as that may seem, it certainly has consequences for the Ndrangheta, with its tradition of keeping as much information as possible within the confines of the family. This criminal organization is based entirely on family relations and an 'honour code' founded on secrecy, discretion and keeping your head down. Unsurprisingly, the Ndrangheta originated in villages deep within the mountains, in communities unfamiliar with exchanging information and experiences with outsiders. On social media, the younger generation share what they've done and who they socialize with – that goes completely against the logic, traditions and foundations of the Ndrangheta's criminal system. For us, it's an additional source of information, increasing the Ndrangheta's vulnerability. Old-school members of the Ndrangheta are aware of the problem, and although they frown upon it, they can't keep their kids off the internet. Ultimately, the needs of those kids to share their lives with the world will change the face of the Ndrangheta profoundly.'

19

THE BATTLE FOR RIACE

In the Netherlands, news of the Ndrangheta's activities within the heart of the Dutch economy quickly faded. The year was 2015, and a million refugees had tried to reach Europe in flimsy boats. Newspapers were full of stories about refugees rescued from rickety vessels and taken to the southern Italian coast, and about others, who tragically hadn't survived the crossing. The need to find a safe resolution for those fleeing hardship became more urgent by the day, but Europe lacked the political will to join forces and show tangible solidarity. The fear of being inundated by helpless refugees influenced public opinion, while an increasing number of violent attacks heightened panic about Islamic terrorism. In 2015, the Italian mafia seemed like Europe's least pressing concern.

A village near where I lived was fast attracting world-wide fame for its creative and hospitable way of accommodating refugees. Riace was an ancient village on Calabria's Ionian coast. Its population was dwindling, and the townsfolk saw the refugees as an opportunity, perhaps even a solution to the growing exodus. Abandoned houses were fixed up to house refugees applying for asylum status in Italy. The streets were once again buzzing with young families out for a stroll. Thanks to newcomers from Africa, the Middle East and

Asia, primary schools reopened and customers filled the shops and cafés. Locals and asylum seekers sat side by side every day, hoping to revitalize the Calabrian handicraft traditions, including weaving, glass blowing and pottery making. They then sold the fruits of their labours to Riace's tourists as souvenirs. It sounded quite appealing, and I was eager to learn more. So I paid regular visits to Riace with N, my then-boyfriend, before the international press descended on the village in the summer of 2015.

In a small pottery studio tucked along one of Riace's alleyways, we met Umme Kulsoom, originally from Pakistan. 'I fled Pakistan with my family because the Taliban, the mafia, was threatening us,' she explained while carving wavy curls into a stoneware cup. 'We owned a shop in Karachi, and the Taliban kept coming around, demanding money. When my husband said we had no more to give, they opened fire on our house and threatened to kidnap our children. I was always terrified when the kids left for school. Ultimately, we sold all our possessions and embarked on our journey, which lasted three months.'

I hadn't known that Taliban fighters, like members of the mafia, extorted money from small businesses, but Kulsoom equated the two organizations as if the similarities were obvious. She probably didn't have to explain it here in Riace, because a criminal organization that combines religious devotion with diabolical savagery is nothing new in Calabria. Near the pottery studio, two bullet holes in the window of a restaurant stood as poignant reminders of the terrorist ambitions of some local thugs. Those bullet holes dated from the run-up to the 2009 elections, before Kulsoom had arrived in Riace. That year, Riace's mayor, Domenico Lucano – a champion of Riace's refugee support system – was running for re-election. The bullets were his opponents' reaction. Local clans can't stand it when public funds are used to realize ideals, especially when there's nothing in it for them.

However, Domenico Lucano won the mayoral election time and time again. The bullet holes in the window of the restaurant of his foundation, Città Futura, or 'City of the Future', were triumphantly covered with white, yellow, green and blue handprints. The words 'We paint to oppose the Ndrangheta' were scrawled in Calabrian dialect on a nearby wall to make the message even more clear.

It began many years ago when a sailboat filled with Kurdish asylum seekers from Turkey ran aground on the beach of Riace. A group of residents immediately opened their arms to them. I spoke with Bahram, who'd arrived on that boat. 'Before the government had organized any official shelter, people fed us and gave us a place to stay,' he said. Many slept in a building belonging to the local parish, but the asylum seekers desperately needed permanent housing. One of the Kurdish refugees looked around and wondered, 'All these old, abandoned houses. Maybe we can live there?'

Bahram showed me his first Italian dwelling on the edge of the village. 'Three of us lived there. I remember waking up in the morning to birdsong and goats bleating. I would stand on the balcony and gaze at the sea, the mountains, and the valley below, filled with animals. It's beautiful here, and the air is clean. I love this landscape; it reminds me of home.'

Most of Bahram's fellow asylum seekers moved on to Germany, but he stayed in Riace, finding work as a carpenter. He was granted a residence permit as a political refugee, and ten years later, he became an Italian citizen.

The grass-roots facilities that had sprung up in Riace became the model for an official government programme that spread across more than a thousand villages in southern Italy and other sparsely populated regions. For inspiration, visitors continued to flock to Riace, where everything seemed possible. The donkeys were one example: fifty years ago, they'd been vital to daily transportation in Calabria; now, they had been reintroduced to collect separated waste along the steep alleyways. Twenty-five per cent of Riace's sixteen hundred residents came from abroad.

I interviewed Mayor Lucano at the offices of the Città Futura Foundation, housed in a building dating from the nineteenth century. He'd hung a framed photo of the Kurd's shipwreck on the wall behind him. 'Historically, we are a community of shepherds, farmers and artisans, and we live with all the age-old problems facing southern Italy. We have traditionally coexisted with others, including the Romans, Saracens, Normans and Spaniards. That background connects us with the wider world; moreover, we all have family members who live abroad for economic reasons. And the people who arrive here with traumatic experiences can sense that. Maybe their first thought is, what a drag! I'd rather live in a bigger city. But some eventually settle here. They're looking for peace and a place to restore their faith in others.'

In Italy, asylum seekers' financial safety net is withdrawn almost immediately upon completion of the application procedure. Was it even possible for the newcomers to stay in Riace? 'For most of them, this is just a stopover,' Lucano said. 'You can't expect everyone to stay here. There isn't enough work in Calabria.'

Despite the constraints facing Riace, the village's fame continued to grow. In 2016, Mayor Lucano ranked among *Fortune* magazine's fifty most influential international leaders. The following year, the RAI network filmed a television series in the acclaimed multicultural village, with star actors appearing alongside Riace residents.

Around the same time, a colossal centre with fifteen hundred beds appeared on the Ionian coast of Calabria; it was an example of the other extreme of asylum seeker reception, as it's known. No cameras were allowed there, and the business model was radically different. As it turns out, a local Ndrangheta clan was behind the massive reception centre in Isola di Capo Rizzuto. They acquired thirty million euros in European subsidies over eleven years and ran the facility with an apparent strategy of systemic neglect. According to the public prosecutor, the centre wasn't kept clean and people were expected to eat animal feed. In 2017, nearly seventy people were arrested on suspicion of collaborating with the Ndrangheta, including the local priest who managed the asylum centre through his Catholic aid organization, Misericordia.

Italy tightened its asylum procedure dramatically after a several years of dealing with large numbers of boat refugees and a lack of clear-cut solidarity from other European governments. In Calabria, refugees who were not eligible for a residence permit often ended up in a veritable ghetto: an improvised tent encampment near the port of Gioia Tauro. Becky Moses was one such refugee. She was a 26-year-old Nigerian who had to leave Riace after the Italian immigration and naturalization service denied her application. One cold January night shortly after she arrived at the tent encampment, Becky Moses died after a fire she or others had lit to stay warm engulfed her tent. Her friends and neighbours buried her body in Riace.

The political dilemmas surrounding the reception of asylum seekers arriving in Italy by boat proved a boon to right-wing populist parties. In 2018, Matteo Salvini, leader of the Lega party, was sworn in as deputy prime minister and minister of the interior. For years, relatively few Calabrian votes had gone to Salvini's party, but the 2018 elections saw a remarkable jump in the number of votes from Rosarno and

Reggio Calabria. It was hardly surprising when it later emerged that the Lega party's campaign teams in those cities had links with the Ndrangheta.

A day after Salvini took office, there was another death connected to the tent encampment. Soumaila Sacko, a 29-year-old man originally from Mali, was shot while searching for scrap corrugated metal at an abandoned factory. The metal roofing material wasn't for his own use, but for a friend living in the informal tent camp who was in need of a safer and more fire-resistant shelter. The grounds of the abandoned factory didn't exactly warrant armed protection. The authorities had found 134,000 tons of dumped industrial and toxic waste on the site, and it was still awaiting decontamination

The victim, Soumaila Sacko, did have a residence permit. He was also an active member of the trade union advocating for rights for seasonal workers, many of whom lived in the tent encampment. The workers earned a pittance picking citrus fruit in Rosarno's orchards under inhumane conditions; they had little choice.

In an unexpected twist, while Italy's immigration policy was becoming increasingly harsh in the hands of the outspokenly intolerant minister Salvini, Riace's Mayor Domenico Lucano was suddenly facing criminal proceedings. In 2018, a district court even banished Lucano from his village. According to the charges, in administering the hospitality programme for asylum seekers Lucano had allegedly facilitated 'clandestine immigration' and acted in violation of the law. Wiretapped conversations revealed that the mayor had been willing to issue a fake identity card to a desperate individual whose asylum application had been denied. Lucano admitted that was the case and said he didn't regret it. It's likely that Becky Moses's recent death by fire in the tent encampment had still been fresh in the minds of both the mayor and the rejected applicant.

Italy didn't turn its back on the mayor after he was arrested. Crowds arrived from across the country to champion Lucano's cause and serenade him with resistance songs like 'Bella Ciao'. And the abrupt closure of Riace's refugee programme after the mayor's arrest was met with fierce protests.

Eleven months later, the former mayor was allowed to return to his home in Riace. But by then, Riace had a new mayor, Antonio Trifoli, whose party enjoyed the support of the right-wing populist Lega party. The name of Trifoli's candidate list was 'Transparency and Legality', which is ironic, considering one of Trifoli's council members had to resign almost immediately due to a previous conviction for bankruptcy fraud. The court also ruled that the new mayor had not been lawfully eligible to run for election. However, Trifoli appealed the verdict and was allowed to remain in the position temporarily.

In the early days of his term, Trifoli wasted no time eradicating any reminders of the world-renowned hospitality programme for asylum seekers. He removed a prominent welcome sign at the entrance of the village. Beneath the words 'Riace: village of hospitality', the sign bore a reference to Peppino Impastato, the iconic anti-mafia activist, who was represented by the words *cento passi*, or one hundred steps – an allusion to the famous film about Impastato's life – and a painting of a black figure with 'Radio' on his T-shirt. The new mayor removed the sign with the help of a cooperative priest and replaced it with a different message: 'Riace: village of the sacred martyrs Cosimo and Damiano'.

RAI put their television series about the village on hold pending the outcome of Domenico Lucano's trial. In 2020, an administrative court ruled against the Ministry of the Interior's decision to close Riace's asylum-seeker support programme, making it retrospectively unjustified, but by then, most of the village's asylum seekers had been transferred to large-scale reception centres.

The last time I visited Riace, the streets were practically deserted, but otherwise, the village looked much as it had when R AI was filming its television series there every day. Colourful murals still adorned the streets, filled with messages of hope and stories of revolutionaries. In the recently opened petting zoo, new-born donkeys stood in the sun, being nursed by their mothers. A few animals ambled over and nuzzled my hand. Like the weaving looms, crafts workshops and abandoned houses, they seemed to be waiting for a fresh start.

20

LYING TO TELL THE TRUTH

In the early summer of 2015, N and I broke up. Cultural differences had amplified the friction between our personalities, and maybe we had been too absorbed in my research into the Ndrangheta. The ideological battle against a common enemy had drawn us closer, but in the end, it wasn't enough to support a future together.

That summer, a businessman in my village was put under police protection after reporting that local clans had been extorting him for twenty years. His story – and his sad eyes – made me face facts: once he had agreed to testify in court, he became a social pariah. I asked myself how smart it was to continue writing about the Ndrangheta independently and made every effort to generate enthusiasm for the subject among the editorial staff of Dutch current affairs programmes. But my proposals didn't mesh with their framing, formats or budgets.

It seemed like a good moment to take stock of everything I had experienced in Calabria in recent years. I longed to live closer to my family and old friends, and I found a tiny but relatively affordable place to rent in Amsterdam. But no matter how hard I tried to settle in, I realized after little more than a year that my heart still belonged to Calabria. I missed the sun-drenched colours, the enchantment of the moon rising over the sea, and the locals who like to be surrounded by enough space and quiet to keep them in touch with what's important in life.

So at the end of 2017, I returned to Calabria for an extended period. It was time to put my quiet house, with its panoramic views, to good use. I decided to write a book.

My fellow villagers greeted me with enthusiasm. My return seemed to reassure them, and the pitying looks I'd encountered years earlier were absent. As a woman alone, I would always be slightly at odds with my surroundings. To maintain harmony, I didn't mention the subject of my planned book to anyone in the village.

When people ask me if it's dangerous to write about the mafia, they're usually referring to Roberto Saviano, the best-selling Neapolitan author of *Gomorrah*. He's been under constant protection from bodyguards since the book was published. But I'm more inclined to think of the German writer Petra Reski. She has also needed police protection – not in southern Italy, or in Venice, where she lives, but in Germany. Petra Reski is an investigative journalist who, following the massacre in Duisburg, explored the limits of Germany's freedom of the press and how it pertained to the Ndrangheta. In Germany, her homeland, she has faced threats and legal challenges; a court ordered her to censor her work.

In 2018, as I was flying back to the Netherlands for the festive season, I made a stopover in Venice to meet Reski. I said goodbye to the Calabrian countryside, its days bathed in sunshine and balmy weather, its evenings scented with the aroma of burning olive wood, and boarded a plane headed north. Glimpsed through the clouds, northern Italy looked like a foreign country, with its industry, its sharply delineated parcels of land and the angular style of its residential buildings. On the bus from the airport to Venice, I was astonished by the tidy streets, the bicycles, gleaming cars, luxury shops, villas, clear signage and all-encompassing orderliness. Bus stops displayed up-to-date posters for dance performances and yoga studios. That made quite a change from Calabria's faded announcements of bygone tarantella concerts and ancient posters for the annual summer circus.

My timing wasn't great – the water in Venice had reached its highest level in recent years. Sea water covered two-thirds of the inner city: houses, shops, museums, hotels, churches, restaurants, artisanal workshops and schools were flooded. According to the forecasts, the worst was over, but Venetians still braced themselves for high tide every day. The chance of flooding led many tourists to cancel their visits, leaving the city less crowded than usual. I strolled through the alleyways and observed Venetians diligently scrubbing their walls and floors and salvaging their belongings. I was impressed by the speed of their reaction time: apart from a few damp patches, I saw little evidence of water damage.

Petra Reski lived in the heart of the city, so she had also had to mop up the water in her home. We met in the late morning; she suggested a place near Venice's opera house, the Teatro La Fenice, or the Phoenix. I arrived first and saw her approaching: a striking woman in her early sixties, both charming and hard as nails. I recognized her well-groomed appearance – short blonde curls, bright pink lipstick and a leather jacket – from photos. Unsurprisingly, she even wore her black rain boots with style.

She led me into a quiet café that time forgot, next door to the opera house. An old-school waiter brought us coffee and tea in baroquely ornate porcelain cups, accompanied by a dish of exquisitely delicate biscuits. This Venetian elegance felt like culture shock after months of living in rustic Calabria. Petra Reski knew the waiter, and she looked right at home. She had been based in Venice for nearly thirty years already. But as for Calabria, she said she wouldn't feel comfortable going there any more, due to her run-ins with members of the Ndrangheta.

Sicily was another story. She still enjoyed visiting the island, which many years earlier had been her first destination in Italy. 'In the summer of '79, when I was twenty, I went on holiday to Italy for the first time,' she told me. 'I drove from the Ruhr region in Germany to Corleone with my then-boyfriend.' They skipped Venice, Florence and Rome, taking the shortest route to the Sicilian village made famous by *The Godfather*. 'I had high expectations because I'd read the book and seen the film. But when we arrived in Corleone, I was disappointed. It was a small, dull village, nothing special.'

It was Petra Reski's first encounter with what she thought the mafia was. 'To me, the mafia held an almost folkloric fascination. I was particularly drawn to *The Godfather*'s concept of family and the power of blood ties. My parents were originally from East Prussia and Silesia, areas that today belong partly to Poland and partly to Russia. They fled to West Germany after World War II. Our family culture was very different from the German one, but there were similarities with how Italians experienced the family, at least when their families were still quite large. Very close-knit, and with a moral stance that is sometimes considered to lie at the heart of the mafia: *familismo amorale*, or 'amoral familism'. When it comes to making decisions, what matters most is what's good for the family, not what's good or bad. And that justifies everything. Those sentiments weren't as strong in my family as in mafia circles, but still, I recognized that feeling of pride and honour, and the sense of family as a clan. My friends couldn't imagine it, but it felt familiar to me.'

Ten years went by before Reski returned to Sicily. 'In June 1989, at the start of my journalism career, I was sent to Sicily to cover what was known as the Palermo Spring. I wrote about the fresh energy stirred up by Falcone and Borsellino, who were preparing their maxitrial against Cosa Nostra. I wasn't fluent in Italian but could speak a few words and get by. It was just before the fall of the Berlin Wall, and there was something in the air – it felt like important changes were possible. I asked myself: if the Berlin Wall can be demolished, why can't the foundations of the mafia? Especially with people like Falcone and Borsellino.'

In 1992, however, Cosa Nostra brought the Palermo Spring to an abrupt and brutal end with bombings that ended the lives of the two fearless crime fighters in the space of two months. Investigations are ongoing as to which politicians, members of the police force and secret service agents were involved in those attacks. But no one in Italy doubts that insiders were involved.

During her first journalistic assignment in Palermo, Petra Reski encountered people who could tell her a great deal about the mafia. One was the world-renowned photographer Letizia Battaglia, who relentlessly recorded the bloodshed in Palermo at that time. Battaglia was also an activist intent on liberating the city council from the mafia's self-serving interests. During her Sicilian reporting trip, Reski also met a detective who drove her around Palermo in an armoured car. 'That made an impression: a policeman who needed protection . . . Who was being protected from whom? And who, exactly, were the police representing? That was such a strange experience that the subject has stayed with me ever since.'

After leaving Palermo, Reski went directly to Venice. Her planned interview fell through, but while there, she met her future husband, a Venice native. 'Two years later, I was living in Venice as a foreign correspondent for the German press. In a way, I'd brought the mafia with me as part of my baggage.'

She was taken aback by the lack of knowledge about the mafia in northern Italy. 'Venice was almost as bad as Germany. People felt completely immune to the mafia. To this day, in Venice, as in Germany, many still assume that they will never have anything to do with the mafia. And in general, even in Italy, people are only interested in the mafia when blood is shed. They don't really know what the mafia is about.'

In August 2007, the shocking retaliations in Duisburg awakened the German population. 'A Hollywood-style bloodbath. The Germans were astonished: the mafia, here? Why hadn't we been told?'

For fifteen years, Reski had already made every effort to alert German people to the mafia's little-known European face, but few had shown an interest. 'You could almost say the mafia did me a favour by murdering six people in Duisburg. Immediately, I was asked to write a book.'

When Petra Reski published her book about the mafia (available in English under the title *The Honoured Society*), a wave of controversy was unleashed. Several Italian businesspeople working in Germany were less than delighted by her revelations. Two of them accused her of libel. The German court upheld the charges, and all the passages in her book that dealt with the two claimants had to be censored. The reprint of Reski's book contained sentences that had been blacked out. The English, Italian, Dutch, Spanish and Polish translations that followed also included pages with blacked-out passages. Despite those thick black lines – or perhaps because of them – the censored pages present a sharp insight into the mafia's camouflage.

Until the summer of 2007, many Germans had never heard the word *Ndrangheta*, although the criminal organization had firmly established connections throughout all levels of German society. The drama in Duisburg had attracted a storm of media attention, making it a strategic blunder, an inconvenient bloodstain on the respectable image the Ndrangheta preferred to convey in Germany. Moreover, Reski maintained that the San Luca-based Nirta–Strangio clan's blood vengeance took a back seat to entrepreneurial jealousy. 'Above all, they wanted to damage the commercial interests of the Pelle–Vottari clan and ruin their business. And in that, they succeeded a little bit.'

As early as the 1970s, the Ndrangheta had established roots in German industrial areas such as the Ruhr, which had attracted many Calabrian immigrants. According to Reski, Ndrangheta clans still invest heavily throughout Germany. They own many restaurants, to make money serving customers but above all to launder their income from illicit narcotics trafficking. Duisburg was – and still is – an interesting operational base because it's only half an hour from the border with the Netherlands, a country where much of their cocaine enters Europe.

Reski admits that someone like Giovanni Strangio – the man who baked pizzas in the Ruhr region and later hid with his family in the Netherlands after participating in the Duisburg massacre – would not typically engage in the laundering of cocaine profits. Instead, that job was usually done by Germans, working in close collaboration with Italians. 'They tend to be respectable Germans with spotless reputations, so there are no Italian surnames to set off alarm bells when they set up companies, often shell companies.' Reski's description calls to mind the private companies set up on Vincenzo Crupi's behalf by his associates with Dutch surnames.

I asked Reski about the people who had brought charges against her. 'One is a Calabrian who runs a luxury hotel in Duisburg. He has close ties with German high society, including film stars, football players and politicians. Rather remarkably, his hotel sits beside a small lake, one of the few areas of natural beauty in the Ruhr region. He was granted permission to build a hotel in a nature reserve and even received financial support, including a European subsidy.' In her book, Reski mentioned that the Italian national football team had stayed there, as had a fugitive Ndranghetist and the San Luca priest, Don Pino Strangio.

The other Italian businessman who had brought charges against Reski happened to have died a few days before our meeting. He was from Tuscany and had been one of the previous owners of the Da Bruno restaurant in Duisburg. The man had been convicted of drug trafficking in Germany in 1994. He subsequently ran various upscale restaurants, including one in a historic building on the central square in the former East German city of Erfurt. And, like Reski's other accuser, he was friendly with the upper crust.

'I mentioned both men in a chapter about the relationship between the mafia and politics. I wanted German readers to realize that this wasn't as far-fetched, or far away, as they might think. I gave examples of close links between German politicians and what we might call "successful Italian entrepreneurs". That caused me lot of trouble.'

It wasn't until Reski went to Erfurt to present her book that she fully understood how influential her enemies were. 'Erfurt is a bastion of the Ndrangheta. A clan from Duisburg moved there as soon as the Berlin Wall fell. Those families' businesses had a strong starting position in eastern Germany because of their excellent ties with politicians and the Stasi, the secret police of the former German Democratic Republic. So, when I went to Erfurt to present my book, I was on high alert. But what happened took even me by surprise.'

When Reski arrived at the bookshop in Erfurt shortly before the presentation, someone handed her a letter informing her that certain parts of her book would lead to legal proceedings. 'That's not ideal, from a psychological point of view, right before you present your book, but it turned out that was just the beginning. The journalist they'd asked to introduce and interview me said that he was a close friend of the man who wanted to have my book censored. He said I'd written a pack of lies, that I'd made things up. I said, "That's what you might think, but I have the documents to prove everything. This isn't my personal opinion." '

The room was already packed, so Reski didn't have time to tell the man to forget about introducing the book if he disliked it so much. 'There were quite a lot of people in the audience, but I couldn't see their faces because I was under the lights and they were in the dark. I read some passages from the book, as we'd agreed beforehand. Then, a carefully orchestrated public spectacle began to unfold. First, the former mayor of Erfurt attacked me about a documentary exposing the city's ties with the mafia. He blamed me for making the film or inspiring it. I told him he was overestimating my influence and was way off the mark, but he insisted that he was right. Then a lawyer launched into an extended monologue, claiming it was impossible to launder money in Germany. A few people seconded his opinion, and finally, someone gave a long speech defending the two men who had brought charges against me. He finished by saying that I had damaged their reputations and said, "I admire your courage, Frau Reski. I admire your courage very much." I realized I was being threatened. People had praised my courage before, but not in quite the same way . . .'

Reassuringly, Reski didn't feel particularly bothered about the lawsuit itself. She'd gathered her information from criminal records, official German police reports and interviews with German and Italian prosecutors. Additionally, the men who sued her had already been linked to the mafia in the Italian press. 'The German judge said I should never have written about the two men because the documents in my possession weren't public; they were meant for internal use. I countered that an investigative journalist's responsibility is to reveal potential risks to society, not to wait until something has been clarified or resolved in court.'

In one of the trials, the judge reprimanded Reski because the man who had brought charges against her had never been convicted of mafia membership. 'But in Germany, such a conviction wasn't possible! Under German law, the most this man could be convicted of was drug trafficking. Moreover, I hadn't written that he was a convicted mafia member, but only quoted the assessment of German police investigators and both Italian and German prosecutors. During the hearing, the judge asked the man if he was a member of the Ndrangheta. The man said, "No, I'm not a member." Then the judge asked, "Can you explain why your name was mentioned in the police investigation?" The man replied, "No, I can't explain that." I felt frustrated by the idiotic course of events in the courtroom.' Reski twisted the bezel of her watch. She was too composed to fall prey to nervous tics, but it was clear that the experience in court had stayed with her.

During the hearings, the German judge had arranged police protection. Reski felt that was absurd in a civil court. 'I was amazed when I saw two officers sitting in the courtroom. The judge had clearly ordered them for her own protection, because my safety didn't seem to be much of a concern. For example, the successful Italian entrepreneur who was suing me and my publisher felt free to say to our lawyer in German, so everyone in the courtroom could understand, "Tell her to bring six policemen next time, not two." '

Reski had also faced some threats in Italy, in Corleone and San Luca. But there, she'd taken deliberate risks by entering the mafia's territory. According to her, the threats made in the German courtroom show how comfortable members of the Calabrian mafia feel in Germany. They seem to regard Germany as their domain, where they can do and say whatever they please. For a while, police officers accompanied Reski when she gave readings in Germany, but she no longer believes that's necessary. These days, members of the mafia seem to prefer filing claims for damages to using firearms when attacking journalists.

But you can never be sure. Think of Ján Kuciak, a young investigative journalist from Slovakia. He looked into the relationship between the Slovakian government and members of the Ndrangheta, uncovering the how Ndrangheta clans had pocketed European agricultural subsidies in his country. In February 2018, he and his girlfriend were shot dead in their home. 'It was shocking because it happened in Europe,' Reski said. 'People don't usually worry too much about what happens in Italy because they assume it's always the same old story, but the mafia has spread throughout Europe. Kuciak's murder was a message to other journalists in Slovakia to stop writing about the Ndrangheta.'

Reski received a message a few days after the Italian translation of her book was published. It was from Marcello Dell'Utri, a senator and close political partner of Silvio Berlusconi. He had announced in the media that he planned to sue Reski. 'That day, my telephone never stopped ringing. The callers were primarily other journalists, welcoming me to the club. It was a relief to receive so much support, such a difference from my experience in Germany, where people asked me why I was poking my nose into the mafia. They assumed I'd written something I shouldn't have. It was a different story in Italy, where, right away, I felt immense solidarity. Luckily, Marcello Dell'Utri never had time to sue me, because he was charged with numerous crimes and ultimately arrested.'

In the end, Dell'Utri was convicted of playing a crucial role in negotiations between Berlusconi and the Sicilian mafia. He was sentenced to seven years, some of which he was allowed to serve under house arrest. Several charges are still pending, including one for collaboration with the Ndrangheta.

The annual World Press Freedom Index always ranks Italy far lower than the Netherlands and Germany, which usually score quite highly. I asked Petra Reski if she agrees that Italy's low ranking isn't a true reflection of the high quality of the country's investigative journalism. 'Journalists in Germany tend to feel superior,' she replied, 'even when it comes to the freedom of the Italian press. And Italy certainly has its problems regarding the influence of politics on journalism. But investigative journalism in Italy is much freer than in Germany, as far as I can see. In Italy, if you want to know who runs a mafia business, you can find out. Unfortunately, Italian journalists who reveal such things often face prosecution, but they don't usually lose. Of course, they're not free to write whatever they want, but they are generally acquitted if they can show evidence in the form of documents. Meanwhile, in Germany, it seems like journalists always lose. Even if they can prove their accusations.'

Reski wasn't the only journalist in Germany to face censorship because of the Ndrangheta. Francesco Forgione, the chair of the Italian parliamentary Antimafia Committee, suffered the same fate when the German translation of his book, *Mafia Export,* was also censored. The same happened to a book by German journalist Jürgen Roth. In his case, bookshops also faced threats. 'His accusers told booksellers that they would face charges if they sold the book. And, of course, censorship hurts booksellers, especially if they have stocked a book they can't sell.'

I asked how the censorship had been carried out in Reski's case. 'We'd already printed countless books and lots of them were stored in a warehouse. How did we avoid having to throw them all away? The publisher hired students to spend hours crossing out the pertinent passages with a black marker. I still have a few of those copies.'

Reski didn't leave it at that. In her subsequent book, she sharply criticized Germany's ignorance of and indifference to the Ndrangheta's influence. And yet, she felt herself holding back. She explained, 'While writing my second book about the mafia's interests in Germany, I noticed that I was censoring myself. I had become more cautious about naming names.' In that book, Reski is open about the fear she has felt since she was threatened in Germany. She wrote, 'It's almost as if someone put a few drops of poison into my heart. Just a few tiny drops.'

Despite Reski's increased self-censorship, she recently had to face new charges in Germany, ironically enough because she'd tried to highlight the restrictions German media face when reporting about mafia cases. Someone had brought charges against the German television network that had produced a documentary about the Ndrangheta in Erfurt. The network lost the case. Reski wrote about the case for a weekly newspaper called *Der Freitag*. 'I deliberately limited myself to a publicly available verdict of the court, and only mentioned the name of the man who had sued the German television station. But then, that man – also from Erfurt – sued me. He was a business associate of the man who had brought charges against me earlier.'

Reski's incredulity reached new heights. 'The publisher and editor-in-chief of *Der Freitag* is the son of the late owner of *Der Spiegel*, so he is quite wealthy. But he refused to back me up. And on Twitter, he said I probably hadn't done enough research. That's odd and extremely worrying because when you don't support journalists who are facing accusations from the mafia, you're playing into the mafia's hands. Freelancers like me will think twice about getting burned again on news items that pay a few hundred euros.' Reski wrote about her situation and set up a successful crowdfunding campaign for her legal defence. And for the first time, she noticed growing German indignation. 'People had been under the impression that Germany had a free press.'

Petra Reski decided to stop writing journalistic books and articles about the mafia. Instead, she focuses on fiction and has already published three novels. She calls it 'lying to be able to tell the truth'. 'In my novels, I try to combine the reality of how Italy and Germany relate to the mafia. I write about *la Trattativa*, for instance, the negotiations between the state and the mafia in the 1990s – or rather, since the 1990s, because those negotiations haven't ended. And I write about the German media, who prefer to treat the mafia like something out of folklore.'

Reski's novels also cover the mafia's interests in wind energy and centres for asylum seekers. And while Reski no longer mentions specific names, the Arena clan springs to mind. That's the clan from the Calabrian coastal town of Isola di Capo Rizzuto, responsible for pocketing millions of euros in European subsidy meant for an asylum seekers centre. That same clan has links with a grandiose wind farm across the bay I look out on from my house, a wind farm that was built with German backing. When I met Reski, I told her that those wind turbines are visible from my house, and that on a clear night, I can see their red lights blinking in the distance. 'A German bank did indeed finance those turbines,' Reski said. 'And that bank was subsequently bailed out by the German government. Incidentally, the

Germans are always amazed to hear about something like that, the mafia building windfarms. They tend to think the clans only invest in dirty business, not clean things, like sustainable energy.'

Even though she writes fiction now, Reski still does her research in the same way she did before. 'I read hundreds of legal documents. But now, I am free to write whatever I want. For example, I can describe how journalism works and the difficulties journalists face. Or how the mafia pays or pressures journalists to generate PR. Take mafia music; it's similar to Nazi songs during the war. The mafia has its own music glorifying violent murders, and they also release those songs in Germany. The lyrics are included in German as well as in Italian, so Germans can't claim ignorance about the songs' subject matter. To promote this type of music, a producer invited German journalists to Calabria to convince them that, in the end, the mafia is nothing more than a form of ancient culture. That's complete nonsense, but it's exactly what the mafia would like the world to believe. Because, of course, you can't bring charges against a culture.'

Behind the mask of folklore, the mafia appears less threatening. So, journalists who use folkloric terms to describe the mafia are doing them a favour. 'The mafia was also delighted with the idealized images in *The Godfather*,' Reski said. 'Other films and series focusing on violence are equally helpful because they reinforce the mafia's intimidating reputation. That's something I try to keep in mind, as well, because when you emphasize the brutality – as happens in ninety-nine per cent of mafia fiction – it strengthens people's fear of mafia-related violence, even though most mafiosi no longer need to resort to violence to get what they want.'

According to the German Federal Criminal Police Office, the Calabrian mafia is Germany's largest criminal organization, comprising at least nine hundred members. 'But those numbers mean little', Reski told me, 'because they only represent the ones the Italian authorities are certain belong to a particular clan. And although many other members of the Ndrangheta live in Germany, their official residence is still in Italy. Moreover, in Germany, as elsewhere, all those clan members are surrounded by a vast grey support network.'

Early 2018 saw the arrest of Mario Lavorato, a German-based Ndranghetist who had close ties with Günther Oettinger, who was a European commissioner until the end of 2019. 'In my book, Lavorato was the third example of a Ndranghetist with German political connections; he was the only one who didn't start legal proceedings against me.' In the 1990s, when Oettinger was still a member of parliament in Baden-Württemberg for the Christian Democratic Union, or CDU, he regularly dined in Mario Lavorato's restaurant near Stuttgart. Lavorato even organized an event to raise funds for Oettinger's campaign. Hoping to avoid a political scandal, the German minister of justice – a fellow member of the CDU – warned Oettinger to stay away from the restaurant because, in Italy, Lavorato was suspected of being a member of the Ndrangheta. In 2010, Günther Oettinger became the European commissioner for energy; in 2014, he became the commissioner for the digital economy and society; and in 2017, he became the commissioner for budget and administration. Oettinger maintains he's long been out of touch with Mario Lavorato, who has since been sentenced to eight years in prison in Italy for his involvement with the Ndrangheta.'

The specific crimes for which Lavorato was convicted indicate that the Ndrangheta feels as comfortable in Germany as it does in Calabria. Following current practices in Calabria, the clans in Germany no longer demand protection money directly; instead, they pressure entrepreneurs into buying exorbitantly priced products from their wholesalers. In Stuttgart, for example, Italian restaurants and cafés were forced to buy overpriced wine, bread and pasta exported by Ndrangheta families. 'Prosecutors told me they have proof, although they never received any information from the Italian community in Stuttgart. Apparently, even those who are not part of the mafia are forced to keep quiet,' Petra Reski explained. 'Italians in Stuttgart knew everything but wouldn't talk. They were threatened and often had relatives in Italy they wanted to protect.'

An earlier criminal case uncovered how an Italian senator, who had been elected with the help of votes bought from Calabrians living in Stuttgart, subsequently helped the Ndrangheta launder two billion euros. These examples show that in Germany, Ndrangheta clans not only commit extortion, deal in drugs and smuggle arms, but also silence people and manipulate elections. You might say that they behave as if they were in Calabria. Or, in the words of a Ndranghetist who was quoted in a recent criminal report, 'In Germany, we can do anything we want.'

'It's interesting to note that Germany can only arrest Ndranghetists by using the Italian anti-mafia law and a European arrest warrant,' Reski said. 'A German policeman admitted being pleased with this possibility because, under German law, the police could not have arrested such individuals.'

Petra Reski's next book will be set in Venice, for a change. 'It will touch on the mafia indirectly,' she told me. The MOSE project, intended to protect Venice from flooding, immediately came to mind. 'The flood barrier cost seven billion euros, one billion of which was used for bribes. And by the time construction began, the technology was already outdated.' The idea was to erect a movable steel barrier that would rise out of the lagoon to keep the city from flooding during *aqua alta* tidal peaks. 'But placing steel underwater always leads to problems. The Dutch are specialists in water management and they would undoubtedly have taken a different approach to the project,' said Reski. 'Back in the 1980s, I naively believed that the consortium created for the MOSE project would consist of scientists and experts working to benefit the lagoon and the city. But the project never even went to public tender. Therefore, private construction companies made all the decisions: private companies backed by Italian politicians. It's a form of legalized mafia, a problem created by the neoliberal economy: everything is sold off to private parties. The port of Venice has also been sold – to cruise ship companies, can you believe it?'

According to Reski, the problems MOSE was meant to alleviate, namely decreasing the frequency of severe flooding, had less to do with climate change and rising sea levels than the current city administrators would have people believe. 'The shipping channels have been dredged because the lagoon itself is very shallow and big ships were no longer able to pass through them. If you deepen a channel, then at high tide, the wind will need less time to push more seawater into the lagoon. So, flooding occurs more quickly, and water needs more time to flow back into the open sea.'

In the 1960s, some experts attributed the first catastrophic flood to a channel that had been dug especially for oil tankers docking at the petrochemical plant on Venice's shores. Nevertheless, dredging in the lagoon continued to new depths, partly to enable the passage of cruise ships. 'And when they started building MOSE, they excavated the inlet between the lagoon and the sea. That only made matters worse.'

Thirty-five people, including the former mayor of Venice, were charged with corruption and abuse of power in connection with the construction of the MOSE. 'The mayor admitted partial guilt in exchange for a reduced sentence, but nothing has happened to the other politicians arrested four years ago,' Reski said with a sigh. 'They got very lenient verdicts, a slap on the wrist. That's absurd. Venice, the whole city, is being bought by these kinds of people. That's why I want to write a book about the city.'

By the time our interview ended and we left the café, a few inches of water had covered the square in front of the opera house. Luckily for me, a street vendor appeared, selling knee-high plastic shoe covers. Reski helped me bargain the price down from fifteen euros to ten; then we gently waded off, heading in the same direction for a while until we said goodbye.

I had some spare time in Venice before my flight left for Amsterdam, which was a godsend because the high water meant having to walk through the low-lying areas of the centre at a snail's pace. In one of the drier alleyways, I passed sewing studios producing handmade carnival costumes. I saw children sitting at a long table in a workshop, painting their carnival masks. This made a welcome change from the souvenir shops that dominated much of the city, crammed with selfie sticks and Murano glass in every colour of the rainbow. In the window of one such establishment, next to racks of cigarette lighters, coffee mugs and magnets decorated with the Italian flag, I spotted a child-sized T-shirt. It featured a picture of a baby with a cigar in his mouth, wearing a fedora and a pinstripe suit, surrounded by the words *Italia*, *Venezia* and *I'm the boss*.

21

SEEK AND YOU SHALL FIND

A woman with blonde hair doesn't attract much attention in Amsterdam, and that comes as a welcome relief after six months in Calabria. After my visit to Venice, I found myself appreciating the canals as if I were a tourist. I was reassured to see that the waters in Amsterdam were not lapping the quayside. Feeling a bit homesick for the south, I visited a Calabrian shop where I could buy tangerines and oranges; the fruit came from a network of organic farmers united against the exploitation of seasonal workers.

But I also found myself missing a few simple Dutch delicacies. So I went into a local sandwich shop, where some tourists still wearing their winter coats were drinking coffee from paper cups. I ordered a *broodje kaas*, a cheese sandwich. When the cashier told me the price, I almost cancelled my impulse purchase, but instead, I paid up. Rents in Amsterdam had been skyrocketing, so it's no wonder local businesses have had to adjust their prices. I asked if paying with a fifty-euro note was a problem.

The owner laughed. 'Sometimes guys come in with five-hundred-euro notes!'

'Really?' I asked. 'Can you make change for that, or do you refuse to accept it?'

'It's usually the drug dealers,' he said with typical Amsterdam level-headedness. 'They try it often enough. Sometimes, a five hundred comes in handy, because it makes my stack of takings more manageable. But I can't always accept a large note like that when I don't have enough money in the till.'

I was tempted to tell the owner about Gioacchino Bonarrigo, an unremarkable man in his early thirties who was suspected of smuggling drugs for Ndrangheta clans based in Rosarno and San Luca. In September 2017, he was arrested near Amsterdam's Waterlooplein flea market on a European warrant. In Italy, he still had two years to serve in prison, while the next criminal trial against him was already taking place. Gioacchino Bonarrigo had previously been detained in Amsterdam eleven years earlier, in 2006, and extradited to Italy. Shortly after that, he did a disappearing act and escaped from house arrest in Italy, heading back to the Netherlands.

Bonarrigo clearly liked the Netherlands, and he spoke Dutch. An Italian criminal file contains pictures taken by Amsterdam police surveillance teams; the images show him and his co-defendants, reputed members of various Ndrangheta clans. They were involved in smuggling drugs and weapons into Italy via the Netherlands, Belgium and Germany. A map in the files shows a circle around the tri-border area, where Germany, Belgium and the Netherlands meet. It illustrates how easily the fugitive Ndranghetists could cross from one country into another and stay ahead of the red tape surrounding official requests for international legal assistance. For many years, they scooted across the borders to sabotage efforts to arrest them.

Gioacchino Bonarrigo was sent back to Italy as a fugitive. But if a Ndrangheta defendant has been a registered resident of the Netherlands for more than five years and has proof of legally earning an income, he or she can stand trial before a Dutch court. That turned out to be good news for Rocco Gasperoni, who ran a popular pizzeria in the Dutch seaside town of Scheveningen. He was allowed to stand trial in the Netherlands, even though in Italy in 2001, he'd been handed a sentence of fourteen years for smuggling hashish between Italy, Spain and the Netherlands. In addition, Gasperoni was also accused of sheltering the suspected murderer of a public prosecutor from Turin, Italy. Although Gasperoni was openly living and working in the Netherlands under his own name, the Italian authorities had had little success in having him arrested and extradited. That changed in May 2016, when Gasperoni was already in his seventies. His extradition didn't go through because he'd spent so many years living in the Netherlands. The Dutch commuted his sentence to reflect local standards, and as if by magic, fourteen years in an Italian prison became eighteen months of house arrest with an electronic tag in the Netherlands.

All in all, European and Dutch efforts to combat the Ndrangheta seemed somewhat lacklustre. Nevertheless, the Dutch version of Santa Claus was on his way, bringing me a big surprise. In 2018, on the morning of 5 December – the Dutch holiday of St Nicholas' Eve – I woke to the news that more than eighty simultaneous arrests had been carried out the previous night in the Netherlands, Germany, Belgium and Italy. Operation Pollino was the largest joint European police operation against the Ndrangheta to date. I rushed to The Hague to attend a press conference at Eurojust, the European Union Agency for Criminal Justice Cooperation.

There, police and justice authorities from the cooperating countries sat in a row, recounting their story for the cameras and microphones of dozens of journalists. I was surprised to learn that the Netherlands had initiated the investigation; the Dutch Fiscal Intelligence and Investigation Service (FIOD) had decided to follow some suspected Ndranghetists they thought were using restaurants in the Dutch province of Limburg to launder money. It soon became clear that drug traffickers were meeting at these restaurants. And one restaurant owner made regular trips to Germany, where he owned more restaurants and ice cream parlours. He also paid frequent visits to Calabria. That prompted the Dutch FIOD to contact German and Italian authorities, creating a European Joint Investigation Team, the first-ever wide-ranging international partnership to tackle the Ndrangheta. The greatest benefit of the collaboration was that it enabled participating countries to circumvent the slow practice of requesting official legal assistance. Instead, information was shared directly between the countries involved, giving the European investigative agencies an edge in outwitting the country-hopping Ndranghetists.

At the press conference, I heard that five people had been arrested in the Netherlands. Authorities had searched eight locations throughout the country: Amsterdam, Amstelveen, Velsen, Zoetermeer, The Hague, Rotterdam, Tegelen and Sittard. Belgium also reported four arrests, but most of the other suspects – there were more than seventy – were nabbed by Italian and German police. Those arrested were accused of collaborating with or being members of the Pelle–Vottari clan from San Luca – what you might call 'the usual suspects'.

I didn't pay much attention to details about the kilos of coke or ecstasy pills that had been seized, or the number of cars and Rolexes. But I did tune in when Cafiero De Raho, Italy's national anti-mafia public prosecutor, started to speak. 'You must not assume the Ndrangheta is represented in the marketplace by its own people,' he said. 'Instead, they always involve respectable professionals – accountants, lawyers and so on, not only in Italy but also in other countries. The people who represent them have good reputations and are all highly respected in their fields. They make up the Ndrangheta's civilized and well-educated citizenry, which remains invisible while enabling the far-reaching pollution of the economy to take place in Italy and throughout Europe, including in your country.'

At the end of the press conference, I asked him if these white-collar Ndrangheta criminals linked to the Ndrangheta could be adequately combated in Europe at this time. 'To do that, we must pay much closer attention to how illicit funds are invested in society,' he replied. I asked Operation Pollino's other spokespeople if they believed Europe's current laws, rules and resources were strong enough to tackle the Ndrangheta's entourage of 'grey area' accomplices. They all said no.

A few weeks later, I caught up with two people I'd met backstage at the press conference. One was the man from the Dutch FIOD, who had initiated the investigation; the other was the public prosecutor he had been working with. For reasons of safety, they asked to remain anonymous. Let's call the man from the FIOD Fred. He's got an athletic build and hails from the southern Dutch province of Brabant. The public prosecutor is a tall, blonde woman; we'll call her Daphne. She's level-headed and sharp-witted, making her the perfect partner for the enthusiastic Fred, who has an excellent memory for anecdotes.

Fred explained how he started the investigation in April 2014. The Dutch FIOD, together with the Dutch tax authorities and police, had just completed a new report about the Italian mafia in the Netherlands. The second report's rather unsatisfactory conclusion was that the Netherlands still had little insight into the size and nature of the problem. At the time, the Netherlands had never conducted an independent criminal investigation into the Ndrangheta, responding instead to Italian requests for judicial assistance. The Dutch report was titled *Cerca Trova*, a reference to the proverb 'seek and you shall find' in Italian. Fred explained that the Dutch investigative services were ordered to set up two investigations to gain more insight. 'One was the investigation into the FloraHolland flower auction in Aalsmeer, the other was our investigation.'

Cerca Trova listed twenty-two restaurants whose owners were suspected of having links with the mafia. Fred focused his probe on two in the Dutch province of Limburg. One was called Botticelli, located in Venray, and the other was La Vita in Horst. 'From the start, I sensed that something was wrong there, but of course, you have to find proof.'

Both restaurants were owned by Giovanni Giorgi, who was born in San Luca, Calabria. He and his business partners had direct links with Ndranghetists just across the nearby German border. 'We quickly realized that we couldn't conduct this investigation without the help of Italy and Germany,' Fred said. 'Our three prime suspects often crossed the border into Germany and then the hands of the Dutch police were tied. We also noticed that some suspects regularly travelled from Calabria to the Netherlands or Germany. They may very well have been carrying large amounts of cash to open new restaurants. But we could never prove that because we couldn't risk giving ourselves away at that time.'

Daphne described how the Dutch investigation ran into a brick wall at the German border. 'We'd wiretapped phones, but we couldn't use conversations we'd recorded in Germany without German permission. The same applied to surveillance: we wanted the Germans to handle that across the border.'

In Germany, Fred's team had uncovered several suspicious

restaurants, including a few in Duisburg. 'We asked the police in Duisburg for assistance a dozen times, but they were powerless to help.'

Daphne explained that there was no equivalent in Germany for the type of investigation the Dutch were carrying out, in which authorities can follow a group because of their suspected involvement in organized crime, so German police were not permitted to assist. 'But by then, we'd gathered a lot of information and tried, for the sake of the collaboration, to focus more specifically on one person,' she said. 'We went back to the German police when we had enough evidence to charge Giovanni Giorgi with suspected money laundering, but that was still problematic because our German counterparts said they couldn't do much about that crime. In money laundering cases in the Netherlands, it's enough to suspect the money has criminal origins. But German law is much more complex: you must state the specific crime from which the money originated, otherwise you can't prove money laundering. But of course, it's almost impossible to prove where the money comes from.'

Nevertheless, the police in Duisburg realized they couldn't dismiss the Dutch appeal for assistance out of hand. 'Don't forget, Duisburg is where the murder of six people took place. There were people there who knew a lot about the subject,' Daphne said. Fred mentioned an associate in Duisburg who had valuable insights into the various clans that were active in Germany. 'She'd type in a name and say, "Oh, that's so-and-so." She knew them all.'

Daphne added, 'The Germans didn't find money laundering very interesting. But they were *very* concerned about drugs. Narcotics weren't our initial objective because we wanted to try a financial approach. So we tried to strike a healthy balance.'

The Italians, however, did take an immediate interest in the investigation. 'We made our first trip to Italy in January 2015,' Fred said. 'We told the police in Reggio Calabria that we'd found a few restaurants run by certain business partners. They knew who they were and agreed that we should work together.' Nicola Gratteri, the world-famous Ndrangheta adversary, took charge of the case for the Reggio public prosecutor's office. 'Gratteri told us to send our findings in a report,' Fred explained. 'That way, we wouldn't have to submit a formal request for judicial assistance. The Italians could start their own independent investigation and we could join forces. I sweated bullets trying to finish that report in February, on the first morning of Carnival, a major holiday in my home province of Brabant. Gratteri was adamant: he needed it that day. Then, after I sent it in, we heard nothing until early in 2016, when we got word that they'd started their investigation in August 2015.'

At one of the meetings in Italy, Fred showed a PowerPoint presentation that included a plate of spaghetti bolognese balancing on the scales of justice – Gratteri and his associates were not amused. However, the Dutchman's irreverent approach did pay off, gradually breaking down the walls between Italian law enforcement's various branches, which seemed unnecessarily competitive and attached to formalities.

'We submitted a request for judicial assistance when the public prosecutor and the national police started the investigation because we wanted to know if they could tell us the size of the Duisburg group's financial assets. But, in Reggio, that request got sent to the Italian financial police and not the national police. Those two departments had offices less than two kilometres apart, but they had no direct contact. So, one Monday, we were in the offices of the national police in Reggio, and our judicial request was over at the financial police, where we had an appointment the following day. I said, why don't we

SEEK AND YOU SHALL FIND

all get together? Isn't this all about the same story? They made a few calls and invited a few people over. That night, we ate dinner with the whole group, and we've worked on the investigation together ever since.'

All in all, it took two and a half years from the start of the Dutch investigation until all parties officially committed to the creation of the Joint Investigation Team in October 2016 at Eurojust. 'Italy had already started their investigation, but Germany had not. The Germans wanted to focus on drugs, but we hadn't looked into that yet,' Daphne explained. 'It was difficult to convince our higher-ups to shift focus. Tackling narcotics offences meant including the police and the Dutch National Criminal Investigation Department. So, everything was going to take more time, and additional personnel was needed.'

I asked why there was so little interest in investigating drug trafficking in the Netherlands. 'We can seize illegal drugs without much effort, but it doesn't help our cause,' Daphne replied. 'We know that drugs from South America are usually shipped to Rotterdam or Antwerp. Of course, during our investigations, we hoped we'd intercept a large shipment, and we made every effort to do so. We know which types of cargo are commonly used to conceal drugs, and that helps us decide which containers to inspect. We had requested judicial assistance in South America, we'd collaborated on surveillance and phones had been tapped in all the countries involved. Using those methods, we once targeted a boat carrying 3,500 kilos of cocaine, a real jackpot. But we could not link that boat's cargo to our suspects, because they never came to collect the shipment.'

That reminded me of the corrupt Rotterdam customs officials who had recently been arrested. They had earned extra cash by offering their services to narcotics dealers. With the push of a button, they could ensure that a cargo escaped inspection – or they could tip off the Ndrangheta's errand boys by phone that the police were about to inspect their container.

Fred was happy to report that they had been able to link a smaller shipment of ninety-five kilos in the Port of Rotterdam to their suspects. He and his team had also intercepted smaller amounts of Ndrangheta cocaine being transported over land in rental cars. 'Just ten or fifteen kilos each time. There's a video of one instance. After the courier had presumably dropped off the payment in Amsterdam, he continued on to Rotterdam. There, a man is seen walking into a flat and reappearing with a supermarket shopping bag. He walks to the rental car, which has a secret storage area that can be opened electronically: you press a button, turn another switch and then, bleep, the lid of a shallow compartment opens, just big enough to hold ten to twenty packages. The video shows the man getting into the car, fumbling for a few minutes and then leaving for Italy. The authorities caught him in Switzerland.'

The first Ndrangheta informer the Dutch ever questioned, Giuseppe Tirintino, turned out to be a crucial source of information for the investigation into drug trafficking by the Pelle–Vottaris and other affiliated Calabrian clans. 'In 2015, our surveillance teams were monitoring one of the restaurants in Limburg, La Vita, in Horst,' Fred said. 'Business was slow, but the restaurant was still operational. At one point, our team saw a man arrive: he checked the door, but it was locked. Then he sat on the terrace, lit a cigarette, grabbed his phone and made a phone call. The surveillance team took his picture. Our team spent a year trying to figure out who the man might be, with no success. Until one day, in Italy, we were allowed to talk to a former

Ndrangheta associate who had become an informer. When he walked in, we found out he was the guy from our picture, Tirintino!'

Shortly after Giuseppe Tirintino visited the pizza restaurant in Limburg, he decided to turn himself over to the justice department in Italy. It seems the 36-year-old clan member didn't have much choice. The authorities had confiscated a few consignments of coke and within the clan, people suspected Tirintino of being a rat. By 2015, he had been living in the Netherlands for over a decade, primarily in a suburb of Amsterdam. He made frequent trips to Colombia, Germany and Italy. 'He worked for several clans, arranging the shipment of coke from South America to Europe, then on to Southern Italy,' said Fred. 'Tirintino explained that a front company usually sent the container holding the drugs to a location in the Netherlands or Germany. That's assuming bribed personnel hadn't already removed the narcotics from the container in the port.'

A group of Ndranghetists in Germany had set up a dummy company, importing and exporting wood and coal, specifically to hide the transport of narcotics. Cocaine was hidden in hollowed-out timber or pressed into charcoal using a chemical process. 'According to Tirintino, the cocaine was then extracted from the coal at a location in the Netherlands,' Daphne said. 'But he couldn't tell us exactly where.'

Giuseppe Tirintino was related to Gioacchino Bonarrigo, the Ndrangheta fugitive from Rosarno who had been arrested in Amsterdam in 2006 and again in 2017. Tirintino's testimony helped ensure his cousin's most recent arrest and the arrests of many others.

The Dutch were grateful for all the information Tirintino gave them. 'During the questioning, the Italian prosecutor sometimes gave us a look, like, that's common knowledge. But a lot of his information was new to us,' Daphne said.

Tirintino was also close to Giovanni Giorgi, the owner of the pizza restaurants. He shed light on some tricks Giorgi used to make sure investments in the restaurants turned a profit. 'We were blown away when he told us about a fire they set to claim insurance money,' Daphne said. 'But Tirintino just shrugged and said it was common practice in his world. And he knew specific details about the fire in that restaurant.'

Fred continued: 'Based on what he told us, we should have started our investigation back in 2010. According to Tirintino, that's when somebody took a member of their clan hostage in Colombia. They had to come up with 200,000 euros to pay the ransom, and decided to set the restaurant on fire. Two guys from Rome were summoned to drive to the Netherlands and torch the place at four in the morning, when the fire department has its slowest response time. Tirintino said the arsonists acted a bit too soon. Luckily, the people living above the restaurant, their own people, had already been relocated, so no one was hurt.'

The international investigation team gradually gained more insight into how the various Ndrangheta clans collaborated through the figure of Giovanni Giorgi. 'Giorgi facilitated the clans' money laundering, and he set up the restaurants. He felt at home in the Netherlands and Germany, spoke German, had the right connections and was familiar with how things were done', Fred said. 'Giorgi wasn't involved in narcotics himself, but of course, he understood where the money was coming from. He arranged airline tickets and rental cars, made sure people were picked up at the airport and facilitated meetings at his restaurants.'

Giorgi lived in the Netherlands with his girlfriend but still went home to Calabria every three months to see his wife and children.

When Fred was in Reggio, he asked about Giovanni Giorgi's holdings in Italy, which were said to be a modest house in Bovalino and a small orchard. 'We drove past that orchard and spotted a roof that was just visible above the treetops. We got out and filmed what we saw. It turned out to be a villa the size of a palace! With an estimated value of a million, but built illegally. When officials returned with a search warrant in December, they saw that the house was lavishly furnished.' When Fred added the words 'according to their tastes', I immediately pictured ornate baroque furniture, plenty of marble surfaces and crystal chandeliers.

Giorgi had long lived in the Netherlands with Birgit, a woman from southern Germany who helped him run his restaurants. 'Birgit was a woman with a lot of experience in the hospitality industry. She spoke Dutch, knew her way around municipal bureaucracy and had plenty of contacts. They'd opened a new restaurant under her name on the Dutch side of the border, as Giorgi could no longer pass the stricter Dutch integrity screening requirements.'

At the time of his arrest, Giorgi was living in the Dutch municipality of Tegelen with a new girlfriend, who had worked in the kitchen of one of his restaurants. Neither of the women was arrested. But the police did pick up Giorgi's two nephews. Both in their twenties, they made pizzas in Giorgi's restaurants in the Netherlands and Germany. Fred told me that their uncle had warned them about behaving like gangsters while living in northern Europe. 'We overheard Giorgi telling his girlfriend that he'd taken them to task. "I said they shouldn't act like they do in the movies! They're just here to work." He didn't want them to wear sunglasses or pricey clothes. Giorgi himself usually drove a practical, economy-sized Fiat Panda in the Netherlands.' Daphne couldn't resist pointing out that Giorgi had however paid cash for a Mercedes in Germany.

The restaurant's staff and cooks always came from Italy. 'Sometimes they were housed in Dutch holiday parks near the border town of Venray,' Fred said. 'Six of the eight employees would work for cash-in-hand; only two would be registered for income tax purposes. Customers often paid cash for takeaway pizzas, and Giorgi frowned on contactless payment. He preferred the German business model, where, at that time, customers paid in cash for almost eighty per cent of transactions.'

Ultimately, Giorgi sold all his Dutch restaurants and the new ones he opened were all in Germany, preferably close to the Dutch border. He also bought some ice cream parlours. 'A German project developer would find the locations for him,' Daphne explained. 'And a solicitor in Duisburg who would take care of the paperwork'.

The money-laundering laws in Germany made it impossible to bring charges against Giorgi's white-collar associates. 'In the Netherlands, we definitely would have arrested that solicitor,' Fred said.

To avoid paying taxes, every two years the restaurants would either be sold or put in the name of a different person within the criminal network. 'If they operated a restaurant for two years and then walked out, their unpaid taxes would lapse after five or six years,' Fred explained. 'This way, they ended up not paying taxes anywhere. And since their earnings are fictitious anyway, they try to play them down.'

Despite Giorgi's activities in the Netherlands and Germany, he was extradited to Italy to stand trial there. Of all the people who were arrested, only four would be brought to trial in the Netherlands. Two of them, a Dutch father and son, were in direct contact with the Ndrangheta. With help from two other Dutch citizens, they had been producing ecstasy pills, among other things, for the Calabrian clans.

'In the Netherlands, we observed the suspected Ndrangheta members regularly meeting the father and son in an Amsterdam café. When we followed them, we discovered escstasy labs,' Daphne explained. They manufactured the pills in Amsterdam and Velsen-Noord, just north of the capital. 'Apart from supplying ecstasy to the clans, they also provided them with contacts and transferred money to South America,' Fred said.

I wondered how long the Dutch suspects would be held in pretrial detention. I was reminded of the case of Marc B., the Italian living in Amsterdam who'd fled after being arrested on suspicion of supplying cocaine to the Ndrangheta. He hadn't been considered a flight risk. Fred got my drift and reassured me: 'We'll probably keep them in custody for a long time.'

The Belgian investigative services joined the international police operation at the eleventh hour because suspects often travelled to Belgium. Fred said hardened criminals were crossing the border between the Dutch province of Limburg and the Belgian province of the same name.

As the date of the simultaneous arrests drew near, the four countries involved in the investigation couldn't agree on the timing. 'The Italians insisted on picking up the suspects at 4am because the people they were planning to arrest in Calabria were known to have a large cache of arms,' Fred explained. The Italian police wanted to strike in the middle of the night to avoid the risk of retaliative fire. 'In Germany, however, agents couldn't be ordered to report for duty at that time of day and in Belgium, they preferred to make arrests after 5am. Thanks to official intervention from Italy, we finally agreed on the time.'

The night of the arrests, Fred and Daphne were at Eurojust in The Hague, watching the action as it unfolded. I asked Fred about their main concerns. He replied, 'We were hoping to find Giovanni Giorgi at home. We'd been listening in on his phone calls in the Netherlands, Germany, and Italy, so we had a pretty good idea where he'd be. We sent him a silent text message to ascertain his whereabouts at a specific time. Fortunately, he was at his home in Tegelen, in the Netherlands. It might not have mattered so much if we had been planning to arrest twenty other Italian suspects in the Netherlands, but he was our only one, and a very important one, too.'

'Eurojust had set up a screen listing all the players,' Daphne continued. 'We were in continuous phone contact with our police so that we were kept up to date and could discuss the next steps. At a time like that, everyone's responsible for their own actions. In Italy, almost all the arrests took place in Calabria. Within thirty minutes, many of the lights next to the list of names had switched from red to green. We were relieved everyone was safe, that there had been no violence and nothing unexpected had occurred.'

Later that day, another search was carried out in Suriname. And in the days that followed, there was an arrest in Madrid, two in Luxembourg, one in Switzerland and one in England.

The investigation had also led to the unexpected capture of the fugitive Antonio Pelle. Pelle was the man referred to as '*la mamma*' in the phone call made by the brother of one of the victims of the Duisburg massacre – the clan leader who needed to be notified about the attack on his men. Pelle was thought to be responsible for the Christmas assault targeting the Nirta–Strangios in which Maria Strangio had perished, and he had briefly been incarcerated. But after being diagnosed as anorexic, he was transferred to a hospital in Locri, from which he later escaped. In recent years, while he was a fugitive, Pelle had paid regular visits to the Netherlands and Belgium, and he'd financed some major drug deals tracked by the international investigative team.

'Pelle's son Domenico was in one of the restaurants we were watching in Germany,' Fred explained. 'He had brought cash to install an ice cream machine there. That's when authorities began listening in on his phone calls and eventually, they overheard him say that papa was home. In October 2016, officers began a search of the family home. And, indeed, he turned out to be hiding there.' The Italian police posted a video of the arrest online, showing the fugitive Antonio Pelle crawling out of a narrow space above a wardrobe.

I paused to reflect on the incredible results of investigating just two of the twenty-two suspicious restaurants in the Netherlands listed in the *Cerca Trova* report. All in all, the teams made nearly ninety arrests and shared much information about the seemingly effortless workings of this pan-European criminal network. For over ten years, in my home in Calabria, I'd been pinning my hopes on such an operation. Full of optimism, I asked Fred and Daphne about the future of these sorts of investigations.

Daphne burst my bubble. 'It will be almost impossible to convince our steering committees of the need for a follow-up. They're not really interested in our overall international achievements. Whereas I believe that when your country proves to be a reliable partner, that translates into gains in other investigations. The police are different from the fiscal investigation department in that they're more concerned about how many suspects are arrested in the Netherlands, how much money has been seized, and how much jail time an investigation yields – although the effects can be much broader.'

'If you look at it from the perspective of our tiny country, the results of our investigation are nothing special,' Fred said. 'And managers are often fixated on their own department, their turf. They thought we were crazy because this investigation went on so long. We even came close to wrapping it up much earlier. We had been planning our raids for September 2016, hoping for nine arrests. We wanted to finish things here in the Netherlands. Done, *finito*.'

Finito. That would have meant one-tenth the number of arrests carried out by the international team two years later. But for the Dutch, on the surface, nine arrests would have seemed more impressive. 'When the Joint Investigation Team was launched, we decided to carry on,' Fred added. However, there was little chance that the remaining twenty Dutch restaurants on the list of suspected eateries would be investigated. Perhaps some had already changed hands, but Fred believed a few were still ripe for scrutiny.

He briefly summarized the importance of the Netherlands for the Ndrangheta's narcotics dealers: 'The Ndrangheta continues to use the Netherlands as a logistical hub. There are harbours and various locations where they can store and transport cocaine, and the Netherlands is small, so clan members are in and out fast. This doesn't mean our country isn't important to them. On the contrary, the Netherlands is an indispensable link. In fact, we have shown how Europe is being explored and used by the Ndrangheta as though it were one country, and we achieved a lot by bringing that to light.'

22

THE INVISIBLES

From the outside, Reggio Calabria's Palace of Justice looks sleek and somewhat daunting. Although I've been there many times, I continue to be struck by the massive courtyard you must cross to reach the various entryways. In the colonnade, where all sounds turn into shrill echoes, I feel out of place. But once past the security checkpoint, the mood shifts and I'm reminded of how human the atmosphere is inside the building. The security staff are helpful and friendly. Their warm welcome stands in contrast to the untidy, fluorescent-lit hallways and the WCs where the lights never work, the taps drip and the cubicle doors don't lock, never mind the corridors stacked with countless bulging binders crammed with files, all covered in dust.

This building houses the workplace of Giuseppe Lombardo, a public prosecutor. Although he isn't as famous as Nicola Gratteri, he's known for conducting investigations into national and international Ndrangheta networks with unparalleled zeal. In 2015, when Gratteri was appointed chief prosecutor in the Calabrian capital of Catanzaro, Giuseppe Lombardo succeeded him in Reggio. For the past few years, as deputy prosecutor, Lombardo has grappled with some of the thorniest criminal cases. After police discovered that the Ndrangheta had earmarked two hundred kilos of explosives for Lombardo, they tightened his personal security.

Lombardo's investigations focus on the links between the Ndrangheta and politicians, and reconstruct the threads connecting historical relationships from previous decades to the present. While his colleagues in Palermo investigated the deals made between the Sicilian mafia and the Italian government around the time of the attacks on Falcone and Borsellino, for example, Lombardo examined the Calabrian mafia's role in those events. I once attended a hearing in Reggio during which Lombardo questioned an informer about that period. I was astonished at how quickly the former Ndranghetist could shift from a polite apology for coughing (*'scusi, signor pubblico ministero'*) to fond recollections of friendly contacts with hit men from the Sicilian mafia. He described how his Sicilian allies had once wined and dined him at a luxury beachfront resort they owned. In return, he offered them his family's comfortable mountain cabin when they needed a place to hide from the authorities. After that, in a seemingly indifferent tone, the witness answered Lombardo's questions about trading cocaine for weapons and supplying tons of explosives needed for Cosa Nostra's openly declared war against the state.

The Ndrangheta is currently more powerful than Cosa Nostra, a state of affairs that is often explained by a favourable strategy set forth by the Calabrian bosses in the 1980s and '90s: they decided not to attack the government head-on, if at all. As a result, the Ndrangheta could remain comfortably under the radar and steadily build its criminal empire, while Cosa Nostra was using bombings as a means of blackmail to gain, for example, a more lenient regime for imprisoned mafia members. But recent state's witness statements reveal a more nuanced reading of past events. It seems that the

Ndrangheta may have started making deals with representatives from the national government as early as the 1970s. Judicial authorities refrained from prosecuting certain clans, provided they didn't target government institutions. Could that be why major mafia families were spared judicial reckoning for so long, and cases against the most powerful bosses so often ended in acquittal due to 'lack of evidence'?

Lombardo investigates these issues and delves into the more recent history to uncover links between the Ndrangheta and local, national and European politicians. According to Lombardo, such links are essential to understanding how this criminal multinational is organized. He suspects there must be a layer of senior administrators pulling the strings above the 'military' top management, which is made up of prominent clan leaders. Informers refer to those operating on this higher level as *gli invisibili*, 'the invisibles' – their identity is hidden from practically all the Ndrangheta's men. Lombardo believes it's this secret upper level of governance that makes all the decisions regarding the Ndrangheta's economic strategy, and that it also selects political accomplices, both in Italy – from Reggio Calabria to Rome – and further afield, at the European parliament in Brussels and Strasbourg.

At the time of my visit, Lombardo had just brought charges against people suspected of membership in the Ndrangheta's secret upper management level. Lombardo gave his trials charismatic names like 'Mammasantissima' and 'Gotha'. In his closing arguments, he quoted the German philosopher Schopenhauer: 'All truth passes through three stages. First, it is ridiculed. Second, it is violently opposed. Third, it is accepted as being self-evident.'

I noticed that the vestibule leading to Giuseppe Lombardo's office was tidier than the rest of the building. He arrived looking upbeat, with a spring in his step, and was accompanied by two bodyguards.

Once I had taken my place in the seating area of his spacious office, my eye was drawn to the film poster from *The Untouchables* hanging on the wall. This Hollywood classic describes how mafia boss Al Capone, played by Robert De Niro, held Chicago in his corrupting iron grip a century ago. Kevin Costner plays a tireless investigator whose colleagues shamelessly thwart his efforts to prosecute Capone. Costner's character can't rely on his colleagues, but in the end, he triumphs over the seemingly invincible gangster.

When we met, Lombardo was in his late forties and had been fighting his battle for twenty years. I suspected his self-confidence was drawn at least in part from his family's background. 'My father was a mafia prosecutor during the era of the kidnappings,' Lombardo explained. 'And his father, in turn, had also been a *magistrato*, a public prosecutor, in the 1950s and '60s. At that time, he was one of only a handful of prosecutors in Calabria. Back then, the Ndrangheta was a criminal organization with strong roots in its original territory, mainly involved with agriculture, livestock farming and forest management. Ndrangheta families primarily forged alliances with the nobility, the landowners of the day. Clan membership grew toward the end of the 1960s, and the Calabrian mafia experienced a dramatic transformation. Studying that period holds the key to understanding the Ndrangheta today. We still know so little about the Ndrangheta's history, especially when compared to Cosa Nostra's. Nowadays, it may seem like we are facing an enormous criminal organization that has come out of nowhere, but that's not the case. The Ndrangheta's number of families and clan members has always been relatively high compared with the mafias in Sicily and Campania. And to prevent conflicts, vendettas and wars between the clans, the Ndrangheta needed an organizational structure allowing a more flexible and efficient administration. In the Ndrangheta, no matter how notorious or prominent an individual criminal is, he is just a cog in a much larger criminal machine.'

It took the Ndrangheta two wars to fulfil its organizational transformation. Giuseppe Lombardo grew up in Reggio Calabria during that era of bloodshed, which followed on the heels of a massive uprising that had to be quelled by the army. He described seeing tanks rolling through town when he was growing up. The disorder arose when the Italian government decided to reorganize the country in the early 1970s, creating larger administrative regions to replace the traditional smaller provinces. Catanzaro was designated as the capital of the region of Calabria, and therefore as the administrative centre for distributing government funds. Reggio Calabria, however, was the largest Calabrian city, and its inhabitants were outraged by the government's preference for Catanzaro. The ensuing uprising, supported by the Ndrangheta, lasted ten long months. In the end, military tanks were called in to end the protests, and the factions agreed to a compromise. From then on, the regional government would meet in Catanzaro, but a regional council based in Reggio Calabria would decide on administrative policy.

The government made further concessions by allocating extra redevelopment funds to the city and province of Reggio Calabria. It earmarked funds for the economy, employment and the improvement of the region's logistical position through the construction of the port of Gioia Tauro, among other things. Disappointingly, some funds went to building industrial castles in the sky – enormous factories that never became functional. And, as often happens in Calabria, the clans enjoyed more benefits from government investments than the average citizens.

'The De Stefano family based in Reggio and the Piromallis from Gioia Tauro soon realized that to take full advantage of government funds, the Ndrangheta needed to become more efficient. It had to become an organization based on the same logic as a company, without territorial boundaries, and less recognizable as a criminal organization. The two families drafted the rules for the new Ndrangheta. And by establishing the high-level secret branch called La Santa, the Ndrangheta could forge new contacts in Italy's most prosperous regions. By the 1970s, the Ndrangheta had already become the strongest and most important criminal organization in Lombardy, one of Europe's wealthiest regions. The Milan stock exchange gave Ndrangheta clans access to enormous economic opportunities in Europe's most prosperous areas, and clan members settled in southern France, Switzerland, and Germany.' According to Lombardo, the Ndrangheta also strengthened its foothold in Australia, the US and Canada at that time.

Lombardo described the internal power struggle that claimed the lives of two hundred victims in the 1970s. Ndrangheta bosses had several of the De Stefano brothers murdered because they were threatening to usurp power. Some events were reminiscent of a Greek tragedy. For example, when Paolo, the most reasonable of the De Stefano brothers, was asked to take over from his murdered brother Giorgio, he was handed the murderer's head on a platter. 'The Ndrangheta became the organization we know today between 1977 and 1985, during Paolo De Stefano's reign. The same handful of families from Reggio and Gioia Tauro, San Luca and Rosarno, still make up the criminal management. At the end of the day, the Ndrangheta's power lies in the hands of no more than ten or fifteen families, who preside over hundreds of others.'

Lombardo listed some of the ways in which Paolo De Stefano had improved the workings of the Ndrangheta. 'He had good connections with Sicily and understood that the alliance needed to go beyond individual, ad hoc deals. To ensure steady growth, the Ndrangheta held talks with Cosa Nostra, the Camorra and the Sacra Corona Unita, one of the youngest mafias, based in Puglia, originally a branch of the Ndrangheta. They met in Milan and avoided saying things like, "I'm stronger than you" or "I have more money than you." The Ndrangheta also had to adopt a different style of dress to avoid looking like classic mobsters. At that time, immense sums were also being laundered. Informants later reported that sacks of money were crossing the border, primarily over the Alps and into Switzerland. And that much money creates problems, because other people become envious.'

Paolo De Stefano had expanded his territory to include Nice and Cannes. Those left in Calabria became especially jealous when he bought a villa on the Côte d'Azur near Saint-Tropez. According to Lombardo, the Ndrangheta couldn't afford to lose sight of its Calabrian roots while it was growing and globalizing. 'After all,' Lombardo continued, 'once people in Calabria started realizing how much money was at stake, they wanted to know why the profits weren't flowing back to the Ndrangheta's home turf. In this case, De Stefano's right hand in Reggio Calabria, Pasquale Condello, was the one who became increasingly displeased. He was under the impression that his family wasn't getting its fair share. So, in 1985, he mustered other disgruntled members and started another clan war, leading to seven hundred deaths in Reggio and beyond. The hostilities ended with a reconciliation in 1991. What had that war accomplished? It forced the Ndrangheta to stop repeating certain of its mistakes. The words of the highest boss still mattered, but his decisions were first checked with an advisory board.'

Since then, the organization has enjoyed a balance of power. '*Grande capi*, or prominent leaders of the Ndrangheta, have stopped throwing their weight around,' Lombardo said. 'Instead, there's an organizational system in place, and decisions seem to be made jointly. This modern way of doing business calms the people back home because no single individual holds all the power or benefits from all the wealth. The Ndrangheta had always had a similar structure, but occasionally, more domineering figures would come along.'

Lombardo took a moment to catch his breath. 'Over the years, the Ndrangheta has used their connections with other crime organizations, government institutions, politicians and international financial networks to accrue massive power, what we call "social capital". That gives them huge criminal clout in Italy and Europe. The clans of the Ndrangheta have been earning billions, especially since they began dominating drug trafficking in the 1990s. They can influence certain political choices with that money because they can pump their earnings directly into the market: money equals influence.'

According to Lombardo, a criminal organization like the Ndrangheta passes through three phases. 'During the first phase, as wealthy individuals, they become preferred customers at banks and within the financial system. Then, as the clans become more ambitious, they invest directly in the financial system by supplying a product – in this case, money – needed by other entrepreneurs, and they become stakeholders. And, in the final phase, they become the bank, no longer someone else's negotiating partners, but autonomous decision-makers.'

Lombardo believes the Ndrangheta had reached the third stage in the 1990s. 'During a credit crisis, you can benefit from an increased demand for money while exerting influence over the market; that creates political leverage. Unfortunately, until just a few years ago, people mistakenly believed that the Ndrangheta consisted of a handful of families with strong roots in a particular region, whose business dealings were limited to particular sectors. Although they had some money to invest, the interconnection between the families wasn't apparent. However, the public prosecutor's office has known since the 1970s that that image didn't add up, and we have been able to prove it since.'

Lombardo was, of course, referring to the Crimine investigations. 'That maxi-trial proved that the Ndrangheta is a Calabria-based organization with tentacles across Italy and the rest of the world. Since then, it's become easier to recognize Ndrangheta clans abroad as part of a larger collaborative entity. And that's crucial because for years, people assumed that the Ndrangheta's operations in other regions represented the work of a handful of individual families. The challenge for our investigative associates in the Netherlands, Germany and Belgium was understanding who they were dealing with: were those criminals members of the mafia, or did they belong to a criminal group outside the mafia? Beyond Italy's borders, it's no surprise if clans behave differently than they do in Calabria, but they are still part of the Ndrangheta, and they need to be fought as such. We also explained to our foreign associates that clan members don't necessarily travel in packs. All you need to carry out a major financial operation is one individual. Therefore, a single person with Ndrangheta connections can potentially have a network of thousands of criminals at their fingertips.'

After the Crimine trial in Reggio Calabria ended, the public prosecutors wanted to gain more insight into who was pulling the strings behind the Ndrangheta's strategic policy. 'It seemed likely that the Ndrangheta had some managing directors who didn't fit into the organizational structure as we had pieced it together up to that point. We'd pictured a pyramid consisting of specific ranks and duties. However, it became clear that key decisions were being made on a different level. You must have the right capabilities to dictate certain strategies. It's not just about shifting large amounts of capital; you must also understand the finer points of timing. And when you look at the men who make up the board of the Ndrangheta, especially if you have a critical eye, you can't help realizing they are incapable of making such complicated decisions. We've listened to their wiretapped conversations for ages and have a pretty good idea who we're dealing with. There aren't many people about whom you'd say, "This person could manage an investment in Central Africa", for instance. And that's when we started wondering if people on that level could represent the highest criminal ranks of the Ndrangheta. Suppose that Capocrimine Domenico Oppedisano – a man driving around Rosarno in a three-wheeled pick-up, selling his parsley at the market – really is the biggest boss, do we really believe his strategies shape the Ndrangheta's criminal holdings?'

With this, Lombardo hit the nail on the head. 'If, after serving as a public prosecutor for ten years, the individuals we've identified as the organization's leaders have such a limited cultural education – they might have enough charisma to inspire other members to want to imitate them as killers, extortionists or loan sharks, granted, but these individuals are completely lacking in specific competencies to justify this criminal organization's annual turnover of tens of billions – then I suspect there must be another layer above, an upper tier of managers who can map the criminal pathways and communicate with individuals who've attained a certain social standing.'

Operation Crimine revealed that the Ndrangheta's top management, which meets annually near San Luca, is tasked with guarding the organization's unity and respect for rules that characterize it in Italy and abroad. When Ndranghetists break those rules, they face reprisals. 'But who makes decisions about the larger strategic issues?' Lombardo drew a pyramid on a blank sheet of paper. 'Is it conceivable that on top of the pyramid there's another tier where a different management layer begins?' He extended the pyramid's lines to create the image of an hourglass. 'Could there be an upper space reserved for people who are known only to the bosses at the top of the pyramid?'

He drew a horizontal line through the centre of the hourglass. 'From the bottom, you can only see so far,' Lombardo explained, pointing to the narrow neck where the bottom pyramid flows into the smaller inverted pyramid above. 'The rest is screened off, so only the upper echelon knows what's happening above it. My colleagues and I drew up this organizational chart during the Mammasantissima trial. We began that investigation when we overheard that apart from the segment of the governing board that was visible to everyone, there was another mysterious, invisible, secret layer. Decisions were made on that top level, criminal business activities were planned and orders were passed down to the major bosses.'

However, most informants could only describe this upper branch in the vaguest terms. 'The size of this upper boardroom seems flexible, as it were, unlike the rest of the Ndrangheta's structure, which is relatively rigid. The secret board does not necessarily need twenty members; it can manage with a variable number, depending on the matter at hand. And that makes this board very difficult to investigate. The only thing we can do is investigate issues that involve a specific person belonging to this secret board.'

Moreover, Lombardo had to devise a legally sustainable way of trying this powerful group within the framework of 416bis, the Italian criminal code's anti-mafia legislation. The law, which criminalizes participation in mafia-type organizations, hadn't been in effect yet during the career of Lombardo's grandfather and was only enacted halfway through his father's term of office, but Lombardo's work heavily relies on it. 'We had to determine if the individuals in the upper, smaller pyramid were Ndrangheta members or simply external facilitators who appeared on the criminal scene only in certain instances. You may have heard the term *concorso esterno*, referring to an individual who contributes by being complicit without being part of a criminal structure. If convicted, such actors receive lower sentences than insiders, and in the past, anyone who had not been formally inducted was treated as an outsider. So, a financial expert who arranged an investment, for instance, was viewed as an outsider and could only be convicted as a minor accomplice. But something wasn't right, because investigations had revealed a stable network of participants available on an on-call basis to help make certain decisions.'

According to Lombardo, the 'visible' layer of provincial bosses, at the tip of the pyramid, acts as a protective shield for members of the secret advisory board. 'This keeps such advisors separate from the Ndrangheta itself, when, in fact, they are the organization's chief administrators.'

He continued, 'Let's imagine that ten years or so of global economic stability allowed the Ndrangheta to infiltrate a particular sector. During that decade, the person in charge didn't need to show his face. But, when circumstances change, perhaps the strategy needs to be tweaked. And that's when the person in charge would suddenly reappear.'

Certain actors would re-emerge when a shift in the criminal path was called for. These individuals were often involved in setting the political course of action. Lombardo explained that the Ndrangheta doesn't have fixed political leanings, but the organization likes to bet on the winning party, whether it's to the left or right of the centre. 'But who decides which party to back? Someone must have access to relevant information and a broad political overview.'

What the clans care about is whether their political representatives have the power to safeguard their economic interests. 'That's crucial because the criminal organization must always stay in tune with residents living in its territory. They must pump some of the earnings and stability back into the home front. Otherwise, chaos breaks loose, as we've seen in the past. However, such funds can't take the form of direct investments; that would set off alarm bells with investigators, who could then seize the capital. And investors who pump private money into areas like Calabria or Sicily are subject to intense scrutiny. Government funds, however, are allocated through procedures that can be manipulated to justify a particular investment. That's why the Ndrangheta can't exist without politics.'

In other words, it's essential for the Ndrangheta to influence voting behaviour. 'In fact, the organization has an army of voters under its command,' Lombardo said. 'But voters want something in return, it isn't enough to buy their vote. Because if they accept a hundred euros to vote a certain way, that's all they'll get. So they don't want handouts; they want financial benefits. They want work, employment.'

The Ndrangheta's businesses can guarantee their supporters' loyalty by providing construction jobs, for example. But while these workers may be under the impression that instructions come from figures they may know, it's the invisible puppeteers operating on a higher level who are really pulling the strings. 'Those higher-ups don't present themselves as mafia figures. They don't give direct orders, they don't handle day-to-day decisions about criminal activities – they appear to be above it all. That's why it's so difficult to prove that someone who only shows their face every two or three years is part of the Ndrangheta, a member of its secret higher level. Ultimately, it's a wonderfully simple and efficient system. And thanks to our state's witnesses, we have assembled enough evidence to prove it.'

These state's witnesses, suspects who had chosen to collaborate with the authorities, had recently climbed to higher ranks within the Ndrangheta, but strangely, they had seen little or no increase in power to accompany their new status. 'They assumed they'd garner more authority and money, but it didn't materialize. When they asked for a reason, they were told there was a tier on top of what was visible to them, a place they could never reach.'

According to Lombardo, many of the highest-ranking Ndranghetists also belong to Masonic lodges. The province of Reggio Calabria, with its population of 500,000, has 180 such clubs, a disproportionately large number, with around 9,000 members. The Italian Parliamentary Antimafia Commission recently confiscated a list of registered Freemasons. The list apparently contained the names of members who had been convicted of mafia-related crimes or were still embroiled in mafia trials, but the commission has not made it public.

Lombardo is cautious about besmirching the reputations of all members of registered, legal Masonic lodges. When criminals mention Freemasonry, he believes they are primarily referring to what is called in Italian the *massoneria deviata* or *coperta* lodges, literally the 'stray' or 'hidden' lodges. In other words, Freemasons who meet clandestinely and have deviated from the lawful path. 'Such meetings allow the leaders of prominent families to meet with the Ndrangheta's accomplices, and to align their common interests to keep power in the hands of the Ndrangheta. The two worlds meet in this circuit and find a perfect opportunity to exchange favours between those who have money to invest and those who want to influence the outcome of elections.'

The initial verdicts of Lombardo's Gotha trial have now been handed down. The courts found a number of suspects guilty of rigging elections between 2001 and 2010 on behalf of the Ndrangheta, which had influenced political representation in its favour on the Reggio Calabria municipal council, in Calabria's regional governing board, in the Italian national government and in the European parliament. Lombardo had also charged several lawyers from Reggio Calabria, as well as Father Pino Strangio, the San Luca priest who, before his indictment, oversaw the Sanctuary of the Madonna of Polsi. In the first instance, the priest would be sentenced to nine years and four months in prison for assisting the Ndrangheta. Among those who had to appear with him before the court were regional councillors, mayors, a journalist, a former member of parliament and a judge of the supreme court of cassation. Lombardo had also charged a senator, who had visited Ndrangheta boss Giuseppe Pelle at his home in Calabria, presumably hoping to win his support for an upcoming election. Pelle was in hiding then, but the police surreptitiously filmed the visit.

Witnesses in Lombardo's cases revealed ties between parliamentarians who fled to Dubai to avoid being jailed for collaborating with the mafia, board members of Italy's largest construction companies and consultants helping construct Venice's MOSE flood barriers. A massive protective web of bribes and impunity seems to connect all these Italian scandals. As the Italians say, *tutto torna* – it all adds up.

A few years ago, experts estimated the Ndrangheta's annual

revenue at about forty billion euros a year, but that estimate has since grown to over fifty billion euros. Lombardo believes that the yearly turnover is closer to 150 billion euros. One possible explanation for the Ndrangheta's ever-growing income is its strong competitive position within both the legal and illegal global economies. 'Don't underestimate the importance of the European Union,' Lombardo urged, 'which is another rich source of public funds. Once you have European-level representatives, you can focus your investments there. Wealth attracts more wealth, and that also applies to businesses. If a company is financially stable, maybe because there is dirty capital involved, the European Union is more likely to reinforce that financial stability with subsidies.'

Lombardo stressed the importance of remaining alert and preventing such criminals from determining the fate of our entire economic system. The danger, he believes, is that the Ndrangheta is well on its way, together with Cosa Nostra, the Camorra and other criminal organizations, to becoming a service provider within a global system based on mafia-type methods but intertwined with legal realities. Once that happens, it will be too late, and we won't be able to rectify the situation. Then our democracy will be in trouble, because if the economy becomes conditioned to mafia-type organizations, those organizations will also influence our political choices.

My mind turned to the frustration I felt when Giuseppe Scopelliti, the governor of Calabria, ran for a seat in the European parliament. Before he became governor, he'd been elected mayor of Reggio for a second term, after winning seventy per cent of the vote. When Scopelliti was campaigning for a seat in the European parliament in May 2014, he had not yet been convicted of colluding with the De Stefano clan, as would happen later, but he had already been charged with fraud and abuse of office. That's because more than 170 million euros had mysteriously vanished from Scopelliti's municipal treasury. A member of the municipality's financial staff died in her car after drinking hydrochloric acid.

I'd pitched a story about Scopelliti's shady candidacy to some Dutch newspapers, but their political editors weren't interested. Fortunately, Scopelliti failed to receive enough votes for a seat in the European parliament. In hindsight, it seems likely that the powers that be decided to back a better candidate from their stable of winners.

After my intensive, two-hour interview with Lombardo, I headed to Reggio Calabria's stunning waterfront promenade, the *lungomare*, to clear my mind. The seafront walkway is the crown jewel of a city otherwise characterized by faded glory and poor governance. Some even refer to the waterfront as Italy's most beautiful mile. Majestic Indian ficus trees and historic palazzos stand opposite the silvery water of the strait of Messina, which was glittering in the midday sun. The silhouette of Sicily's Mount Etna was visible on the horizon. There was a small ice cream parlour at the end of the promenade with divine flavours, served with a smile. Once I'd reminded myself that, thankfully, this city and the entire region have much more to offer than a history of criminal families who have oppressed it for a century and a half, I felt ready to face the two-hour drive home.

It was getting dark, so I decided against taking the old road, past the 'wine-dark' sea of the Costa Viola, by the fishing village of Scilla. If it had been earlier in the day, I might have crossed the Aspromonte, passed through the deep green mountain range and emerged near the bergamot orchards on the Ionian coast. But a poorly lit, single-lane road winding through dozens of villages didn't appeal to me. Instead, I headed for the longer but faster route, the motorway along the Tyrrhenian coast. When I passed the Palmi exit, I silently saluted Gaetano Saffioti and his diggers. At Rosarno, I remembered Maria Concetta Cacciola's radiant smile. And, in between the long tunnels, I tried to catch glimpses of the rocky shore around Tropea, one of Calabria's more famous tourist destinations.

In the car, I listened to music by Rino Gaetano, an immortal Calabrian singer who died young and wrote warm-hearted, sharply ironic songs in the 1970s. People still sing them at the top of their voices. One of my favourites is 'Fabbricando case': 'Building schools / you make a personal contribution to education / Building schools / sub-contracts and corruption, bribes of a million . . .'

23

THE SILENT ANTI-MAFIA

Shortly before Christmas in 2019, the largest operation in history targeting the Ndrangheta took place, on the back of a 13,000-page arrest warrant. Public prosecutors from Catanzaro, the Calabrian capital, were on edge until the last minute, because conversations they had wiretapped indicated a leak. So they got together 2,500 carabinieri a day earlier than planned and the raids went ahead, with success. Except for a handful of fugitives, all 330 planned arrests in Germany, Switzerland, Bulgaria and eleven Italian regions could go ahead.

More than four hundred people would stand trial for collaborating with the Ndrangheta's Mancuso clan and other clans in and around the Calabrian city of Vibo Valentia. The arrest of Giancarlo Pittelli, a former member of parliament from Berlusconi's Forza Italia party, was by far the most sensational. Pittelli was a member of Italy's oldest and largest Masonic society, the Grande Oriente d'Italia. He had also been the attorney for clan leader Luigi Mancuso, and the prosecutors made the case that he had opened many doors for his client to contacts in government institutions, banks and foreign companies, thereby safeguarding Mancuso's interests and privileges.

The investigation was given the almost utopian code name

Rinascita, meaning 'rebirth'. It expressed a desire to liberate the population, to give people a chance to live in a region that wasn't ruled, exploited and suffocated by the interests of the clans. Many residents of Vibo Valentia saw the wave of arrests as an opportunity to start over with a clean slate. More than a thousand people gathered outside the police station the day before Christmas to give authorities a ten-minute standing ovation. Calabria had never seen such a massive, overt show of gratitude for the arrests of Ndranghetists.

In January, there was further evidence of support and appreciation as hundreds gathered in front of the stately Palace of Justice in Catanzaro to celebrate the results achieved by chief prosecutor Nicola Gratteri and his team through their daring and perseverance. People used megaphones, encouraging each other to continue breaking the omertà, the fearful code of silence. Everyone had to persist in openly showing distaste for mafia-related behaviour, until such disdain became increasingly normal.

But then, February 2020 rolled around, and the first Italian cases of Covid-19 appeared in the Lombardy region. Soon, the coronavirus had spread throughout northern Italy. Those living in Italy's deep south gradually realized it was time to stop shaking hands and hugging. Social encounters became increasingly awkward; maintaining distance was difficult for the warm and physically demonstrative members of Italian society. In early March, the inevitable happened: Italy became the first country in Europe to announce a national lockdown.

We were were no longer allowed to leave the house, except to buy essentials. We not only had to wear face masks but also carry special documents attesting to the necessity of our errands – the situation was without historical precedent. And yet, during those first weeks of lockdown, my anxiety reminded me of something. My worries were fuelled by the vast difference of opinion between Italy and the Netherlands as to whether this virus posed a general health risk. It seemed that the Netherlands found it difficult to believe people could become fatally ill, not just in China and Italy, but throughout the world. The two weeks it took the Dutch government to impose measures against the spread of the virus felt like an eternity. It reminded me of the many years that had passed before the Netherlands made curbing drug crime a priority.

The Dutch authorities had not exactly been galvanized into action when they heard about the number of fugitive Ndrangheta hitmen and narcotics smugglers who viewed the Netherlands as a favourite hideaway destination. After all, Ndranghetists knew how to blend in. It wasn't until the violence of other groups of drug criminals got entirely out of hand, making it impossible to ignore, that the Dutch felt compelled to pay extra attention to the fight against organized crime.

In recent years, investigators have uncovered quite a few corrupt employees at the Port of Rotterdam. And each year, tens of thousands of kilos of cocaine are found in shipping containers, in increasingly large consignments of a tonne or more. However, police believe these record hauls represent only the tip of the iceberg, because the street price of the drug doesn't seem to fluctuate, meaning there's still plenty to go around.

For over a decade, I have listened to Italians warning me that the miserly, indifferent Dutch policy was a great gift to organized crime, leading to irreparable harm. Perhaps that criticism didn't convince the Dutch, coming as it did from a country where the mafia had originated and was still thriving, a country whose own house was hardly in order – they considered it a case of the pot calling the kettle black. And, despite my native land's popularity with the Ndrangheta, which, according to experts, was the centre of Western cocaine trafficking, I tried to avoid becoming unnecessarily alarmed. Yet I couldn't help noticing more and more symptoms of a diseased society, of ills familiar to me but to which Dutch public opinion seemed immune.

For example, a fruit company in the Dutch province of Gelderland faced extortion for not allowing cocaine to be smuggled with their shipments of bananas and pineapples from South America. After repeated threats to the lives of their employees, the company was given protection from a special police unit. Agents armed with machine guns guarded the entrance to the company's premises. Was Gelderland becoming the next Gioia Tauro, a place where companies that failed to cooperate with drug smugglers needed protection from heavily armed soldiers?

According to a 2019 report about drug crime in Amsterdam's underworld, called *De achterkant van Amsterdam* (which roughly means 'Amsterdam's backside'), approximately two kilos of pure coke are consumed daily in the country's capital. That translates to four kilos of cut cocaine, or tens of thousands of lines, with a total street value of approximately two hundred thousand euros. Those estimates are based on traces of the drug found in sewage water, and these levels have remained constant for many years. In the study, researchers described Amsterdam as the hub of the European drug trade, and a significant amount of dirty money is laundered in the Dutch hospitality sector and real estate. There's a plausible link between the recent astronomic rise in Amsterdam's house prices to investments from the criminal milieu. The genuine figures, however, remain anyone's guess, because it's almost impossible to trace illicit money. The study also revealed that over a third of hotel and restaurant financiers have criminal records, but sham management companies allow criminals to bypass permit checks.

In 2017 – better late than never – Dutch police finally set up a small specialized team to tackle the Italian mafia. Let's hope that targeting criminals with Italian backgrounds isn't counterproductive, because the Ndrangheta likes to collaborate with other criminal groups. When laundering money, Ndrangheta families are careful to avoid attaching their names to any trail of illicit funds. And, when smuggling narcotics, they prefer to leave the high-profile dirty work to others too. Members of the Calabrian mafia use their base in the Netherlands to arrange so-called cocktail shipments, combining marijuana, hashish, pills and coke. The Calabrian clans order their ecstasy pills from Dutch production labs, and they often use Dutch, Antillean, Surinamese and Colombian contacts to organize supplies of cocaine.

It's no surprise that in recent years Moroccan and Albanian names have sprung up in judicial inquiries into the Ndrangheta's activities in the Netherlands, because the Ndrangheta prefers to use outsiders when removing cargo from containers arriving in Dutch ports or transporting drugs to Italy. And in the European narcotics market, the number of Albanian and Moroccan groups has grown in recent years. They seem to have have picked up a few tips from the Italian mafias and have started joining forces to form international criminal networks.

But even the Italians were shocked by the murder of a Dutch attorney representing a state's witness in the Marengo trial. The violence was traced back to Ridouan Taghi, the alleged boss of the so-called Mocro Mafia, a network of drug criminals operating in the Netherlands and Belgium, many but certainly not all of whom are of

Moroccan descent. This criminal organization undoubtedly learned a thing or two from the Ndrangheta, although they seemed to have missed the crucial lesson of avoiding violence and blending into the woodwork. In fact, if the group doesn't change its ways, there's little chance it will still pose a threat to the Dutch legal order in a hundred years. As the Italian mafias have shown, long-term success is easier to achieve by joining forces with the state, rather than waging war against it. The smartest strategy is to focus on those interests that are shared with the ruling classes and to blend into society, and it seems implausible that other criminal networks in the Netherlands haven't figured this out long ago.

Often, we don't realize how vulnerable we are until we come face to face with distressing images. That was also the case with the pandemic. The distance between Calabria and the dramatic situations in Lombardy, where coffins were piling up, was roughly equal to the distance between Lombardy and the Netherlands. Because of this distance, during those first few weeks, my village still seemed quite safe from the virus. At the same time, we knew we'd be wise to exercise caution because of the relatively large number of older people living among us, and the uncertain quality of Calabrian healthcare.

Although I was neither particularly panicked nor deluded into thinking I was immune, I did feel painfully aware of a sad situation that had existed here long before the pandemic. Namely, not every patient could count on receiving the same hospital care as everyone else. In Calabria, it is customary, sometimes even necessary, to use your contacts to gain access to things that are seen as fundamental rights elsewhere. I have always intensely disliked the degrading overdependence this system of preferential treatment fosters. But I also realize it's easy for me to talk because I was born into the kind of context where I could afford the luxury of self-reliance. Life is different in southern Italy. Here, a weak government with a tendency towards corruption and clientelism often forces people to seek solace in an informal social safety net. Whether it involves a job application or a hospital stay, you won't get far without the right person putting in a good word. And that plays into the hands of mafia organizations, which consist of networks of opportunists doing favours for one another.

Luckily, Calabria was spared the sight of overflowing intensive care units. In fact, during the first three months of the pandemic, the coronavirus claimed the lives of fewer than a hundred people in the region. The largest outbreak occurred in a nursing home, and I knew one of the victims. She had lived in the street at the bottom of the hill where I'd spent my first year in Calabria.

At first glance, life in my village seemed to go on as it had before the pandemic. The pace had always been slow, and most activities were centred in and around the home. The town was of course even more quiet than usual, because the lockdown meant fewer cars and people on the streets. No groups of elderly men gathered on park benches, youngsters no longer chatted in the town square after school, and the cafés and pizzeria were closed. The only queues formed at the supermarket down on the coastal road, and although it offered a much wider selection of products than the small village grocery stores, I managed to do without, for weeks on end. There wasn't any evidence of hoarding; instead, residents raised money and bought groceries for villagers who had trouble providing for themselves.

The lockdown did give me an unexpected glimpse into some of the restrictions that are a permanent part of daily life for people under police protection. Even before lockdown, they were forced to weigh the safety and necessity of every step outside the home, every meeting. But for them, there would be no post-lockdown lifting of restrictions to look forward to.

I realized how lucky I was to be in such a verdant part of Italy, in a house with a balcony that allowed for endless views. Every week, more and more swallows circled above my head. I would watch how they swooped over the rooftops and hills towards the sea, and then returned over olive and citrus groves, parasol pines and cactuses.

My neighbours sometimes rang my bell, surprising me with pasta, tiramisu, biscuits, cakes, *frittelle* – fritters still warm from the pan – fresh lettuce from their vegetable patch, and sausages and wine from their cantina. Comfort food.

Totò was the last person with whom I'd had physical contact. He's the villager who has been singing hymns and preaching the gospel on the streets since he woke up from a coma. On the uncomfortable first day of the national quarantine, I ran into him at the door of the village shop. He proffered a hand and I took it, smiling. After all, Totò is Totò. 'Those who do harm hate the light,' he said, clutching my hand and looking me in the eye. 'Look towards the sun, Sa, look towards the sun!'

In the early days of the lockdown, a policy of strict roadside controls yielded a few unexpected results for the Calabrian police, when some fugitive Ndranghetists were apprehended in their cars. They also uncovered one fugitive's hideaway when officers observed someone delivering groceries to a seemingly abandoned house – a cigarette could be seen glowing behind a dark window.

Concerns about the spread of the virus in prisons meant benefits for some mafia bosses serving life sentences, who to the dismay of many Italians were temporarily sent home for their own protection.

But when it later emerged that some were holding court at home, despite the ban on visitors, the prisoners went right back behind bars. During one such police raid, one of the boss's visitors even tried unsuccessfully to hide under a bed.

Most Ndrangheta clans survived the pandemic unscathed, thanks to their large cash reserves. A few may have tried setting up new illegal side jobs, such as selling worthless hand sanitizer. But the Ndrangheta prefers to operate in essential sectors, like food distribution, waste disposal and healthcare, which remain stable in times of crisis. There was, of course, a temporary slump in drug trafficking. During the pandemic, the supply of Chinese fentanyl, an ingredient in synthetic drugs that can be lethal in tiny quantities, temporarily dwindled. Ndrangheta clans in Canada had been eagerly importing the substance for years, but they were forced to make do with their reserves.

In March 2020, one Ndranghetist in Gioia Tauro was apparently at his wits' end, wondering what to do with the 537 kilos of cocaine and 24 kilos of marijuana he had in his possession. He was burying the cache in his family's orchard when the police arrived to arrest him.

According to Europol research, the lockdown in Europe turned out to have been especially inconvenient for distributing drugs and selling them to users. Although the pandemic meant that cocaine shipments by air to Europe weren't possible, drugs continued to arrive at favoured ports in the Netherlands, Belgium and Spain. In some countries, local shortages caused the street price of cocaine to rise. Some areas experienced shortages of other hard drugs, such as heroin, but according to Europol, substitutes were usually available. Furthermore, organized crime quickly adapted to the restrictions, coming up with inventive ways to deliver drugs to users, some of whom turned to the darknet to place their orders and pay for them digitally.

*

In Italy, it's hardly breaking news that a state of emergency often allows criminals to increase their profits and strengthen their position. This was painfully reinforced a few years ago by an intercepted text message from Salvatore Buzzi, a criminal based in Rome, who had connections with a few Ndrangheta clans. In his New Year's greeting, Buzzi wrote, 'Let's hope this will be a year filled with garbage, refugees, immigrants, evacuees and displaced children. Let us pray it rains heavily so a lot of grass must be mowed, and if we're lucky, we'll also have a few snowstorms. Long live support for the common good.'

Members of mafia organizations are not only adept at profiting from random crises, lining their pockets with public funds released during disasters, but they also benefit from the more or less permanent financial crisis in southern Italy. It's no surprise that the origins of Europe's most successful mafia can be found in one of Europe's poorest regions. Unemployment in Calabria affects one in four people; the figure is almost double among young people. After finishing their studies, only a third of college graduates find employment within three years of graduating. Ndranghetists exploit this economic hardship by making people dependent on their poorly paid jobs.

In the spring of 2020, newspapers reported that the mafia in southern Italy profited from the coronavirus crisis by lending money to businesses and subsequently charging exorbitant interest, with the goal of taking over those businesses. In addition, members of the mafia were said to be offering families food assistance, anticipating that such a dependency relationship would help secure votes in the next election for the mafia's candidate of choice.

By mid-May of that same year, over two-thirds of people throughout Italy who'd lost jobs because of the pandemic had yet to receive any government benefits. For many months, businesses that had suffered losses because of the lockdown also failed to receive state aid. Solving problems faster than the government is one way to earn trust and quickly gain popularity, and for the past hundred and fifty years, Ndrangheta families have built their empires on such social consensus. Particularly but not exclusively in Calabria itself – wherever they want to extend their sphere of influence, by acting as a formal employer, informal temping agency or a service provider.

Public prosecutor Giuseppe Lombardo predicted that the mafias might lie low temporarily during the lockdown, but that they would ultimately use the Covid crisis – in Italy and beyond – to get businesses hooked on their 'financial doping'. And because of the ready supply of dirty money, these companies do not have to show an immediate return. That fact strengthens their competitive edge against other businesses that do depend on market forces.

During the first two months of the lockdown, tens of thousands of Calabrians left their homes in other parts of Italy and returned to Calabria, a place they usually only visited during the summer holidays. Most of them were young people who could no longer go to work or had to follow their college lectures online. They preferred staying with their families in the rural south to being cooped up in small flats in the city. In the south, they would breathe cleaner air. And although only short walks were permitted, they might get a glimpse of the sea, the mountains, or both from their gardens or balconies. I am sure I'm not the only one who wished these young people would settle here permanently, making use of digital opportunities for work or study.

Fortunately, Calabria has seen a sharp rise in hopeful initiatives for making local communities more robust and economically resilient. People are standing up to mafia-related exploitation, sometimes with success. For instance, a colossal hole was dug a few years ago about forty kilometres from my home. It was intended to become one of

Europe's largest landfills, but a group of locals occupied the area and planted vegetable gardens. Their protest action proved successful. And while the gaping hole is still visible, plans for a landfill site have been shelved.

In another case, African migrants and Italians have joined forces on the Gioia Tauro plain to combat modern slavery in the agricultural sector. Mayors, small businesses, priests and local activists also stick their necks out because they believe change is possible in Calabria. For many, it's a struggle, but they persist despite repeated threats and sabotage. They are convinced that a stronger, more empowered Calabria can counterbalance the toxic influence of the Ndrangheta – at least at a local level.

For years, people in Calabria have been saying that an ethical economy is the only way to stop the mafia. The enemy is not necessarily 'the mafioso' or someone with a particular surname, but anyone who behaves with mafia-like disregard for other people. Often enough, that's also standard behaviour among people who aren't formal members.

This is one of the reasons why Calabrian initiatives aiming to strengthen community resilience prefer to avoid the 'anti-mafia' label. Another is that such a label might encourage an aggressive backlash from the clans. What's more, many people consider the qualification 'anti-mafia' to be meaningless, or at least without guarantees, because members of the mafia have often been shown to make money from organizations or events bearing the 'anti-mafia' label.

Even when the actions are subtle, every deed aimed at appreciating the natural and cultural beauty of a fragile region is, in fact, a fist raised against mafia-induced degradation. And, in Calabria, it's this silent anti-mafia that impresses me the most.

24

DRAGONS AND DOLPHINS

Not far from my village, right by a lighthouse and a little-used railway line, there is a vast grassy field with archaeological excavations. In this field, freely accessible via the railway underpass, you can wander among the remains of a Greek temple dating from the fifth century BC, when this area was known as Kaulon. Here, for fifteen summers, an archaeologist volunteered his time to teach students from all over Italy. The municipality provided the group with modest accommodation and generous residents brought tasty food. Year after year, the archaeologist and his students excavated the ruins of houses, uncovering coins, bones and pottery in the process. While working, they would make jokes about the chances of stumbling across a spectacular mosaic. In 2012, on the day before the students were due to leave for home, a glimmering white mosaic tile emerged beneath the sand, the first piece of what turned out to be the floor of an ancient bathhouse. Two summers later, the entire floor had been restored and it turned out to be the largest and most figurative mosaic ever discovered in Italy's Ancient Greek colonies.

I visited archaeologist Francesco Cuteri, whose dedication to the excavation project made this unique discovery possible, in early 2020. Authorities had just taken down a clandestine network of nearly two hundred people who had plundered a vast quantity of Hellenistic archaeological finds in Calabria and sold them via British and German auction houses. 'They looted the place,' Cuteri told me. Archaeologists had collaborated with the criminal network to determine the age and market value of the artefacts. 'These criminals clearly understood how profitable archaeology can be when archaeological finds are not preserved for the community where they are excavated.'

I was impressed by the calm moral lesson the archaeologist derived from the events. 'Beauty and culture are essential in fighting against people who devastate territories at various levels,' he said. 'We must continue telling stories about the beautiful objects that belong to everyone and make us better people.'

I still vividly recall the story of the mosaic floor that he and his students discovered. In recent years, the unique excavation site had been re-hidden under tarpaulins and a layer of sand, awaiting the construction of a shelter to protect the mosaic from the elements, thus making it accessible to visitors in all seasons. No funding had yet been secured, but the largest mosaic discovered in Magna Graecia deserved to be admired during peak tourist season, at the very least. And so, one day in August, I joined visitors of all ages on the edge of what had, in the fourth century BC, been a communal place to bathe. With the sea whispering behind us, we listened to Francesco Cuteri as we gazed down at a space measuring roughly five by eight metres, sunken into the dry field. The scorching August sun meant that it was only possible to view the site late in the day, but even in the slightly cooler hours, imagining the heat of the ancient sauna's rising steam was fairly easy.

The mosaic had once filled the room like a carpet and now gently followed the contours of the ground; Francesco Cuteri's bare feet were familiar with every detail of the surface. According to the archaeologist, the space hadn't had windows. Oil lamps had provided the only light, and the walls and vaulted ceiling had been stained dark red. Water would flow past a copper shield heated by a flame: an ancient kettle shaped like a tortoiseshell. Before entering the room, visitors would have had to wash their feet. Then, at the threshold, they would have stepped over a mosaic of a flower bearing twelve leaves, representing the twelve gods of Olympus, reminding them this was a sacred space. The rest of the floor was decorated with animals.

'The elites of Kaulon had grown rich thanks to their proximity to the sea, which facilitated trade,' Cuteri explained. 'Perhaps out of gratitude for this economic prosperity, the floor of the thermal bathhouse depicts sea creatures, but that may not have been the only reason. Like the other elements, water was sacred to the ancient Greeks, and the mosaic's sea creatures protected those who entered this space from evil.'

A dragon was displayed prominently by the entrance, greeting visitors with tiny fins and a gracefully curling tail, split like a scorpion's. The archaeologist explained that in Ancient Greece, dragons were incorporated into the mosaic floors at the entrances to houses and rooms to guard valuable spaces. 'This dragon's smile is a reminder of his sharp teeth, with which he can protect himself, and others.' The creature had a friendly and trustworthy expression. Two dolphins swimming alongside the dragon were wearing the same watchful smile. 'Dolphins symbolize playfulness and cheerfulness, and they represent the harmony between humans and the sea. They are our ideal travelling companions.'

Finally, Cuteri showed us a lovely seahorse. 'We also find seahorses near cemeteries,' he said. 'According to the Ancient Greeks, seahorses hold the key to the bodily cage that imprisons our soul. They let our souls fly away, not only after death but also during life. They help us choose to go after our desires.'

As the sun set behind the lighthouse, the sky turned a deep, reddish-orange and in the east, the moon rose above the sea. Cuteri used a plant mister to spray the entire mosaic, hoping to bring out the colours and contrasts. At this hour, the drops of water posed no danger to the small, fragile stones that time had faded to pale shades of red, white and purplish black, as they would not burn off in the sun. Now, the droplets on the tiles of the mosaic reflected the warm evening light and with a bit of imagination, some of the ancient hues reappeared: cobalt blue, golden yellow and vermilion red.

'This mosaic tells us that we must all choose a space where evil will never be allowed,' said Cuteri. 'Sometimes, we can only see our enemies, but if we take a closer look, we can also recognize the travelling companions who protect us during our lives and inspire us to continue exploring.'

From my house, I watch the sea every day. I know there are dolphins swimming near the coast, sea turtles laying their eggs on the beach and seahorses breeding in the sheltered warmth of the bay. Calabria's natural beauty and timeless grace have inspired me to explore situations that are dark and far from pretty. Yet despite everything I have discovered, my love for this place has only grown. I have a better idea of what the rest of the world may have to lose by looking away, and – thanks to the courageous people I have met – I know what we have to gain by opening our eyes and taking action.

AFTERWORD – THE GLOBAL REACH OF THE NDRANGHETA TODAY

The Ndrangheta has its roots in Calabria, but it has sent up new shoots around the world, especially the English-speaking parts of it. By chance, the events that led to the most specifically British Ndrangheta-related criminal case to date unfolded right before my eyes. It all started during my first years in Calabria. As I was settling into my hilltop village and getting to know my new neighbours, I couldn't help noticing the abundance of houses springing up along the Ionian coast. It was hard to see the appeal of these relatively pricey, boxy, cramped holiday homes, charmed as I was by the panoramic views from my ancient *borgo* high in the hills, the quiet village life and my proximity to a rushing river complete with waterfalls. From an architectural standpoint, most of these newly built holiday homes were neither refined nor very original: glaringly white cement cubes constructed cheek by jowl in an otherwise barren holiday resort. But they all had one unique selling point – they were right by the sea.

Foreign tourists were the intended buyers of these units. They were offered for sale primarily in England and Northern Ireland, and business was brisk. Direct Ryanair flights from London Stansted to Lamezia Terme and other convenient air links had turned Calabria into a desirable holiday destination, easily accessible multiple times a year – making these small residences a home away from home that could also be let to other holidaymakers.

Unfortunately, the quality of the completed buildings left a lot to be desired, as home buyers I ran into at summer parties in the village were sad to report. For example, the electrical wiring couldn't cope with the demand, resulting in regular power outages in dozens of homes at once, even when only a few of the houses were inhabited. The developers showed little interest in resolving the problem and left their clients to their own devices. The homeowners grew more and more dissatisfied, and the resorts felt increasingly desolate.

Shortly after construction had begun, the property developers had asked me if I was interested in working for them. They were looking for an English speaker who lived nearby and could act as a local contact for interested parties and new owners from Britain and Ireland. Luckily, I trusted my intuition and declined the offer.

Many people's suspicions were finally confirmed a few years later, in March 2013, when police arrested twenty men suspected of laundering money for the Ndrangheta by investing in the construction of no fewer than 1,343 holiday homes worth 450 million euros, at seventeen different locations spanning more than a hundred kilometres of coastline. The public prosecutor's office linked most suspects to the Morabito and Aquino clans from the Calabrian villages of Africo and Gioiosa Ionica, respectively. Spanish entrepreneurs and a former IRA bomber were also charged in the proceedings.

For buyers, the situation at construction sites further afield was often even more dire than for those who had bought holiday homes on the beach visible from my house: construction on some houses hadn't even started yet. Some of them were supposed to have been built in a protected breeding area for sea turtles, where construction was illegal. Dozens of buyers had already transferred half the purchase price, ranging from thirty thousand to one hundred thousand pounds, to Giambrone & Partners, an intermediary law firm with offices in London and Palermo. Gabriele Giambrone, the law firm's founder, was born in Sicily and had studied law in both Palermo and London. In addition to speaking Italian and English – with an upper-class accent – he was fluent in Spanish and French, and occasionally, he commented on Italian criminal cases for news programmes on British radio and television.

In 2013, Giambrone was struck from the Solicitors Regulation Authority's Register of European Lawyers for his connection with the Calabrian holiday homes. A British judge ruled that his firm was liable for damages incurred by his clients as buyers. According to the ruling, Giambrone had been aware of the widespread involvement of mafia clans in the Calabrian construction industry, but he had failed to warn his clients of the risks. In 2020, the High Court in London ordered the law firm to pay 3.5 million euros in damages to forty-one holiday-home buyers. In an earlier case against the same law firm tried before the High Court in Belfast, a group of sixty-six aggrieved Northern Irish buyers were awarded settlements totalling five million pounds.

When the case was tried in Italy in the court of first instance, it seemed like a fiasco for the public prosecutor's office because only a fraction of the suspects was convicted. Nevertheless, during the appeal, most of the convictions were upheld, and the court handed down prison sentences ranging from three to twelve years. There wasn't enough evidence, however, to convict the former IRA member.

The case illustrates the ways in which the Ndrangheta typically works, because the clans involved not only used their territorial power to buy land, including some plots where construction was prohibited, but also generated goodwill by hiring local workers in their construction companies. What's more, the scheme helped the clans launder revenues from drug trafficking – the Morabitos are major players in the cocaine market – and some of their international accomplices went unpunished, even though they profited from the fraudulent business. Much of the money lost by investors, including deposits paid to the sellers and property developers, has never been traced or refunded. According to the Italian public prosecutor's office, the money vanished into various tax havens and Swiss bank accounts.

In recent years, Gabriele Giambrone has been allowed to resume his work as a lawyer. And in the meantime, the law firm bearing his name has received numerous awards and opened offices in major cities in Spain, Morocco and Portugal.

Many properties in the holiday parks are still available to let online. The units often get good reviews – it seems likely that the problems with the electricity, for example, have been resolved by now – and the pictures don't reveal the buildings' complex criminal history. The trees and shrubs outside have grown, and the summery interiors exude the calm and simplicity of ordinary seaside rentals. But overall, this case reinforced Calabria's reputation within the UK as a bad place for making serious investments, and it also resulted in a few otherwise beautiful stretches of coastline being scarred by unsaleable cement carcasses.

A relatively large number of Calabrians have moved to the UK in the past decade. Of course, that doesn't mean they brought Ndrangheta-type problems with them – on the contrary, many will have wanted to leave behind the poor economic conditions related to the mafia's influence. At the moment, there isn't much evidence of the presence of actual Calabrian clans in the UK – but that doesn't mean their money isn't flowing through the country's capital anyway. Investigations by the Italian justice department point to economic crimes linked with the City of London. The culprits are usually intermediaries who set up shell companies for Ndrangheta clans or launder money on their behalf through other companies. One example is the owner of a popular South London restaurant, who was jailed in 2018 because of long-standing money-laundering activities for the Ndrangheta through a currency exchange office. He had also collaborated with German-based Ndrangheta members in an extensive wine-smuggling racket.

Thanks to a lack of local judicial and follow-up investigations, the picture of the Ndrangheta's interests and influence in the UK is still far from complete. When it comes to the highly lucrative UK drugs trade, the Ndrangheta does not appear to play a major role locally. Various other criminal organizations take an active part in drug trafficking here, including many Albanian-speaking groups. In 2021, the British National Crime Agency reported that more than 1,700 criminal groups in the UK were collaborating with international players like the Ndrangheta to import ever-larger amounts of cocaine into the UK. In 2023, members of the Gallace clan from Calabria were convicted in Italy of large-scale cocaine trafficking from Colombia to destinations including the UK and Australia.

Australia is a very different story as far as the Ndrangheta is concerned: Calabrian clans have been active there for over a century. In December 1922, three prominent members of the Ndrangheta arrived on the continent by way of the same ship. Today, Australian Ndrangheta clans are spread throughout the country, and still maintain contact with the clans in Calabria. Ransom money from kidnappings that took place in the 1970s, '80s and '90s was brought into the country, sometimes literally in the luggage of Ndrangheta migrants, and used in part as start-up capital for drug trafficking. In present-day Australia, thousands of clan members engage in international cocaine and synthetic drug trafficking, manage large cannabis plantations, are involved in extortion and operate businesses in sectors ranging from construction, hospitality and transportation to retail, agriculture and the fruit and vegetable trade. According to the Australian Federal Police, the Ndrangheta clans are 'pulling the strings' of Australia's many outlaw motorcycle gangs, which are much more visible and violent than the Calabrian gangs themselves.

There was, however, a time when the Ndrangheta in Australia was very violent and eliminated some of its enemies. In 1977, for example, a politician who had called for measures to curtail the Calabrian clans' drug crimes was murdered, as was a prominent Australian Federal Police officer who, in 1989, had followed the trail of successful clans and raised the alarm about them in the media. These two murders remain unsolved, and bring to mind the murder of a young detective named Geoffrey Bowen that went unsolved for decades. Bowen was killed with a parcel bomb in his office in Adelaide in 1994, one day before he was due to testify in a major cannabis criminal trial targeting a member of the Perre family, who had immigrated from the Calabrian village of Platì and was suspected of large-scale illegal cannabis production.

It wasn't until twenty-eight years later, in 2022, that there was enough evidence to convict Domenic Perre for Bowen's brutal murder. By the time Perre was convicted, he was already serving a prison sentence for drug trafficking, and he died of heart disease one year later. The long funeral procession leading to the Catholic church in

Perre's former hometown included limousines decorated with Italian flags. Hundreds of family members, friends and acquaintances came to pay their respects.

Another revealing and long-drawn-out Australian case involves the charge of illegal immigration brought against Francesco or Frank Madafferi, a man from Oppido Mamertina, Calabria. In Italy, he had been a suspect in the five-month-long kidnapping of a young woman as well as an attempted murder, and he had spent time in prison in the 1980s for extortion, assault by stabbing and possession of drugs and weapons. He then evaded another arrest by fleeing to Melbourne, where his brother lived. Once there, Frank Madafferi married, had children and built an extensive network among the local Calabrian community. In a conversation overheard by police, he shouted in Calabrian dialect: 'Melbourne is mine!' Madafferi seemed to have everything – except a residence permit.

When the Australian government began deportation proceedings against him, Madafferi challenged them in every way he could. In 2005, after years of litigation, Australia's newly appointed minister for immigration, Amanda Vanstone, stepped in: she allowed Madafferi to stay in Australia and become a citizen. And, although Italy's National Anti-mafia Directorate heavily criticized her decision in the Australian press, calling Madafferi a danger to society, no one intervened. There was nothing to prevent Madafferi from investing in the import of fifteen million ecstasy pills from Italy to Melbourne, shipped in cans labelled 'peeled tomatoes'.

At 4.4 tonnes, it was the largest amount of ecstasy seized up to that point, and led not only to the arrest of Frank Madafferi, but also to that of Pasquale Barbaro, a prominent drugs criminal and the son of a wealthy Calabrian family. Not long after the arrests, in 2009, it came to light that the party of Amanda Vanstone, the minister who had intervened on Frank Madafferi's behalf, had received a healthy donation from Frank's brother. By the time of this investigation, Vanstone herself had moved to Rome, having been appointed, surprisingly enough, as Australia's ambassador to Italy. In the end, the Australian courts sentenced Pasquale Barbaro to life in prison, with a minimum term of thirty years, and Frank Madafferi to ten years. He is due to be released in 2024.

For several years now, Australian police have heightened their focus on the Ndrangheta. In 2021, a massive international police operation known as Ironside/Anom proved an eye-opener. Central to this operation was a special type of smartphone called Anom, which was used by drug criminals to exchange encrypted messages. These phones had in fact been secretly brought onto the market by the FBI and the Australian Federal Police, to enable them to read over the criminals' shoulders. A total of twenty-seven million messages were exchanged between 9,000 users in a hundred different countries, resulting in 800 international arrests, including 340 in Australia. Among those arrested were many Ndrangheta members, who were often obeying orders from Calabria and, in turn, were giving orders to Australian motorcycle gangs. In this part of the world, as elsewhere, the Ndranghetists' relatively discreet lifestyle has become a notorious trademark of their success.

Anna Sergi, professor of criminology and organized crime studies at the University of Essex, is undoubtedly the foremost academic expert on the global business affairs of the Ndrangheta. Sergi was born and raised in Calabria and makes regular trips to Australia for her research. She writes extensively on the subject, not only for academic audiences but also for outlets such as the Italian 'slow journalism' website iCalabresi.it. There she describes how 'the

Ndrangheta in Australia, accustomed as it is to political proximity, with influence and interests even at the highest national levels', is 'still able to victimize certain parts of Calabrian, southern and Italian communities' and is 'fully integrated into the country's economic and social history'. That's why, according to Sergi, the Ndrangheta in Australia 'has always seemed one of the most successful formulas of mafia mobility'.

Canada is another country reputed to be a Ndrangheta stronghold. Although Ndrangheta members began emigrating from Calabria to eastern Canada in the early 1900s, it wasn't until the 1950s that they successfully reproduced the Ndrangheta's classic organizational model there. Internationally, the 'Siderno Group' attracts the most attention. It was created when Antonio Macrì, the renowned Capocrimine from Siderno, joined forces with affiliated criminals in Canada, the US and Australia. Macrì was known for his preference for old-school mafia-related crimes like extortion and cigarette smuggling. But when he died in 1975, the Siderno Group in and around Toronto soon moved on to smuggling heroin and cocaine. In more recent years, as described earlier in this book, this group also had close ties with the Ndranghetists from Siderno based at Royal FloraHolland, the Dutch flower auction.

In Canada, as in Australia, a separate Crimine had been set up to monitor the local balance of power between the clans and to prevent vendettas. But the Siderno Group, now in the hands of a younger generation of Ndranghetists, always maintained close ties with Calabria. Italian prosecutors have told me they'd noticed that suspects who had settled in Canada often wore flashy, expensive, clothes, as if to emulate the image of Hollywood gangsters. However, when they visited Calabria, they adapted, chameleon-like, to the local environment. Perhaps by wearing less showy attire, they were hoping to escape the attention of the police or the evil eye of their business partners and former neighbours.

What's worrying but not entirely surprising about the Calabrian clans in Canada is that they go beyond drug trafficking, illegal gambling, loan sharking and fraud by also extorting money from members of the Italian community and illicitly procuring public funding. In 2019, the Superior Court of Justice in Ontario explicitly recognized the Ndrangheta as a foreign criminal organization active within Canada. Giuseppe Ursino, a Canadian citizen born in Gioiosa Ionica, Calabria, was sentenced to eleven and a half years in prison for cocaine smuggling and leading a local Ndrangheta clan, marking the first time a court outside of Italy convicted someone explicitlyfor their role in the Ndrangheta. For the time being, however, it remains challenging to convict specific individuals in Canada for membership in the Ndrangheta, because much of the evidence is usually gathered in Italy.

In addition to Toronto, the Canadian city of Montreal also has links with the Ndrangheta. For the past fifty years, bloody vendettas have been waged there between mafia figures with Sicilian and Calabrian roots. It seems their specific regional origins aren't always relevant to the alliances they have formed. In the United States, where Sicilians first introduced the mafia concept, the distinction between the American Cosa Nostra and the Ndrangheta is certainly not as clear-cut as in most other parts of the world. For example, representatives of the Ndrangheta are included in the ranks of the notorious 'five families', traditionally associated with Cosa Nostra. Ndrangheta clans also collaborate with these families in and around New York when trafficking narcotics.

*

It's tempting to try to present an overview here of all that is known about the Ndrangheta's global activities, but that would take quite a while. According to Interpol, Ndrangheta clans are active on at least five continents and in forty countries. In early 2020, Interpol launched a project optimistically called I-CAN to target the Calabrian mafia more effectively worldwide. In the three years Interpol's Cooperation Against the Ndrangheta has been active, more than forty Ndranghetists have been arrested thanks to the initiative. One was the fugitive Francesco Pelle, who was convicted of ordering the armed attack on the Christmas party at the Nirta family's house in San Luca – the attack that took the life of Maria Strangio. At the time of his arrest, Pelle was recovering from Covid-19 in a Lisbon hospital.

Rocco Morabito was another Ndrangheta fugitive who had long eluded authorities. This 'king of Milanese cocaine' had been untraceable for more than twenty years. It turned out that he had been living in Uruguay, dealing in property and running soybean plantations under the assumed name of Francisco Antonio Capeletto Souza. Authorities picked him up in Brazil and extradited him to Italy, where he faced thirty years in prison for drug trafficking.

Although Project I-CAN also led to the arrest of three Polish women suspected of money laundering for the Ndrangheta in Poland, the focus of law enforcement outside Italy tends to remain on the usual suspects: Calabrian men with notorious surnames, descendants of families who have represented the Ndrangheta's interests for more than a hundred and fifty years and who seem to have thought they could outwit the authorities abroad. There isn't much enthusiasm for apprehending accomplices of the local nationality – especially in places facing shortages of police and judicial staff, which means practically everywhere. And so, the network of people who facilitate the Ndrangheta's criminal affairs remains uncharted. Because proving the guilt of such facilitators is relatively complicated, and the maximum sentences they face aren't very long, there is less incentive to pursue them among ambitious police and prosecutors hoping to advance their careers.

In Calabria, however, prosecuting white-collar criminals has become integral to significant mafia trials. The Rinascita maxi-trial, the largest case against the Ndrangheta ever mounted, is a good example. Among the more than four hundred defendants were a former member of the Italian parliament and senator, attorneys, mayors, entrepreneurs, regional administrators, a colonel and a captain from the carabinieri, a former secret service agent and a municipal police commander.

Hearings in the maxi-trial were held nearly every weekday from early 2021 until late 2023 in a massive, purpose-built bunker courtroom in Lamezia Terme. It was a fascinating trial to observe from the sidelines, and not just because of the fierce debates between prosecutors and the defence, or the involvement of witnesses who had only recently begun to cooperate with judicial authorities. It was interesting, for example, to observe squabbles flaring up between criminal defence lawyers and the local press, and then see them cool down just as quickly. The maxi-trial's unprecedented number of defendants also attracted unprecedented interest from foreign news channels, who occasionally swooped in to report on developments in the Calabrian courtroom.

After seventy-three of a total of ninety suspects had been convicted in a parallel, so-called abbreviated, trial, around two-thirds of the other suspects from the network of clans from the Calabrian province of Vibo Valentia were sentenced to more than two thousand years in prison – for murder, extortion, usury, the rigging of elections, money laundering, all manner of fraud, abuse of office and, of course, for being members of or aiding the Ndrangheta. The most eagerly awaited verdict was that of Giancarlo Pittelli. This seventy-year-old politician and criminal lawyer had been a member of the Italian parliament and senate for Berlusconi's Forza Italia and Popolo della Libertà parties, and had subsequently joined the right-wing, populist Fratelli d'Italia (Brothers of Italy), the party of Giorgia Meloni, Italy's current prime minister. The team of public prosecutors had demanded a sentence of seventeen years for favours Pittelli had granted to the Mancuso clan, including leaking secret information and facilitating access to government institutions, banks and foreign companies. Pittelli was sentenced to eleven years and has appealed the verdict.

For years, Giancarlo Pittelli had represented the head of the clan, Luigi Mancuso, who was tried separately but has recently been sentenced to thirty years in another case. Among Pittelli's other clients – he has also called them 'friends' – were other prominent Ndranghetists, such as members of the Piromalli family from Gioia Tauro. In a different ongoing court case, Pittelli is facing charges of collaborating with the Piromallis in illegal waste dumping.

When I finished writing the original version of this book in 2020, I implied that the Netherlands, my native country, had a lot to lose – and to gain – in the realm of organized crime and its prevention. When I wrote those words, I had no idea how true they would be. In July 2021, on a sunny evening in the historic centre of Amsterdam, Peter R. de Vries, the most famous crime journalist in the Netherlands, was murdered. He had just left a TV studio after a live broadcast and was walking to the garage where he'd parked his car when he was approached by an assailant who shot him in the head at close range. De Vries was rushed to hospital in a coma and died nine days later.

Suspicions are that drug criminal Ridouan Taghi, leader of the so-called 'Mocro Mafia', who is alleged to have worked with the Italian mafia and the Irish Kinahan cartel while hiding in Dubai, ordered the murder of De Vries from his high-security prison cell. The motive for the murder was presumably the journalist's role as an advisor to the state's witness who was testifying in a trial in which Taghi was the prime suspect. Since this state's witness has started giving testimony, his brother has also been murdered, as has one of his lawyers. In February 2024, Taghi was sentenced to life imprisonment.

When Peter R. de Vries was killed, many said that the Netherlands was turning into another Italy, although murdering a public figure is not in keeping with the way today's Italian mafias tend to act. The mafia hasn't murdered an Italian journalist in decades – although some Italian journalists do unfortunately still face death threats and are forced to live under police protection. In any case, the Dutch government decided to sharpen their tactics when battling organized drug crime. In doing so, the government specifically emphasized its desire to learn from Italy's approach in fighting the mafia. Soon, the Dutch adopted some Italian-style restrictive measures to prevent high-risk prisoners from continuing their criminal activity behind bars.

The exchange of knowledge and experience is essential when dealing with something as international as the battle against organized crime, and Italy has valuable lessons to offer in this area, not least in terms of social awareness and resistance. At the same time, I believe we must avoid falling into some of the traps that Italy fell into. Suppose repression does not go hand in hand with sufficient investments in prevention, including poverty reduction and youth social service? In that case, criminal organizations will continue to find fertile soil in which to grow.

When it comes to favourable conditions in northern Europe, Ndrangheta clans have the advantage that other, more violent groups of narcotics criminals with whom they collaborate often divert the authorities' attention. Nevertheless, in recent years, there have been some innovative developments in combatting the Ndrangheta in Germany and Belgium. Authorities managed to crack encrypted messaging services – in this case, Encrochat and SkyEcc – providing a wealth of information about the international network of the Nirta–Strangio and Morabito clans. More than a hundred people were arrested in May 2023, including thirty in Germany and thirteen in Belgium. They are suspected of smuggling twenty-three tonnes of cocaine, money laundering (including through companies in Portugal and France), arms trafficking, fraud and tax evasion.

More Ndrangheta arrests soon followed in locations around Germany. In the by now familiar city of Duisburg, the police stumbled upon Antonio Strangio, who had been working at the Da Bruno restaurant on the night of the multiple murders in 2007. More recently, Strangio had been living as a fugitive in that same city, and even managed to find a regular job at DHL, delivering packages.

By chance, the first place I gave a talk about the German translation of *Mafiopoli* was Erfurt, the capital of Thuringia. Erfurt has a somewhat fraught reputation regarding the Ndrangheta's influence. The subject has finally made it onto the political agenda in this eastern German state: a parliamentary commission is trying to find out why, twenty years ago, a promising investigation into money laundering was suddenly halted. During that investigation, police discovered substantial investments made by Ndrangheta suspects in the hospitality industry in the picturesque centre of Erfurt. Preliminary findings seem to suggest that the quashing of the investigation was linked to cordial relationships between successful Ndrangheta entrepreneurs and local politicians, administrators and the judiciary.

Sadly, the omertà, the implicit code of silence, still seems widespread among Erfurt's citizens today. The people organizing the conference at which I was invited to present my book, and at which members of the parliamentary committee and several other experts were asked to speak about the working methods of the Calabrian mafia in the region, said they had great trouble finding a welcoming venue in the city.

One thing I can't help noticing is that my invitations to speak in Germany usually come from members of the Italian community there. Are they simply more interested in the subject, or perhaps also less afraid?

In recent years, the production, import and consumption of cocaine has only increased. More and more criminals are making money from the drugs trade, even though the police are seizing ever larger quantities. As a result, more and more crime fighters have grown tired of fighting a losing battle. They can see no end to the war on drugs.

Thanks to the illegal drugs market, criminal organizations amass vast amounts of capital, whether it's through cash, cryptocurrency or underground banking transactions. What's more, conflicts relating to drug trafficking result in horrific violence in many parts of the world. An international group of police and justice officials has become so dissatisfied with the situation that they've set up the Law Enforcement Action Partnership, or LEAP, to explore alternatives to current drug policy. They argue for gradually decriminalizing the production and use of illegal drugs and, with an eye to public health, finding ways for governments to regulate their use. Those involved admit doubting whether their goal is achievable in their lifetimes, but they remain committed to the debate.

In addition to important questions relating to the effectiveness of the current war on drugs, we might also ask ourselves how the growth of organized crime is linked to our global impasse in trying to resolve other pressing issues, such as economic inequality and the climate crisis. To what extent, for example, would a more effective detection and prosecution of financial and environmental crimes help curb the activities of international criminal organizations? The Ndrangheta, with its global operations, could provide us with revealing test cases.

A NOTE ABOUT THE CONVICTIONS

Several of the court cases mentioned in the preceding chapters still await a final ruling. All the people mentioned in this book are innocent until proven guilty. At the time of going to press, the status of the Italian criminal cases that are relevant in the Netherlands, insofar as that is not specified in the preceding chapters, is as follows:

Giovanni Giorgi, arrested in the Netherlands in December 2018 and charged in Italy with money laundering and collaborating with the Ndrangheta, was sentenced in February 2022 to fourteen years and eight months in prison by a court of first instance. On appeal, his sentence was reduced to eleven years and two months. The supreme court of cassation has yet to consider the case.

Vincenzo and Rocco Crupi were arrested in Italy in September 2015. During the 'Krupy' trial in 2018, the Latina court of first instance convicted them of drug trafficking. The court of appeal in Rome acquitted them of those charges in 2019.

In June 2020, the court of appeal in Reggio Calabria gave a verdict in the 'Acero' proceedings. The judge found both Vincenzo Crupi and Giuseppe Crupi guilty of membership of the Ndrangheta. Vincenzo Crupi's prison sentence was reduced to eight years, after the court of first instance had initially sentenced him to twenty, and Giuseppe

Crupi's sentence was reduced to eight years and six months, although the court of first instance had sentenced him to fifteen.

Massimo Dalla Valle was sentenced by the court of appeal to eight years for collaborating with the Ndrangheta, after the court of first instance had initially imposed a sentence of sixteen years. Rocco Crupi was sentenced in 2017 by the Reggio Calabria court of first instance to fourteen years in prison for membership of the Ndrangheta, but the court of appeal later acquitted him.

In September 2021, the court of cassation ordered the court of appeal to retry the cases against Vincenzo Crupi, Giuseppe Crupi, and Massimo Dalla Valle. In March 2023, the court of appeal sentenced Vincenzo Crupi to eight years in prison for membership of the Ndrangheta, and acquitted both Giuseppe Crupi and Massimo Dalla Valle. It is not yet known if the public prosecutor's office will appeal this verdict.

In 2019, the Calabrian court of first instance in Locri sentenced Vincenzo Macrì to twenty years for membership of the Ndrangheta. In 2021, the court of appeal reduced the sentence to fifteen years. The court of cassation has upheld the conviction.

Marc B. was arrested in Amsterdam in 2014 on suspicion of supplying cocaine to the Ndrangheta and was subsequently released from pre-trial detention. In March 2021, he was arrested in the Dominican Republic and extradited to Italy. In 2023, the case against him was dismissed for lack of jurisdiction.

BIBLIOGRAPHY

The criminal reconstructions in this book are based on information found in the associated criminal records. Articles in Italian newspapers and interviews with prosecutors helped me to find my way through thousands of pages of legal documents. For this book, I researched, among others, the following cases: Crimine, Fehida, All Inside, Onta, Mauser, Acero-Krupy and Pollino, also known as the European Ndrangheta Connection.

OTHER LITERATURE AND DOCUMENTARIES CONSULTED

Badolati, Arcangelo, *Santisti e 'ndrine: Narcos, massoni deviati e killer a contratto*, Cosenza: Luigi Pellegrini Editore, 2018

Baldessarro, Giuseppe, *Questione di rispetto: L'impresa di Gaetano Saffioti contro la Ndrangheta*, Soveria Mannelli: Rubbettino, 2017

Camarca, Claudio (editor), *Dizionario enciclopedico delle mafie in Italia*, Rome: Castelvecchi, 2013

Canepari, Claudio and Gabriele Gravagna (directors), *Ilaria Alpi: L'ultimo viaggio*, Rome: RAI, 2015

Cataldi, Federico (director), *Peppino Impastato: Omicidio di mafia*, Rome: RAI, 2008

Ciconte, Enzo, *Storia criminale: La resistibile ascesa di mafia, Ndrangheta e camorra dall'Ottocento ai giorni nostri*, Soveria Mannelli: Rubbettino, 2008

Ciconte, Enzo, *Ndrangheta. Edizione aggiornata*, Soveria Mannelli: Rubbettino, 2011

Ciconte, Enzo, *Riti criminali: I codici di affiliazione alla Ndrangheta*, Soveria Mannelli: Rubbettino, 2015

Ciconte, Enzo, *Dall'omertà ai social: Come cambia la comunicazione della mafia*, Pavia: Edizioni Santa Caterina, 2017

De Jong, Stan and Koen Voskuil, *Maffiaparadijs: een onthutsend beeld van Italiaanse maffia in Nederland*, Amsterdam: Boekerij, 2017

Dickie, John, *Mafia Republic: Italy's Criminal Curse*, London: Sceptre, 2013

Dutch National Police Corps, *De Ndrangheta in Nederland: Aard, criminele activiteiten en werkwijze op Nederlandse bodem*, The Hague: KLPD/Dienst Nationale Reche rche, 2011

European Monitoring Centre for Drugs and Drug Addiction and Europol, *EU Drug Markets: Impact of Covid-19*, Luxembourg: Publications Office of the European Union, 2020

Forgione, Francesco, *Maffia Export: Hoe 'ndrangheta, cosa nostra en camorra de wereld hebben gekoloniseerd*, Amsterdam: Ambo, 2010

Gratteri, Nicola and Antonio Nicaso, *Fratelli di sangue*, Milan: Mondadori, 2009

Gratteri, Nicola and Antonio Nicaso, *Dire e non dire: I dieci comandamenti della Ndrangheta nelle parole degli affiliati*, Milan: Mondadori, 2012

Gratteri, Nicola and Antonio Nicaso, *Fiumi d'oro: Come la Ndrangheta investe i soldi della cocaina nell'economia legale*, Milan: Mondadori, 2017

Gratteri, Nicola, Marta Maddalon, Antonio Nicaso and John B. Trumper, *Male lingue: Vecchi e nuovi codici delle mafie*, Cosenza: Luigi Pellegrini Editore, 2014

Iantosca, Angela, *Onora la madre: storie di Ndrangheta al femminile*, Soveria Mannelli: Rubbettino, 2013

Ingrascì, Ombretta, *Confessioni di un padre: Il pentito Emilio Di Giovine racconta la Ndrangheta alla figlia*, Milan: Melampo, 2013

Landman, Cecile, 'Van gangsterliefje tot politieagent', Amsterdam: *Nieuwe Revu*, 8 September 2010

Maurizi, Stefania, 'Armi chimiche siriane a Gioia Tauro: I cablo di WikiLeaks spiegano perché', Milan: *l'Espresso*, 16 January 2014

OCCRP, IRPI, Miami Herald and Al Qatiba, ''Ndrangheta-Linked Broker Banked at Credit Suisse', OCCRP.org, 21 February 2022 [https://www.occrp.org/en/suisse-secrets/ndrangheta-linked-broker-banked -at-credit-suisse]

Project Cerca Trova, Antonius Spapens, Cerca Trova: *Een analyse van de Italiaanse maffia in Nederland*, The Hague: Dutch Ministry of Justice and Security, 2017

Reski, Petra, *Enkele reis Corleone*, Amsterdam: Lebowski, 2011

Reski, Petra, *The Honoured Society: The Secret History of Italy's Most Powerful Mafia: My Journey to the Heart of the Mafia*, London: Atlantic, 2013

Sales, Isaia and Simona Melorio, *Le mafie nell'economia globale: Fra la legge dello Stato e le leggi di mercato*, Naples: Guida editori, 2017

Sauviller, Raf and Salvatore di Rosa, *Maffia*, Brussels: Manteau, 2016

Sergi, Anna, 'Australia, la 'ndrangheta della porta accanto', I Calabresi, 8 June 2022 [https://icalabresi.it/rubriche/australia-ndrangheta-porta-accanto-an0m-e-100-anni-ndrine/]

Sergi, Anna, 'The evolution of the Australian 'ndrangheta. An historical perspective', *Australian & New Zealand Journal of Criminology*, 48(2), 155–174, 2015

Sergi, Anna, *Chasing the Mafia: 'Ndrangheta, Memories and Journeys*, Bristol: Bristol University Press, 2022

Sergi, Anna and Anita Lavorgna, *Ndrangheta. The Glocal Dimensions of the Most Powerful Italian Mafia*, Palgrave Macmillan, 2016

Sergi, Anna and Alice Rizzuti, *C.R.I.M.E. Countering Regional Italian Mafia Expansion*, Report, University of Essex, 2021

Tops, Pieter and Jan Tromp, *De achterkant van Amsterdam: Een verkenning van drugsgerelateerde criminaliteit*, Amsterdam: The Municipality of Amsterdam, 2019

Trimarchi, Giuseppe, *Calabria Ribelle: Storie di ordinaria resistenza*, Naples: Città del Sole, 2012

FURTHER INFORMATION

Roberto Di Bella, a juvenile court judge in Reggio Calabria, has set up an educational programme for children from Ndrangheta families who have experienced run-ins with the law. Sophia Luvarà made a fascinating documentary about the project, called *Sons of Honour* (2020).

A Chiara (2021), an Italian film directed by Jonas Carpignano, is also about children who grow up in a Ndrangheta family. It is the most moving film about the Ndrangheta I have ever seen.

The documentary *But Now is Perfect* (Carin Goeijers, 2018) focuses on the turbulent final years of the asylum seekers' programme in Riace and includes the tragic story of Becky Moses.

Visitors to Calabria who are eager to see the mosaic floor that Francesco Cuteri uncovered with his students should know that the Archaeological Museum in the Municipality of Monasterace manages the site. The museum also has a much smaller mosaic depicting a dragon on display, but visiting the remains of the ancient bathhouse, especially with Cuteri as a guide, is highly recommended. Hopefully, a suitable shelter will be built in the future so that Calabrian residents and visitors can view the mosaic floor year-round.

ACKNOWLEDGEMENTS

First, I would like to thank Jake Lingwood, publisher at Monoray, for believing in this book. I am also very grateful to my editors Mala Sanghera-Warren and Alex Stetter for taking great care of this publication, and to Chloë Johnson-Hill, Charlotte Sanders, Peter Hunt and the rest of the team at Octopus. Futhermore, I am indebted to my literary agent Lisette Verhagen at Peters, Fraser and Dunlop for her professionalism and enthusiastic support.

I want to express my gratitude to the people I was privileged to interview and who appear in this book, either at length or briefly: Gaetano Saffioti, Alessandra Cerreti, Lirio Abbate, Nicola Gratteri, Luigi Bonaventura and his family, Enzo Ciconte, Tonino Saraco, Antonio De Bernardo, Petra Reski, Giuseppe Lombardo and Francesco Cuteri.

Many of the other experts I consulted in Italy and the Netherlands inspired me and provided valuable information and insights. I would especially like to mention and thank Roberto Di Palma, Giovanni Bombardieri, Vincenzo Capomolla, Hester van Bruggen, Giap Parini, Isaia Sales, Simona Melorio, Anna Sergi, Zora Hauser, Marta Maddalon, Laura Aprati, Antonio Nicaso and Arcangelo Badolati.

I admire and am grateful to all the Calabrian journalists who write about the Ndrangheta and give me my daily dose of information about this subject.

I am also indebted to Janneke Louman, my Dutch publisher, to my editor Melle van Loenen and to everyone else at Park Uitgevers/ Nieuw Amsterdam who has worked to make this book a success in the Netherlands.

And I would like to thank my dear family and friends. Some of the friendships I've made in Calabria make me feel like I have family there, too. I am grateful to Patrizia, Sonia, Alba, Ilaria, Sergio, Maria Isabelle, Sandra and Erika for their encouragement, care and nearness. *Grazie per il vostro prezioso incoraggiamento.*

ABOUT THE AUTHOR

Sanne de Boer is a Dutch journalist who has lived in Calabria, southern Italy, since 2006. She is the first foreign journalist based in Calabria to write about the 'Ndrangheta, and regularly appears on TV and radio as a mafia expert. *Mafiopoli* was originally published in Dutch in 2020 and nominated for the 'Brusseprijs', a prestigious award for the best book of journalism.